CL 118

D1140099

Landmark

Cornwall

& the Isles of Scilly

Editor's Note

In Chapter 4 mention is made of the Tregellas Tapestry, now on display at the Cornwall Centre (Kresenn Kernow) in Redruth. The 58 panels of the tapestry tell the story of Cornwall in pictures, each individually designed and produced using a variety of techniques such as embroidery, appliqué and collage. The inspiration for this fascinating work came from the Cornish Bard, Tregellas an Bluven – Rita Tregellas Pope, the author of this book. She researched the subject matter and under her direction it was designed and executed by a team of skilled craftspeople. Indeed she embroidered the final panel, 'Plen-an-Gwary'. For some years no place had been found to display all the panels of the tapestry together but with the opening of the Cornwall Centre this has now been made possible. This work of art is a truly remarkable achievement and well worth a visit.

Acknowledgement

The editor would like to thank all those people in Cornwall, especially the staff of the Tourist Information Centres, for the help and kindness received during the revision of this book.

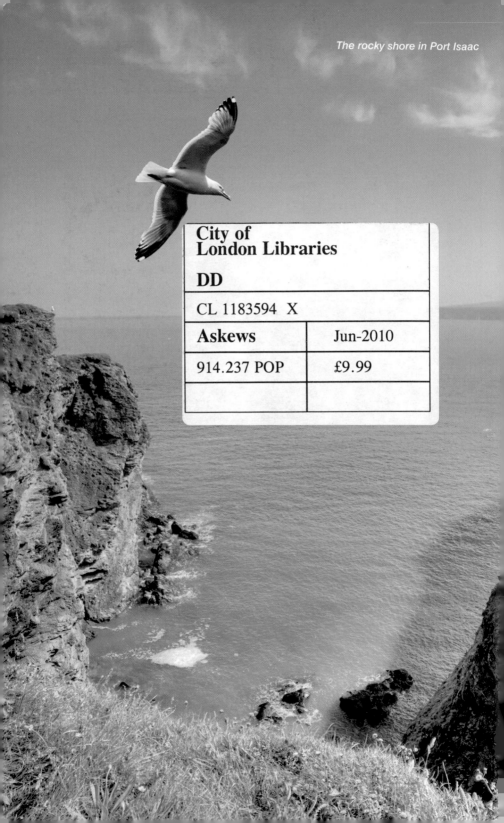

The rocky shore in Port Isaac

City of London Libraries	
DD	
CL 1183594 X	
Askews	Jun-2010
914.237 POP	£9.99

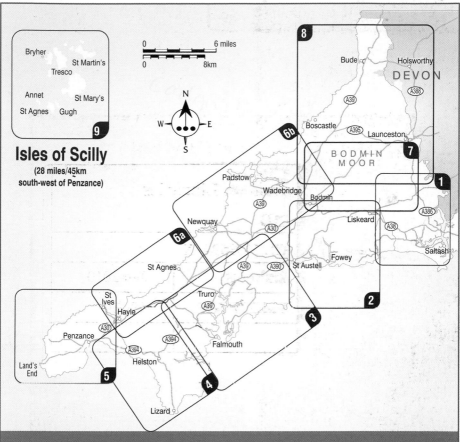

Bryher
St Martin's
Tresco
Annet
St Mary's
St Agnes
Gugh

9

0 ___ 6 miles
0 ___ 8km

N
W ─── E
S

Isles of Scilly
(28 miles/45km
south-west of Penzance)

8
Bude
Holsworthy
DEVON
A388
A39
Boscastle
A395
Launceston
6b
**BODMIN
MOOR**
7
Padstow
1
Wadebridge
Bodmin
A39
Newquay
A30
Liskeard
A38
A386
6a
St Agnes
A39
A390
St Austell
Fowey
Saltash
St
Ives
Truro
3
Hayle
A39
2
Penzance
A30
A394
A394
Falmouth
Land's
End
A394
Helston
5
4
Lizard

Cornwall & the Isles of Scilly

Key for Symbols

Listed below are symbols used in the 'places to visit' section at
the end of each chapter.

Ⓟ *Parking Available*

 ♿   *Disabled Facilities*

ᴪ *Family Attraction*

<Nᵒ *Concession for under age shown*

 ☂   *Suitable in Wet Weather*

🐕 *Well-behaved dogs on leads welcome*

Contents

Welcome to
Cornwall & the Isles of Scilly

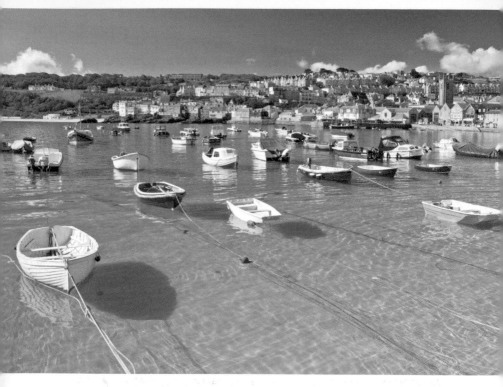

The land of King Arthur – the Cornish Riviera – the Delectable Duchy – call it what you will. Few places have as many facets as Cornwall but this is because the land west of the Tamar is not just a holiday region, it is much more. It is almost a 'nation' in its own right. Look carefully and you will find what you seek, whether it be tales of the past, pleasures of the present or even glimpses into the future.

Until the middle of the nineteenth century, few people visited Cornwall. Roads were dangerous and sea travel largely restricted to packet ships and merchantmen. But this state of affairs ended abruptly in 1859 when Brunel's great railway bridge carried the first train over the Tamar into Cornwall. That historic event was the 'Open Sesame' for visitors. At first they came in a thin trickle, but others soon realised the attraction of the land beyond England and the era of the holiday-maker had begun.

Left: The Eden Project
Opposite Page: Boats in harbour at St Ives

Top Tips

*Left Land's End; Middle top: Newquay Zoo; Middle bottom: Cornwall's Crealy Great Adventure Park;
Right: National Maritime Museum Cornwall*

FAMILY ACTIVITIES

As one of the UK's premier holiday locations, Cornwall has plenty of attractions to keep the whole family happy, but here are a few ideas which would be particularly suitable for families with children:

Land's End

Probably the most famous location in the whole of the south-west, and nowadays the home of a whole host of rides and attractions as well as rugged scenery for the older members of the family to sit and enjoy. Don't forget to have your photo taken by the famous signpost.

The Flambards Experience

Fun and games for kids large and small at one of Cornwall's longest-established theme parks, and a fabulous array of aircraft including a Concorde cockpit. There are also plenty of undercover activities should the weather turn nasty.

Newquay Zoo

Named Cornwall's Visitor Attraction of the Year in 2006, this is much more than just a traditional zoo, with lots of opportunities to meet and learn about a wide variety of animals.

(Continued over page)

DairyLand Farm World

There's something for all the family at what claims to be Britain's leading farm attraction, come rain or shine. There are activities throughout the day, ranging from pony rides and pat-a-pet to the excitement of the Bull Pen.

Paradise Park

Not only is Paradise Park an award-winning wildlife sanctuary, with free-flying bird shows and the ever-popular feeding times, but it now also offers the JungleBarn play area for undercover fun.

Cornwall's Crealy Great Adventure Park

The former Shires Adventure Park offers six different 'realms' with rides, adventures, animals and activities to satisfy everyone from the active to the more relaxed.

Beaches

Cornwall is the home of some of the finest beaches in the country. Grab your bucket and spade (or your surfboard) and enjoy the most traditional of British holiday pursuits.

WHAT TO DO IF IT RAINS

FutureWorld at Goonhilly

The world needs to communicate even if it's raining outside, and there's lots to explore in FutureWorld and the Visitor Centre, although you may still want to take your coat for the tour of the satellite dishes.

Penlee House Gallery and Museum

Both a fascinating museum of the history of Penzance and West Cornwall and the best collection anywhere of the work of the famous 'Newlyn School' of artists.

World of Model Railways

Just a short distance from Mevagissey harbour, this miniature railway world will appeal to young (especially fans of Thomas the Tank Engine) and old alike.

Royal Cornwall Museum

Cornwall's oldest and most prestigious museum, in the heart of Truro, houses both a permanent collection and a changing programme of exhibitions.

Newquay Waterworld/Ships and Castles Leisure Pool, Falmouth

Just because it's wet outside doesn't mean you have to stay dry inside. Both these attractions feature a variety of waterslides and other activities as well as pools suitable for all ages.

National Maritime Museum Cornwall

An award-winning building on the seafront at Falmouth will shelter you from the elements while you explore the history of seafaring through the wide variety of craft on display, but there's also plenty to do outdoors when the weather clears.

Several of Cornwall's leading visitor attractions have recently added covered children's play areas to their facilities, such as Paradise Park's JungleBarn and DairyLand's Bull Pen. See also the suggestions for indoor activities at the end of each chapter.

There are, however, those who say that they can find nothing to do in Cornwall. Perhaps they have not troubled to look. The Cornish motto of 'One and All' has numerous interpretations but the right choice for this guide is 'One Place and Something for All'. S P B Mais said that Cornwall has a 'diversity of riches', and as those are the very treasures that shaped its development, a brief look at the past will show how their mosaic of influences have formed the region as it is today.

Early settlers

With the sea on three sides and the Tamar making the fourth boundary, Cornwall has always been almost an island. So when wandering tribes from Europe arrived, they were able to enjoy a life of comparative peace – scarcely disturbed by the hordes who ravaged the rest of the mainland. That is why, with only wind and weather to affect them, so many Neolithic and Bronze Age monoliths and barrows remain.

The richness of Cornwall's mineral deposits was not exploited until about 350BC when Iron Age tribes from Europe came in search of tin. The people of this fair-haired, blue-eyed race were tall and finely built, probably the originals of the 'giants' in Cornish folklore. They brought their knowledge of tin production with them as well as their culture and a completely new social structure. Evidence of this important occupation is still to be seen in hill forts, cliff castles and the 'trevs' or settlements. The area of West Penwith, beyond Penzance, also retains low drystone walls and unique small fields – the latter having been cultivated continuously ever since Iron Age times.

The much-maligned Druids were Celtic priests who, far from being mere growers of mistletoe, lovers of apples and makers of bonfires, were, in fact, the most highly respected scholars of their day. Men travelled across Europe to learn from them, early Greek was indebted to them and even the great Cicero paid tribute to their knowledge. People who laugh at their customs have only heard about the more sensational aspects and would doubtless be surprised to know that these same Druids were among the first of the so-called pagans to proclaim the doctrine of immortality.

Visitors interested in Roman remains will find few here. Romans did not settle in Cornwall but their merchants came here for tin, so the Romano-Cornish association was mainly through trade.

Arrival of Christianity

The next arrivals were of great importance, for they led the Cornish people away from paganism to Christianity. These were holy men and women from Wales and Ireland who established their 'cells' near water – rivers, wells or streams. Many of these, previously objects of pagan worship, then became shrines and places of pilgrimage. Today about a hundred holy wells still exist, most of them pleasant places to visit, others looked upon as serving a special purpose – turning the affections of a loved one in the right direction, for example! Cornish churches (many near wells or water) are dedicated to those 'saints' and have names not seen in other English counties, such as St Gluvias, St Probus and St Petroc.

Scones, Jam, Clotted Cream and Strawberries with Afternoon Tea

AD926 that King Athelstan finally conquered the Cornish. A few Anglo-Saxons settled in Cornwall, mostly along the eastern border. Some ventured further and there is evidence of this in the scattering of non-Cornish place names found elsewhere – Wicca at Zennor is a good example.

For centuries, Cornwall was entirely Celtic, but once the Anglo-Saxons had overcome England they turned to the west for further conquests. Here they met fierce resistance from Cornish chiefs or kings. One was Arthur, a Celtic ruler born in the late fifth century AD who led the last great Celtic battle against the Anglo-Saxons. The legends that grew up after his death and the medieval romances associated with his name have so obscured the historical figure that it is now almost impossible to discover the truth about him. By the end of the seventh century the Anglo-Saxons had conquered Devon but it was not till after

From the Normans to the Victorians

The Norman Conquest, however, did bring many changes. King William's custom of rewarding his barons with large estates held good in Cornwall – even to Land's End. The *Domesday Book* must have looked impressive with its accounts of groups of manors belonging to this or that Norman overlord. But many of the so-called manors were little more than small farmsteads or 'trevs' run by perhaps two people as they had been since Celtic times. In many cases, these homesteads are still farmed today – to be found almost hidden in a maze of narrow winding lanes. Here Cornwall

St Ives

has scarcely altered for centuries and those who would like to walk back in time need simply take the latest OS map and explore the narrow lanes of a remote parish. These lead to the very heart of Cornwall.

The castles the Normans built for defence – Launceston, Restormel and Trematon – also served to restore the sense of security the Cornish had lost since the Saxon conflicts. By the mid-twelfth century, Cornwall was Europe's largest supplier of tin, and stannary towns grew up at places where tin was tested. Royal charters for markets and fairs also encouraged trade while the building of numerous collegiate and other churches resulted in a more settled way of life. By 1337, Cornwall was therefore a fitting land for King Edward III to bestow on his heir, the Black Prince.

In the Middle Ages, however, there was less need for defensive castles so the landowners built manors with only a degree of fortification. A good example is Cotehele, overlooking the Tamar, one of Cornwall's most beautiful great houses.

At sea, as on land, Cornwall prospered.

Her sailors and fishermen gained renown at home and abroad. Perhaps one of her proudest occasions was when Fowey sent 47 ships to help the king besiege Calais in 1346. This was nearly twice the number mustered by the City of London.

But sad times lay ahead. When the Reformation came, Cornwall's beautiful churches were stripped and most of her collegiate establishments closed. Men no longer travelled from Europe to study at Glasney Collegiate Church in Penryn and the place, which might have been Cornwall's university, is now remembered in a few scattered remains. The final blow came, however, when Bibles were printed in English – a language that Cornishmen did not want to understand and certainly could not read.

Prosperity returned briefly, however, in the eighteenth and nineteenth centuries when underground mining came into its own. The inventions of great Cornishmen like Richard Trevithick, Michael Loam and Goldsworthy Gurney enabled shafts to be sunk deep into the ground and even under the seabed so

The amazing garden at Lanhydrock

Beach Guide

Golden sands, rocky coves, surf, cliffs, blue sea, bracing wind – everyone wants something different from a beach but Cornwall has all of these if you know where to look. No matter where one is on the peninsula the sea and wonderful beaches are not far away. Everyone will have their favourite and these are just a few suggestions:

Safe bathing beaches

East Looe* and Plaidy, Looe
Readymoney Cove*, Fowey
Porthpean*, St Austell
Gorran Haven, south of Mevagissey
Porthluney Cove (by Caerhays Castle)
Pendower, near Veryan
Gyllyngvase*; Flushing; Swanpool*;
Maenporth*; all at Falmouth
Gunwalloe*, near Helston
Praa Sands*, west of Helston
Marazion*, nr Penzance
Porthcurno*, south of Land's End
Porthgwidden*, St Ives
Porth Joke*, near Newquay
Porth*, Newquay
Treyarnon Bay, Padstow
Summerleaze Beach, Bude
Widemouth Bay (North)*
Widemouth Bay (South)

Surfing beaches

Whitesand Bay, Land's End
Godrevy*, Hayle
Perranporth, south of Newquay
Tolcarne, Newquay
Great Western, Newquay
Fistral*, Newquay
Crooklets*, Bude

Rock pools can be found at:

Hannafore, West Looe
Castle*, nr Gyllyngvase, Falmouth
Godrevy*, Hayle
Widemouth Bay*, Bude

Quieter beaches which may be more difficult to reach:

Towan, nr St Anthony Head
Vaulty, nr Gorran Haven
Prussia Cove and Kenneggy Sands, both at Mount's Bay
Peter's Point (Godrevy), Hayle

* Dogs not allowed from Easter Day to 1 October.

Many beaches have lifeguards in attendance but whether this is the case or not, care should always be taken when bathing. Always keep well away from an estuary. Sea conditions can change rapidly and a system of warning flags is used to advise bathers.

When the red flag is flying bathing is not permitted. Red-over-yellow flags at the water's edge mean bathe between these flags. Black and white flags at the water's edge indicate malibu board and surf craft areas.

that the increasing number of engine houses transformed much of the landscape. Fortunes were made and lost almost overnight but Cornwall faced a major disaster once again when cheap surface tin was imported from Malaya.

This time miners emigrated to look for work. Many settled in Canada, Australia, South Africa, Tasmania and the United States and this often meant that whole families died out and Cornwall's glory faded again.

Cornwall today

But there is much of the phoenix in this land. Its story has always been influenced by the rocks of its landscape and its coast. Granite has been the source of shelter in life and protection in death; of prosperity with tin and copper and more recently, china clay. Some feel that Cornwall's granite stones are only subjects for artists and photographers but scientists with vision have already begun to realise the great potential of this vast treasure store. The first dish antennae ever used for intersatellite communication were built on the firm foundation of granite in the Lizard Peninsula. Once they are across the Tamar motorists are soon aware of a subtle change in the atmosphere of the countryside through which they are driving. This can be noticed as they pass groups of granite farm buildings or cottages often built against the shelter of a hilly slope and it is these 'trevs' or homesteads that reflect the way of life in Cornwall since Celtic times. 'Tre', 'Pol' and 'Pen' are first syllables that appear on many signposts as the road heads west. 'Lan' and 'Men' are other indications that this land is both Celtic and ancient.

The Cornish mining industry, and the prosperity it brought, may have declined almost to nothing, but the distinctive landscape it left behind was recognised in 2006 when UNESCO named the Cornwall and West Devon Mining Landscape as a World Heritage Site, a status on a par with the Taj Mahal and the Pyramids. The industry may have gone, but it still plays an important part in Cornwall's unique appeal.

Throughout the year there is an abundance of entertainment with festivals, plays, music and dance to be seen everywhere. The venues range from the unique Minack Theatre in the west, the solemn Gorsedd ceremony in a different open-air site each year, to local arts centres, National Trust properties and halls in every village.

At any place in Cornwall – town, village or hamlet – visitors will be certain to discover outstanding talent in arts and crafts. It is not only artists who abound but others skilled in weaving, pottery, woodcarving, metalwork, leather work and the creation of stained glass items. The list is endless and fascinating to the tourists whose visits form such an important part of Cornwall's economy.

The Cornish language has its living presence in place names everywhere. Perhaps this is one reason why there is such an increase in the number of people studying it. Celtic associations are to be found across the Continent; place names with a Celtic prefix appear even on maps of Slovenia. There is a selection of Cornish words in the Fact File at the end of this book.

The geography of Cornwall offers 'much in little' for visitors who come for an activity holiday. There is rock and cliff climbing at coastal resorts, while sailing, surfing, windsurfing, diving, canoeing and fishing are also to be found here. Golf, walking and riding can be enjoyed throughout Cornwall too.

Archaeology, painting, visits to the many lovely gardens and various summer workshops are only some of the holiday pastimes that visitors can enjoy. Sample the fresh seafood, locally grown produce and of course a true Cornish pasty accompanied by the local speciality ale

Cornish Language

The Tre-, Pol- and Pen- prefixes to family and place names, which are so typical of Cornwall, also stem from the Iron Age period. For those tribes introduced the Indo-European Celtic language which, as Cornish, is the Brythonic branch. Although it seemed to die as the universally spoken tongue more than two centuries ago, it has now come out of hibernation. This revival, which began at the start of the twentieth century, was inspired by dedicated men like Henry Jenner and Morton Nance. Today the language is studied and spoken by linguists such as a former Bishop of Leicester, the Right Reverend Richard Rutt. It is an examination subject for schoolchildren and has recently become the first language in a number of homes. Many bards are fluent Cornish speakers and at their annual Gorsedd, awards are given for literary compositions in the Cornish tongue. Weddings, baptisms and other church services are also conducted in the language.

Hicks Special Draught. The only difficulty is deciding how to spend the precious time.

And now from the general outline of Cornwall to a closer look at the region. It has been divided into eight areas all with different characteristics – avoiding main roads as far as possible. In this way, it is hoped that visitors will see Cornwall's many facets and so appreciate to the full the variety and individuality of this ancient and beautiful land.

Gardens

The gardens of Cornwall are justly famous and many visitors will wish to include some in their visit. Before embarking on an exploration of the county it may be helpful to note some of the finest.

As the Gulf Stream washes the Cornish coast it is not surprising that subtropical and some tropical species flourish in Cornwall. William and Thomas Lobb were the first plant hunters sent overseas for a commercial firm and although some of their discoveries are not well known, many of the plants they found now thrive in their native Cornwall.

Those interested in such matters should note the William Lobb section of **Fox Rosehill Gardens** in Falmouth.

These and other plant hunters of earlier centuries, good soil, landowners seeking ever more exotic gardens to set off their newly acquired mansions, the influence of the Gulf Stream and long hours of sunshine – all have played their part in making Cornwall the 'garden capital of the world'. This was the description used by Tim Smit, Project Director for the restoration of the **Lost Gardens of Heligan**, surely one of the most remarkable garden events in recent years. The 80 acres (32 hectares) of Heligan, abandoned to nature at the outbreak of the First World War, have been uncovered from the overgrowth of ivy, laurel and bramble and restored as a living museum of nineteenth-century horticulture. Magnificent as Heligan is, it is only one of many lovely gardens, large and small, formal and informal that can be seen in Cornwall throughout the year.

Mild winters lead to an early spring with wonderful displays of camellias, rhododendrons, azaleas and magnolias. Many subtropical species flourish and a number of gardens have special plant collections.

The earliest eighteenth-century landscaped garden in Cornwall can be found at **Mount Edgcumbe Country Park** near Saltash, the only Grade I listed historic garden in the south-west. It is a place of romance, magic and delight with follies, a shell seat and temples. If you like to be quiet, there is peace in the wooded areas and gardens full of flowers. Formal gardens in varying styles, a National Camellia Collection, lovely woodlands and stunning views are all to be found here.

Many of the gardens in Cornwall are on the coast and combine wonderful views with outstanding plant collections. **Caerhays Castle**, overlooking Veryan Bay, was once the home of Mr J C Williams, who gave his name to many species of camellia. The garden still houses many fine rhododendrons, camellias and magnolias. **Trelissick Garden** is lovely in all seasons with rare shrubs and plants, extensive parklands, woods and farmland. The superb views include vistas of the Fal Estuary and Falmouth harbour.

The area around Falmouth boasts several fine gardens. Originally planted by the Fox family, starting in the 1820s, but now cared for by the National Trust, **Glendurgan** is a valley garden running down to the Helford River. There are many rare and exotic plants and fine trees here with particularly lovely magnolias and camellias in the spring. The laurel maze dating from 1833 has been restored.

Another garden running down to the Helford River and originally planted by the Fox family is **Trebah**. Trebah Estate was sold in 1939 and the garden neglected and nearly lost over the next forty years. The Hibbert family bought it in 1981 and began the restoration which is being carried on today by the Trebah Garden Trust. This garden will appeal to plantsmen, artists and families, with special attractions for children. A stream running through gives a home to koi carp and exotic plants and eventually runs out on to the private beach which is open to visitors to the garden for picnics and swimming.

Penjerrick Garden, found on this peninsula too, features ponds in a woodland setting and lovely sea views. In addition to rhododendrons and camellias there are bamboos and tree ferns in this subtropical garden, also originally planted by the Fox family.

There are fewer gardens as the far west is approached but **Trevarno** near Helston should not be missed. This too was nearly a lost garden and has been undergoing an extensive programme of restoration. Many rare shrubs and trees are to be found here together with garden features and a fascinating Gardening Museum. The 98 acres (40 hectares) of park and garden at **Trengwainton** near Penzance were given to the National Trust in 1961 by Lieutenant Colonel Sir Edward Bolitho. It is interesting to learn that today's beauty has been created mainly over the last 50 years with help from three great Cornish gardeners – Mr J C Williams of Caerhays, Mr P D Williams of Lanarth and Canon Boscawen of Ludgvan. The walled gardens contain many tender plants which cannot be grown in the open anywhere else in Britain, and although Trengwainton is always lovely it is perhaps only fair to say that it is at its best in the spring.

On Cornwall's north coast there are few gardens of note, an indication of the

Other Gardens

The following list will also reward the visitor

See p.3 for key to symbols

Antony House and Garden

(National Trust)
Torpoint, PL11 2QA
☎ (01752) 812191
Formal garden at Antony House featuring National Collection of Hemerocallis (day lilies). Open: 1.30–5.30pm Tue–Thu and Bank Hol Mon, Apr–Oct; plus Sun in Jun, Jul and Aug.

Ⓟ ♿ ♟

Antony Woodland Garden

Torpoint, PL11 2QA
☎ (01752) 812364
Natural woods and woodland garden including National Collection of Camellia Japonica. Open: 11am–5.30pm daily except Mon and Fri (but open bank holidays), Mar–Oct.

Ⓟ ♿ ♟ <16 Free

Bosvigo

Truro, TR1 3NH
☎ (01872) 275774
www.bosvigo.com
3 acres (1.2 hectares), mainly herbaceous, best in summer. Open: Mar–end-Sep, We–Fri, 11am–6pm.

Burncoose Nurseries and Garden

Gwennap, TR16 6BJ
☎ (01209) 860316
www.burncoose.co.uk
30 acre (12 hectare) woodland garden alongside working nursery. Part of the Caerhays Estate. Open: Daily, all year (except Christmas).

Ⓟ ♿ ♟ <14

Carwinion

Mawnan Smith, Nr Falmouth, TR11 5JA
☎ (01326) 250258
www.carwinion.co.uk
Valley garden with reference collection of bamboos, unusual exotics and The Towan Camellia collection. Specialist nursery within the garden. Open: Daily all year, 10am–5.30pm.

Cotehele

(National Trust)
Nr Saltash, PL12 6TA
☎ (01579) 351346
Valley garden dropping steeply to River Tamar; much of interest throughout the year. Open: 10.30am–dusk, daily all year.

Ⓟ ♿ ♟ ☂ 🐕

different conditions that prevail there. However, there are three further properties which should not be missed on a gardening tour of Cornwall: Lanhydrock, Pencarrow and Prideaux Place. Of these only **Prideaux Place** is near the north coast. It lies on the outskirts of Padstow and offers newly restored areas of garden overlooking the Camel estuary, a formal sunken garden and a deer park.

Lanhydrock, owned by the National Trust, is situated just south of Bodmin. Dating from 1857, the formal garden includes a unique circular herbaceous garden and there is a stunning collection of magnolias, rhododendrons and camellias. With its many rare trees and shrubs this garden offers fine colours right through to autumn.

To the north-west of Bodmin lies

Creed House and Gardens

Grampound, TR2 4SL

☎ (01872) 530372

5 acres (2 hectares) including alpine and herbaceous gardens. Woodland walks. Open: Daily Feb to Oct, 10am–5.30pm.

Fox Rosehill Gardens

Melvill Road, Falmouth, TR11 4DB

☎ (01872) 224377

2 acre (0.8 hectare) garden, many exotic trees and shrubs. Free admission. Open: Daily, all year round, dawn to dusk.

Japanese Garden

St Mawgan Village, TR8 4ET

☎ (01637) 860116

www.thebonsainursery.com

Water and Zen gardens. Bonsai nursery. Open: Daily, all year, 10am–6pm (5.30 in winter).

Lamorran House Gardens

St Mawes, TR2 5BZ

☎ (01326) 270800

4 acres (1.6 hectares). Water gardens. Palms and subtropical plants. Open: Apr–Sep, Wed, Fri, 10am–5pm.

Pine Lodge Gardens and Nursery

A390 east of St Austell, PL25 3RQ

☎ (01726) 73500

www.pinelodgegardens.co.uk

30-acre garden with over 6,000 plants, many rare and unusual. Open: daily, all year, 10am–6pm.

Ⓟ ♿ (In part) 🚻 <5–16 🌂

Tresco Abbey Gardens

Tresco, Isles of Scilly

☎ (01720) 424105 www.tresco.co.uk

A delightful place where an immense number of varied plants are grown. In the spring, arum lilies, camellias and azaleas begin the main flowering season. By the old pump, the Pump Garden leads to the ruins of the old priory, inside which are graves dating from the Dissolution of 1539 to 1820. Pebble Gardens, Neptune's Steps and terraces are other delights in the Tresco Abbey Gardens. Open: 10am–4pm daily all year. Shop shut in winter.

♿ 🚻 <16 Free

Trewithen

Grampound Road, Truro, TR2 4DD

☎ (01726) 883647

www.trewithengardens.co.uk

Open: 10am–4.30pm Mon to Sat, Mar to Sep; plus Sun Mar to May. Rare trees and shrubs. Plants for sale.

♿ 🚻 <16 🐕

Cornwall Garden Festivals

☎ (01872) 322900

www.gardensofcornwall.com

Each year, from 1 Mar to 31 May, the Cornwall Festival of Spring Gardens takes place. Many gardens, not to be seen at other times, open specially for the Festival. The Cornwall Gardens Harvest Festival takes place from 5 Sept to 31 Oct. Full details of gardens participating and opening times may be obtained from the Cornwall Tourist Board, who also publish a handy *Cornwall Gardens Guide*, which includes a map.

Pencarrow, with its formal and woodland gardens laid out in the 1840s by Sir William Molesworth Bt. Over 650 species of rhododendrons can be seen here along with an internationally known specimen conifer collection. A huge granite rockery, formal Italian and American gardens, a lake and woodland walks will all delight the visitor.

Any account of Cornwall's gardens must include the phenomenal success, **The Eden Project**, just outside St Austell. Built in a former china clay pit, this twenty-first-century garden with its eye-catching 'biomes' was attracting visitors even before it opened. Now fully established, it explores both the history of mankind's dependence on plants and how we need each other to ensure our future survival.

1. In & around Saltash

On the Cornwall side of the River Tamar lies Saltash, and visitors generally arrive either by way of the Tamar Bridge or train via Plymouth. The name is a reminder of days when Romans, Anglo-Saxons and Normans used this 'passage' or 'esse' which was the meeting place of salt and fresh water. King John granted Saltash borough status and in 1270 the lords of nearby Trematon Castle owned the ferry. Soon the town held jurisdiction over the tidal reaches of both Tamar and Lynher, extending their claims on oysterage and anchorage till they controlled all tolls as far as the Calstock salmon weirs.

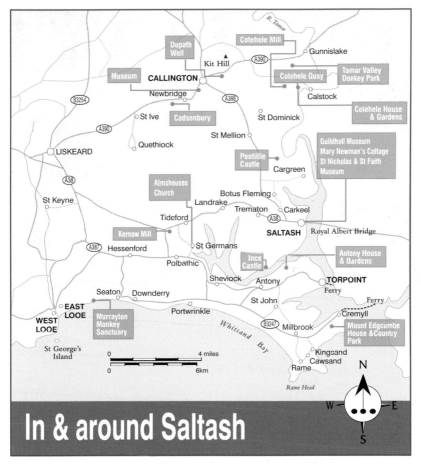

In & around Saltash

By 1752, traders and fishermen rebelled against the Saltash monopoly and refused to pay their tolls. The burgesses applied to parliament for confirmation of rights but were strongly opposed by James Tillie of Pentillie Castle. As he owned Halton Quay, which was a little way upriver, and several trading vessels, he was considerably affected. He gained support from the governor of Plymouth and eventually won the lawsuit brought against him. Finally he instructed the ships' masters to pay only 1s, an act that made them free for ever 'from all encroachments of the unjust and iniquitous Saltashers.'

The town no longer sent members to parliament after 1832 and consequently declined in political importance. It kept its reputation as a great 'nursery' for sailors, however, but even more celebrated were its fisherwomen who

Brunel's Triumph

On 6 May 1859, the Prince Consort opened Isambard Brunel's masterpiece, **the Royal Albert Bridge**, which had taken two years to build. That was the day when the Great Western Railway carried the first holidaymakers into Cornwall. Still an impressive sight today, the handsome structure was the first to be built in a unique combination of suspension and conventional style. It was the great engineer's last work but he was too ill to attend the ceremony. However, although he was a dying man, Brunel had an open truck made especially for him and by the end of that same month travelled in quiet triumph over the Tamar to Cornwall.

frequently beat all comers in the four-oared gig races at various regattas.

This new influx of visitors gave the town of **Saltash** a brief revival but when the Admiralty bought the oyster rights in 1901, its long maritime history came to an end. Today it is a friendly shopping centre with a scattering of historic buildings to remind people of its past and although the bypass in its tunnel gives it the appearance of standing alone, it is proud to know that it is still very much a part of Cornwall.

On the corner of Fore Street and Station Road is the present fine **Guild-hall**. Over the centuries it has been market hall and town hall, now re-splendent inside and out – worthy of its name. The latter building was added at the end of the eighteenth century

and since 1890 has been called the Guildhall. The upstairs assembly hall is used for every kind of meeting from politics to popular markets as well as the mayor-choosing ceremony. The mayoral insignia has a special local interest in that it incorporates three silver oars with maceheads. Almost opposite is the **Heritage Museum**.

Closely associated with the Guildhall is the **church of St Nicholas and St Faith**. A chapel of ease until 1881, it dates from about 1225 (although the tower is earlier), while the clock – probably 1720 – is a rarity in a Cornish church (possibly because the hardness of granite made it awkward to incorporate such a feature). No visitor can overlook the sumptuous memorial to three shipwrecked Drew brothers and that, with a wall tablet, is only one of the interesting items to be found here. The tablet reads: 'This chapple was repaired in the Mayoralty of Matthew Veale, Gent., anno 1689'.

Mary Newman was born here in a small Tudor house on the steep slope of Culver Street, overlooking the Tamar. She would have seen many fine ships anchored in the river, but did she ever dream that one day she would be the wife of Sir Francis Drake?

To celebrate the millennium a **Town Trail** was created that links the main historical features. By the riverside is a striking mural on the wall of the Union Inn, showing characters from the town's past. A bust of Brunel keeps a watchful eye on his bridge from beside the new bridge over the bypass. The new bridge is decorated with mosaics created by local schoolchildren with the assistance of artist Emma Spring.

North of Saltash

Much of Saltash's history has been linked with the villages along the banks of the Tamar. On the A388 Callington road lies **Carkeel** where an industrial estate offers work in Cornwall for local people who do not want to go to Plymouth. A right-hand turn in the centre of the village – so narrow that it can easily be missed – leads to tree-lined lanes winding round to **Botus Fleming**, set high above the Tamar. A memorial to the Symons family is in the church – an unusual wooden reredos which shows the agricultural nature of the area, with its vines, corn and various fruits.

There is also a memorial brass to one of Cornwall's great engineers, Michael Loam, inventor of the 'man-engine' that saved so many lives in Cornish mines. Born in west Cornwall, he died at Moditonham House where only 12 years before, the Prince of Orange had surrendered Pendennis and Plymouth Castles. During World War II, Moditonham suffered considerable bomb damage, but was lovingly restored by the haematologist, Dr John O'Brien.

Cargreen and Halton Quay

Lanes to **Cargreen** are warm with meadowsweet and bright with purple vetch in summer. Linger beside the quiet quay – a pleasant place to watch the small craft. Walkers may prefer to make a bypass to **Landulph church** where Theodore Palaeologus was buried. He was descended from the last of the Greek Christian emperors and has achieved later fame as an ancestor of Prince Philip who, with the Queen, visited the tomb in 1962.

A handful of cottages hug Cargreen quay. The village has a lively yacht club and it is hard to realise that this was once Cornwall's Covent Garden. Market gardeners from all over the valley brought their produce here to be ferried across to Devon. Now only sailing boats and birds make the crossing – a walk beside the Tamar at low tide reveals its beauty. It is little wonder that this riverside area is popular with both birdwatchers and naturalists while a marked increase in the number of nurserymen seems to indicate a revival in a former trade.

Motorists climb gently away from Cargreen, past Coombe Lane, where wool used to be collected from local farmers en route to a mill at Liskeard. The turning to the right, after the church, rises high above the valley and ferny lanes give way to open views. **Pentillie Castle** (not open to the public, but available for hire for conferences and special events), overlooking a wooded sweep of the river, can be seen on the right. It was built in 1698 by James Pentillie, a steward to the Coryton family of Cornwall's Newton Ferrers. When Pentillie's great-niece married a Coryton in 1810, William Wilkins, who designed London's National Gallery, planned the alterations. Further work was carried out after 1965 and by 1970 the castle was almost the same as the original. Granite pillars from Kit Hill make the front look impressive while a statue of James Pentillie in the centre of the courtyard seems to register approval.

Beyond this, narrow lanes climb

Kit Hill

Kit Hill is an outlying eminence of granite, the summit of Hingston Down where King Egbert defeated Britons and Danes in AD835. The Duchy of Cornwall preserved the 85-foot (26m) stack at the summit and it remains a mining monument to the workers who won tin over so many centuries and who, with Devon men, held their Stannary Parliaments there. In 1985 the Duchy gave Kit Hill to the people of Cornwall to celebrate the birth of Prince William.

On a clear day the views extend to Dartmoor's Hessary Tor 12 miles (20km) away, the Eddystone Lighthouse (23 miles/37km) and west to Bodmin Moor and Roughtor (15 miles/24km). There are old mine workings among the heather and many people, choosing their weather, enjoy a whole day here. A circular walk is waymarked by granite posts and riders may follow a horse trail. It is an excellent spot for kite flying and birdwatching or maybe just a lazy picnic.

then dip into the strangely-named Mount Ararat woods before dropping steeply to the peace of **Halton Quay**. The Pentillie fleet ferried Hingston Down granite from here to Devon in the eighteenth century and cargoes of local fruit and flowers downriver. Since the quay closed in 1926, bird lovers and fishermen have taken over so that the chapel of St Dominick beside the water is once again a place of quiet.

From here, even narrower lanes lead up past Chapel Farm to the village of **St Dominick,** home of the intriguingly named **Who'd Have Thought It Inn** where a warm welcome awaits visitors. Between the inn and Cotehele there is the one remaining cherry orchard of the many which used to supply markets all over the country.

Cotehele

In the next valley lie the mill and riverside buildings of **Cotehele** – the manor on the hill overlooking the Tamar. This romantic medieval house, now a National Trust property and one of the least altered in the country, was built between 1485 and 1627 and constructed around three courts on the foundations of an earlier dwelling. The furniture, tapestries and armour have always been where they are today, but if you wish to make a close inspection of the pictures and textiles, avoid dull days early or late in the season, as certain rooms have no electric light. The valley garden has a restored medieval dovecote and on the walk through the woods to the quay is Richard Edgcumbe's chapel, built by the warring knight as a thanks offering for his survival after declaring against the Crown in 1403.

Cotehele is not a place to hurry away from. The whole area is ideal for a day's pleasure with walks, birdwatching and sometimes salmon fishing to watch. Picnic where you will, have refreshments in the old barn or by the river and marvel at the craftsmanship of *Shamrock* and the skill of those who restored her. She is the last surviving stone-carrying Tamar barge and a grand old lady who still makes occasional

Above: Cotehele

Right: The Shamrock, preserved at Cotehele Quay

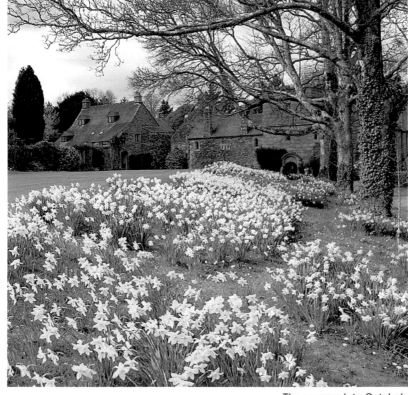

The approach to Cotehele

voyages on the river. **Cotehele Quay** on the Tamar, with its eighteenth and nineteenth-century buildings, houses an outstation of the National Maritime Museum and an art and craft gallery. The former public house at Cotehele Quay, the Edgcumbe Arms, is now a café and is also open to people not visiting Cotehele House. There is a signposted walk from here to **Cotehele Mill**, which now grinds flour that is on sale to visitors. Here there are exhibitions of old tools displayed in the blacksmith's forge, carpenter's, saddler's and wheelwright's shops.

During summer months a regular passenger ferry service operates between Calstock and Cotehele giving the opportunity for a delightful excursion travelling one way by boat and returning via the riverside footpath. Motorists have to follow a more narrow ferny way to the attractive village of **Calstock** – another quiet place now but once a busy shipyard. The handsome railway viaduct brought trains to the village but destruction to its shipping. Today pleasure boats make pleasant pictures as they sail past the place where James Goss built the *Garlandstone* which was Britain's last ketch. Most river and fishing ports have always held regattas; Calstock's, which are as famous as those of Saltash, have recently been revived.

Gunnislake

Gunnislake village climbs to an even steeper slope than Saltash and the road to the New Bridge calls for low gear and

Car Drives

Saltash to Seaton via Torpoint

West of Saltash take the Polbathic road on the B3249 out of St Germans and drive along the A374 towards Sheviock and Torpoint. The river views are delightful and at Sheviock Wood there are picnic areas and well-signed walks. Carry on to Antony where you could stop at the house for a picnic visit but then carry on through to St John village along minor roads, some steep. Join the B3247 in the direction of Portwrinkle, Downderry and Seaton. The coastal views are superb. Turning inland at Seaton a beautiful wooded drive goes to quiet Hessenford and joins the A387 Polbathic road to St Germans and eventually Saltash.

Saltash to Calstock and Kit Hill

Six miles (10km) to the north of Saltash the road from Calstock Station rises out of the valley and very steeply to Norris Green. Now meander along the lanes through Metherell and Harrowbarrow, noting the converted East Cornwall Silver Smelter, to join the A390. Soon after the left turn at that junction take the right-hand B3257 and make your way past historic Hingston Down to Kit Hill Country Park with extensive views. Here is opportune for a picnic before following the B3257 to Kelly Bray when it joins the A388 to nearby Callington and the return to Saltash.

good brakes. Before stagecoaches demanded roads and not muddy byways, the approaching paths to the river went straight down the cliff side – a daunting gradient even on horseback. Piers Edgcumbe of Cotehele built this Tamar bridge in 1520 and in 1644 Sir Richard Grenville did his utmost to defend it against the Roundheads. It was then the chief pass into Cornwall, but Sir Richard's efforts were unfortunately in vain. At this point, the Tamar 'tastes' the tide and as maritime trading interests cease, it is appropriate to turn inland again.

Following the A390 westwards you will come to the **Tamar Valley Donkey Park** at St Ann's Chapel, a popular attraction for children with its cuddly animals, donkey rides, woodland walks and play area. The A390 Callington road runs at the foot of **Kit Hill** but make time to leave it and find the B3257 that takes you to the lane leading to the top (see box on p.22).

Callington to St Mellion

Before entering Callington, take a minor road on the left signposted 'St Mellion'. A short way down, another lane leads to **Dupath Well**, a handsomely covered spring, the largest of its kind in Cornwall. When the canons of St Germans acquired the property, it included 'Theu Path' and they probably had the protective building erected over the holy place. It remained in their possession until the Dissolution. The name is interesting as it is thought to mean 'The Palm of God' in old Cornish: 'Theu' changing to 'Dew' (God) and 'Path' which is a corruption of 'Palf' (palm of

hand); and it then became Dupath as we know it today. Fortunately it was saved from complete disintegration by a rector of South Hill and is now managed by the Cornwall Heritage Trust.

The quiet town of **Callington** was once the centre of a thriving wool industry and possibly it was originally Killiwic where King Arthur had a palace. Pause to visit the **Heritage Centre**, unusually housed in the cemetery, and then drive along the short main street, to see a little lane beside the church. This was Tillie Street (now reduced to one cottage), the birthplace of John Knill, St Ives' well-known and controversial mayor who will be mentioned again later on.

The Liskeard A390 dips down to picturesque **Newbridge**. At this point the River Lynher was spanned by an ancient construction dating from 1478 and the cluster of cottages is typical of a Cornish 'trev' or homestead. The early settlement, however, was once high above on **Cadsonbury**, a prehistoric fort now owned by the National Trust. It is well worth stopping to walk up to it and enjoy the views down the lovely wooded valley.

St Ive ('Eve') hamlet sits clean and fresh beside the busy road from Callington to Liskeard. The church is somewhat unusual as it is a Knights Templar foundation, dating back to 1180. There is more, too, of interest in the compact little village of **Quethiock** (Gwithick) which so many visitors do not know about. Take the narrow lane just opposite the slate-hung Butcher's Arms on the A390 and follow its twists and turns down to the church, content in the protection of the picturesque cottages guarding its history.

The church is one that lovers of brass memorials should not miss. A fine example here is one crafted in 1471 for Roger Kyngdon, his wife and their 16 children. If the church is locked there is a list of keyholders' names on the porch. Look out, too, for the Maids' House before you leave. It was built in a new style of architecture not long after 1633 when a charity of poor spinsters was established. Today this remote parish of twisting lanes and secluded farmhouses leads a busy life of its own and one of the highlights is an agricultural show held in mid-July. Here the standards are good and everyone is made welcome.

From Quethiock to **St Mellion**, the lanes dip and curve in almost impossible configurations, but in high summer they are cool and delightful. It matters little whether you find the clapper bridge at Bramble Wood or take the way to Pilla-tonmill and climb out of the deep valley

Antony House in springtime

from there – both roads are rarely used. Squire Coryton of Pentillie probably originated the Cherry-Pie Feast in the nineteenth-century, inviting local school children to a cherry pie and cream tea on the lawns of his castle. Swings were set up in the 200-year-old lime trees bordering the 1-mile (1.6km) long drive from the road. Everyone enjoyed this event and it was sad when it stopped in 1937. It has, however, now been revived and takes place in mid-July at St Mellion Rectory.

St Mellion has another, though very different, interesting point to note. It was the birthplace of John Trevisa (1412), a Cornishman who was eager to promote the use of English. He translated the entire Bible from Latin to English but in so doing was one of the indirect causes of the eventual decline of his native tongue. Today, this village's claim to fame is as one of the UK's leading golf and leisure resorts. The championship course,

designed by Jack Nicklaus, caters for all handicaps.

The drive round Saltash covers about 44 miles (71km) but the time cannot be assessed so closely as it would depend on how long the stops were and how deep the investigations into such items as the Kyngdon brasses and the manorial watermill at Cotehele.

South of Saltash

The countryside which lies south of Saltash has quite different attractions from those of the Tamarside villages. A glance at the map shows that this area can be explored in two parts, but only by coming back along the same road. The information in the rest of the chapter covers the Torpoint–Rame peninsula.

Trematon

Take the road from Saltash where it dips to **Forder** away from the mother church, St Stephen's. After 2 miles (3km) from the town centre there is instant countryside with Trematon Castle outlined on the far hill. In the valley, mill buildings and a cluster of old Tudor cottages huddle together watching the traffic climb sharply to the lodge gates of Trematon.

Those who prefer may walk the riverside way and perhaps see the train lumbering slowly round from Saltash after carefully negotiating Brunel's Royal Albert Bridge – the engineering triumph of its time. Today, the high granite shafts and unusual tubular arches give it a strange look, but since its opening in 1859 it has been efficient and safe, the first considerations for a railway bridge.

Train passengers, walkers and motorists all enjoy their brief sight of **Trematon Castle** with its romantic shape silhouetted against the sky. Possibly the most extensive in Cornwall, it has a well-preserved keep which is said to be one of the most beautiful examples of the Norman period. Sited 1 mile (1.6km) south-west of Saltash, it was built either by Earl Mortain or the Valletorts, but is now privately owned. It passed into Duchy hands in the fourteenth century and later figured in a particularly distressing incident when Sir Richard and Lady Grenville were captured by treachery. Beyond the castle, where a road descends to the riverside chapel, a stumpy wayside cross marks the important part once played by this now out-of-the-way place.

Viscount Boyd of Merton owns **Ince Castle** which stands beside the Lynher. It is situated 5 miles (8km) south-west of Saltash and can be reached at the A38 Stoketon Cross junction which is signed Trematon, Trahan. If you are fortunate enough to be in Cornwall when the grounds are open you can not only wander through ornamental woods, but see the shell house and dovecote. Tea is also available on these occasions.

The architecture resembles that of a French château but the date of construction is probably early seventeenth century. It is believed that at one time the Killigrew owner kept four wives, one in each of the square towers – a picturesque story that matches the building.

St Germans

There is no way for motorists across the Lynher, but the short distance along the A38 to **Tideford** is not unpleasant. This roadside village takes its name from the River Tiddy, quietly flowing down from the high moors of Caradon until it meets the salt water here. Tideford is still frequently spoken of as Tiddyford.

The riverside walk is a pleasant way to reach **St Germans** but motorists have to turn left onto the B3249 to travel the 3 miles (5km) to the historic but now sleepy village of picturesque cottages and flower-filled gardens. At the slope into the village notice Sir William Moyle's almshouses. Built in 1538, they were skilfully reconditioned in 1967 at the instigation of the National Association of Almshouses. Driving through this peaceful place today it is hard to believe that St Germans was once a 'rotten borough' which sent two MPs to Westminster.

St Germans Church

The handsome parish church, formerly Cornwall's ancient cathedral, is away from the traffic, almost hidden among trees. Consecrated in 1261, the building had formerly been of importance as an Augustinian priory and had been the seat of the Cornish bishopric from the close of the tenth to the early eleventh century. Its great west doorway, Cornwall's finest, is a powerful example of Norman architecture and is constructed of elvan stone from Tartan Down near Landrake, while the church's spacious and lofty interior contains numerous features of interest. Since 1974 the diocese has had a bishop suffragan at St Germans.

The Tudor gateway close by leads to **Port Eliot** where the Eliot family have lived for 400 years. It is probably Cornwall's largest private house. Sir Thomas Elyot bought it from Cardinal Wolsey when he was selling monastery lands for Henry VIII. He was known as an astute businessman, a skilled ambassador and the first person to compile an English dictionary. But perhaps the best-remembered member of this family was Sir John, an MP and vice-admiral of Devon. Unfortunately his interest in maritime affairs proved his undoing as it led him to the Tower and an untimely death. He believed that the king's Bills of Tonnage and Poundage would impose too great a strain on the mercantile community – a group of people with whom he worked closely. His strong feelings in the matter forced him to oppose the new proposals but he paid dearly for doing so.

In 1762, Sir Humphry Repton redesigned the gardens and Sir John Soane made certain architectural alterations which included the addition of a splendid round room, some 40 feet (12m) in diameter. The present Earl of St Germans administers all 6,000 acres (2,430 hectares) and hosts a literary festival each July, while the house and gardens are normally open to the public from March to mid-June.

The view upriver through the thirteen arches of the railway viaduct is a fine sight on a sunny day when seen from St Germans' quay and it is difficult to leave it for the turn to **Polbathic** nearby on the B3249. But once through that village and on to the A374 in the direction of Torpoint there are pleasures of a different kind. A whole stretch of woodland walks and picnic areas beside the St Germans (or Lynher) River await those wanting to explore the paths to the small village of **Sheviock** and the area around Antony House. It is a part of Cornwall which has been called a miniature kingdom.

Antony and Torpoint

Antony House was built in the early eighteenth century and is the most distinguished classic house in Cornwall, with its central block of silver-grey Pentewan stone, and wings of red brick joined to the house by colonnades. Now owned by the National Trust, it is still very much the home of the Carew Poles, a fact that adds warmth to its elegance. The 250 acres (101 hectares) of grounds slope gently to the Lynher – both the contents and the house are well worth a visit. An interesting and unusual feature of this property is the Bath Pond House – 800 yards (400m) from the main building and open only by appointment. It was built in 1789 and has recently been repaired.

Antony church, which was re-dedicated in 1259, is a building which should be visited. It is famous for an early brass of Lady Margery Arundell (1420) which is acknowledged to be the most spectacular in the whole of Cornwall.

Torpoint may seem a mere mass of uninteresting buildings after the elegance of Antony House but it does have its own features to offer the visitor. In 1691, William of Orange's order for the construction of a naval dockyard across the Tamar at Cattewater was followed by such great activity that Torpoint came into existence. Accord-ing to the comments made by Daniel Defoe, not only did the workmen need homes but the entire operation needed 'yards, dry docks, launches and con-veniences of all kinds for building and repairing of ships'!

The small part of that undertaking that is left today is now private housing and business units, near the Torpoint ferry. This has always been an impor-tant crossing and in 1793 the ferryman was obliged to keep three boats for pedestrians as well as a horse boat. His charge for everyone was one penny for the journey there and back. Today, pedestrians travel free from Torpoint but wheeled vehicles have to pay a small charge. Many people use this novel way of commuting to work or school in Plymouth.

Instead of retracing the route use the slightly narrower road out of Torpoint which goes past the shore station of HMS *Raleigh* before cutting sharply across to **St John**. This is a quiet place of contrast, a delightful medieval cluster of narrow lanes in a fold of hills and cottages that match their surroundings. At low tide, the best way is by the road across the ford at the head of St John's Lake. This is a place to tempt birdwatch-ers to linger.

Millbrook to Rame Head

Walk or drive on to the little town of **Millbrook** but take care to negotiate the narrow, winding lane slowly as you pass fine Georgian houses side by side with humble but picturesque cottages.

The road to **Cremyll** goes first through Maker Heights in a steep climb and looks down on Millbrook

The Copley Arms at Hessenford

From here walk into **Mount Edgcumbe Country Park**, 800 acres (324 hectares) of superb parkland, bordered by 10 miles (16km) of magnificent coastline that are open all the year from dawn to dusk with no admission charge. This park is now restored to its Edwardian splendour and the plans have been laid out with such skill that one day is scarcely long enough to encompass everything. From April to September the **Mount Edgcumbe House** and formal gardens, former home of the Earls of Edgcumbe, are open and there are refreshments in the Orangery of the Italian Gardens, with follies and a handsome conservatory not far away.

as a toy town. Then, from the top of the world, the B3247 slides down to quiet Cremyll, a small group of houses at the crossing to Plymouth named the Passage of Crimela in charters of the thirteenth century. Here is a place that retains its individuality and its old houses while the small, modern, passenger ferry crosses regularly to Plymouth. Watching Drake Island and the shipping in Plymouth Sound keeps Cremyll busy all the year round and there is no objection when visitors park and join in their quiet game.

Walk from here to **Rame Head** – about 2 miles (4km), skirting the Park and continuing through Maker parish, Cawsand and Kingsand. There are splendid distant views of Plymouth

Pay a visit to Pele and Pablo at The Monkey Sanctuary near Seaton

Flower Boat Ritual

If a visit to Cornwall coincides with the early May bank holiday stay at Millbrook, near Saltash, because you will be able to see and take part in a centuries-old festival. At some time in mid-morning the Flower Boat ritual begins. A procession of dancers and singers make their way through the narrow ways of Millbrook, Kingsand and Cawsand, stopping at chosen houses and inns en route. This takes up most of the day, for they carry with them a decorated boat – not a large one but one that is beautified with all the available spring flowers.

The finale is an exciting one and when it grows dark, the boat is launched on the water, usually to the accompaniment of fireworks. This ceremony has been known in Millbrook since the fourteenth century but is thought to be pagan in origin.

The story told by an old inhabitant of Millbrook is an interesting one as it has a particular bearing on the name given to the boat – *The Black Prince*. It is well known that the son and heir of King Edward III had a great fondness for Trematon Castle, near Saltash, and whenever possible, stayed there for long periods of relaxation.

He had to reach this haven by way of the ferry crossing over the Tamar from Plymouth to Saltash and apparently had a number of craft to choose from. All those in use, however, were showing signs of wear and, according to the ideas of one of the inhabitants, were completely unsuitable to carry royalty. As a result, the Millbrook ferry disappeared one night from its usual moorings only to be seen a short distance away at Saltash. This outrageous theft caused everyone in Millbrook to declare 'war' on their neighbours and, armed with staves and pitchforks, they marched on the offenders.

It was fortunate for all concerned that the Black Prince himself was there at the time for, had he not intervened, there would doubtless have been bloodshed and quite possibly a considerable loss of life. However, when he decreed that the people of Millbrook should have a new ferry – paid for by him – the tension disappeared and the militant villagers returned home quietly. Their gratitude, though, was not a simple matter of a few words of thanks for they then decided that future generations should know about the generosity and kindness of the king's son. So it was agreed that the May Day Flower Boat would always bear his name, The Black Prince.

An event that probably has the same roots takes place at St Ives on Good Friday – but here it is a less spectacular occasion when model yachts are brought out and sailed. And Cornwall has another story in the same vein, told of the interment of King Geraint. He is said to have been buried in a great tumulus at Carne, above the eastern side of Gerrans Bay on the Roseland Peninsula, after being rowed across the bay in a golden boat with silver oars. This particular royal leader was one of King Arthur's captains in his fifth-century battles against the Saxons and his story sounds more than legend in the light of a discovery at Broighter Bay in Ireland's County Derry. This was nothing less than a gold boat with silver oars.

Breakwater and then across to Heybrook Bay from Penlee Point before arriving at the headland.

Motorists have to climb again to Maker Heights before dropping down narrow lanes to Kingsand and Cawsand Bay at the water's edge. Till 1835 this area did not belong to Cornwall and there is still Boundary Cottage standing as a reminder.

Kingsand is very much a sailor's place – the streets twist like an anchor rope in a storm and the cottages cling to the cliff as seamen to the mast in rough weather. Trying to avoid leaning walls and jutting corners, most drivers miss Halfway House and find themselves in and out of **Cawsand** before they realise it. The *Bellerophon* set out from here under the command of Penryn-born Captain Maitland, who eventually captured Napoleon after his escape from Elba.

Once away from the villages, the road to **Rame** seems to continue for ever and, with land falling away on both sides, gives the strange sensation of driving straight into the sea. But there is a car park beyond the church for those who want to explore the headland. Wander down to the ancient **chapel of St Michael** and wonder at the piety and dedication of the hermits who lived here and kept a light burning to warn ships of the dangerous rocks below. By 1488, however, men were paid for this and they received 4d for 'Keeping of ye bekying'.

Seaton

From here, the road to Seaton keeps close to the cliff top – as does the coastal path and, given fine weather, the views

---

Hero of Trafalgar

Few people know that a young sailor of Cawsand made history at the Battle of Trafalgar. Lieutenant John Pollard, born in 1784, was a midshipman aboard the *Victory* when Nelson was shot. He later became known as 'Nelson's Avenger' because he shot and killed the enemy sailor who fatally wounded Admiral Nelson.

---

are superb. **Portwrinkle's** golf course on the cliffs is almost the only sign of life till **Downderry's** hotels appear. Beyond is **Seaton** – a place of sands and summer enjoyment for those who like crowds. A nearby attraction is the world's first protected breeding colony of Amazon woolly monkeys, the **Monkey Sanctuary**.

The wooded valley which leads from Seaton to **Hessenford** is quiet and magical for lovers of birds and trees. The beauty continues beyond Hessenford until the narrow winding lane opens onto the A38 just east of Tideford, from where it is a short journey back to Saltash.

Before the end of this 40-mile (64km) drive make the short detour into **Landrake**. It was the birthplace of Robert Jeffrye, who went to London in the time of Charles Stuart. There he won fame and fortune and became Lord Mayor. He founded the Shoreditch almshouses which are now a museum but did not forget his native village. As well as establishing its first school, Robert Jeffrye also left money to help Landrake's poor. The villagers remembered his generosity and the hall now bears the name of their benefactor.

Walks

Tamar Valley

4½ miles (7km) • occasionally steep • 2 hours

Map: OS 1:25,000 Explorer Series 108: Lower Tamar Valley and Plymouth

This walk can be enjoyed from Calstock on the Tamar Valley Line, one of the prettiest country branch railway lines, running for 14 miles (22.5km) between Plymouth, Bere Ferrers and Bere Alston in Devon and Calstock and Gunnislake in Cornwall.

Take the train to Calstock Station. Walk downhill to the quay, retrace your steps up the hill for 50 yards (50m) beyond the back of the Tamar Inn and fork left along the lane by the river, under the viaduct which was completed in 1907. The road passes in front of a lime kiln with its characteristic arches and then under a bridge which formerly carried an inclined railway. The path turns away from the river at the former Danescombe Valley Hotel (now a private residence) and branches uphill to the right about 50 yards (50m) further on. Continue up the Danescombe Valley; when the path reaches the road, bear left downhill to the hamlet of Danescombe. Just before the cottages at the bottom of the hill, turn sharp left down a track which takes the walker back along this attractive valley, past the disused and now converted buildings of the Cotehele Consols, a former copper and arsenic mine. As the path nears the valley end the route turns right, uphill to Cotehele House. From the house take the road down to Cotehele Quay. Turn back upstream just inside the woods, and follow the path past the chapel to rejoin the route leading back to Danescombe. At the bottom by the marsh turn right for the hotel and follow the riverside road back to Calstock and up to the station.

Rame Head

10 miles (16km) approx • moderate • 4 hours

Map: OS 1:25,000 Explorer Series 108: Lower Tamar Valley and Plymouth

The coastline of Mount Edgcumbe offers wide views over Plymouth Sound and out into the English Channel where the Eddystone Lighthouse can be seen 10 miles (16km) offshore. Some of the most spectacular scenery of the South Cornwall Coastal Footpath may be viewed along the route from Cawsand to Penlee Point. It continues to another point at Rame Head where St Michael's Chapel is situated. Walkers may then continue along Whitsand Bay to the caravan site where cars may be parked or return to their original starting point enjoying the views in the opposite direction.

Places to Visit

Saltash

Saltash Heritage Museum

17 Lower Fore Street, PL12 6JQ
☎ (01752) 848466
www.saltash-heritage.org.uk
Exhibits depicting history of the area.
Open: 2–4pm Wed. 10am–4pm Sat, Apr
to Nov. Jul, Aug and Sep also open
10.30am–12.30pm and 2–4pm Thu and
Fri. 10am–4pm Bank Holiday Mon
 ℗ (Nearby) ♿ ♟(Free) ☔

Town Heritage Trail

Links historic buildings with the
waterside where there are superb views
and colourful murals depicting local
history. Route is outlined on information
boards around the town.

Mary Newman's Cottage

48 Culver Road
☎ (01752) 843796
Little low Tudor house believed to be
the birthplace of Sir Francis Drake's first
wife. Open: summer months, Wed 2–
4pm and Sat and Sun 12noon–4pm.

Elliott's Store

Lower Fore Street
☎ (01579) 384381
Family-run (1902–73) grocery store
preserved as a museum.
Open: Easter–Oct 2–4pm Wed. 10am–
12 noon Sat.
♿ ♟<18 ☔

North of Saltash

Cotehele

(National Trust)
St Dominick, PL12 6TA
☎ (01579) 351346
A romantic medieval house of grey
granite, built 1485–1627. One of the
best-preserved examples of a squire's
house and for centuries home of the
Edgcumbes. Beautifully furnished with
original tapestries, needlework and
armour. Gardens, and art and craft
gallery at the quay.Open: 11am–4.30pm
daily from mid-Mar–end-Oct. House not
open on Fri. Garden open all year.
 ℗ ♿ ♟ ☔ 🐕(Woods Only)

Cotehele Mill

In woodland near Cotehele house
☎ (01579) 350606
Open: 11am–5pm (4.30pm in Oct)
daily, mid-Mar–Oct. Open every day
Jul and Aug.
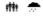 ♟ ☔ 🐕(Woods Only)

Cotehele Museum & Shamrock

The Quay, Cotehele
☎ (01579) 350830
Branch of National Maritime Museum.
Open: 10am–6pm daily Apr to Oct.
Small admission charge in honesty
box.

Tamar Passenger Ferry

Calstock to Cotehele and return.
☎ (01822) 833331
Runs from early Apr to late Sep.
Depends on tides: see
www.calstockferry.co.uk for details

Places to Visit

Kit Hill

2 miles (3km) NE of Callington beside the A390

☎ (01579) 370030

An outlying eminence of granite, the summit of Hingston Down where King Egbert defeated Britons and Danes in AD835.

Dupath Holy Well

About 1 mile (1.6km) from Callington between the A388 and A390. The largest well building in Cornwall.

Callington Heritage Centre

Liskeard Road, PL177HA

☎ (01579) 382697 or 382119

www.callingtonheritage.org.uk

Open: 10am–4pm Fri, Sat, Sun and Bank Holidays, Apr to Oct.

Tamar Valley Donkey Park

St Ann's Chapel, Gunnislake PL18 9HW

☎ (01822) 834072

www.donkeypark.com

Donkeys and other animals. Adventure playground. Café. Open: 10am–5pm daily, Easter to end-sept; Oct Thur–Sun and Half Term. Nov to Easter, weekends and school holidays only, 10.30am–4.30pm.

 Ⓟ ♿ ♟<2 Free ☁

South of Saltash

St Germans

The church was the seat of the Cornish bishopric from the close of the tenth to the early eleventh century. Its great feature is the Norman west door. The almshouses were built by Sir William Moyle in 1538. They were restored in 1967 through the National Association of Almshouses.

Port Eliot

St Germans, PL12 5ND

☎ 01503 230211

www.porteliot.co.uk

Home of the Eliot family, and probably Cornwall's largest private house. Open: 1 Mar to 30 Jun, 2–6pm (last admissions to house at 5pm).

Ⓟ ♿

Antony House

(National Trust)

Torpoint, Cornwall PL11 2QA

About 15 miles (24km) from Saltash

☎ (01752) 812191

A Carew Pole property since the fifteenth century, but this house was built in the early eighteenth century. The Bath Pond House can be seen on written application to the Property Manager. Extensive grounds slope to the River Lynher. Fine paintings are to be seen in the house.

Open: 1pm–5pm Tue, Wed and Thur. In Jun, Jul and Aug these times apply to Sun also. Open all Bank Holiday Mon.

 Ⓟ ♿ (In parts) ♟(Family Ticket) ☁

Antony Church

Rededicated in 1259, this church is mainly remarkable for its spectacular early brass to Lady Margery Arundell (1420).

Mount Edgcumbe House & Country Park

Cremyll, Torpoint, PL10 1HZ
☎ (01752) 822236
www.mountedgcumbe.gov.uk
Originally built in 1547–53 for Sir Richard Edgcumbe but destroyed in 1941 blitz. Rebuilt 1960. Home of the present earl and open again since 1988. Open: 11am–4.30pm daily except Fri and Sat, from Apr to Sep.
Country Park: 800 acres (324 hectares) of parkland on magnificent coastline are open, all year, free admission.
Ⓟ(Nearby) ♿ ♟♟♟<15

Rame Head

Stretching into the sea beyond Rame church (St Germans) with expansive views east and west.

Ince Castle Gardens & Grounds

5 miles (8km) South-west of Saltash: from A38 at Stoketon Cross take turn signed Trematon, Trahan.
☎ (01752) 842672
5 acres (2 hectares) with lawns and ornamental woods; shell house and dovecote. Open: on occasional Sun in spring and summer.

The Monkey Sanctuary

Nr Looe, PL13 INZ
☎ (01503) 262532
www.monkeysanctuary.org
Amazon woolly monkeys seen in garden and tree setting. Daily talks.
Open: 11.00am–4.30pm, Sun to Thu, Easter to the end of Sep and autumn half-term. Open Fri and Sat for Easter and May Bank Holidays.
Ⓟ ♿ (Limited/No Guide dogs) ♟♟♟<15

Kernow Mill

Trerulefoot, junction of A374 and A38.
☎ (01752) 851898
Working watermill housing craft centre with associated shopping complex and coffee shop. See the Cornish National Tartan. Open: 9.30am–5.30pm Mon to Sat, 11am–5pm Sun all year.

What to do if it rains

Saltash
Heritage Museum

Cotehele
Cotehele Manor
Cotehele Museum
Cotehele Mill
Cotehele Gallery

Torpoint
Antony House

Callington
Heritage Centre

St Germans
St Germans Church

Kingsand
Mount Edgcumbe House

Seaton
The Monkey Sanctuary

Trerulefoot
Kernow Mill

Gunnislake
Donkey Park (indoor play barn)

2. Liskeard to St Austell

Between Saltash and Lostwithiel lies Liskeard, once a prosperous town trading in tin and wool. Minerals from Caradon Hill brought a charter and subsequent wealth in 1240. Stannary privileges followed in 1307, when Liskeard became a coinage town. Later the flourishing wool trade added to the prosperity. The increasing demand for tin in the eighteenth and nineteenth centuries led to the opening of the Liskeard–Looe Canal, which carried ore and stone supplies to the coast for export. Webb's Hotel in the Parade was built in 1833 as a coaching inn. It has now been restored to reflect its listed building status and is in use again, though not as a hotel.

Left: The Fishing village of Polperro

Opposite page: Eden Project

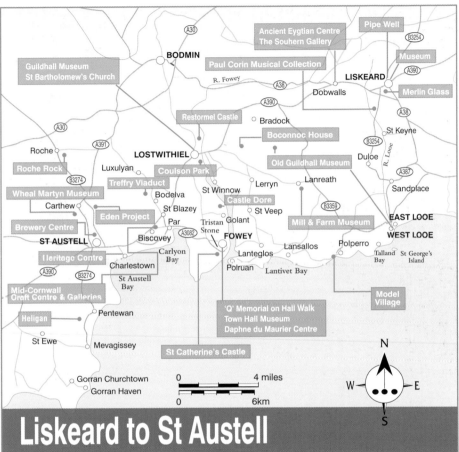

Pipe Well

Ancient Eygtian Centre
The Souhern Gallery

A30

BODMIN

Guildhall Museum
St Bartholomew's Church

Paul Corin Musical Collection

R. Fowey

A38

B3254

Museum

A390

LISKEARD

Dobwalls

Merlin Glass

A390

A38

Restormel Castle

Bradock

St Keyne

A30

Boconnoc House

B3254

Duloe

R. Looe

Roche

A391

LOSTWITHIEL

Luxulyan

Roche Rock

Coulson Park

Old Guildhall Museum

A387

B3274

Treffry Viaduct

St Winnow

Lerryn

Lanreath

Sandplace

Wheal Martyn Museum

Bodelva

Castle Dore

B3359

Carthew

St Blazey

St Veep

EAST LOOE

Eden Project

Par

Tristan
Stone

Golant

Mill & Farm Museum

WEST LOOE

Brewery Centre

Biscovey

A3082

FOWEY

Lansallos

Polperro

ST AUSTELL

Carlyon
Bay

Lanteglos

Talland St George's
Bay   Island

Heritage Centre

Charlestown

Polruan

Lantivet Bay

A390

B3274

St Austell
Bay

Model
Village

Mid-Cornwall
Craft Centre & Galleries

Pentewan

'Q' Memorial on Hall Walk
Town Hall Museum
Daphne du Maurier Centre

Heligan

St Ewe

Mevagissey

St Catherine's Castle

N

Gorran Churchtown
Gorran Haven

0   4 miles

W   E

0   6km

S

Liskeard to St Austell

The **Church of St Martin** is the second largest in Cornwall, its history dating from the mid–thirteenth century. **Stuart House** in Barras Street is attractively slate-hung, as it must have been when King Charles stayed there (1644–5). Restored in the early 1990s it is now a local arts and heritage centre used for exhibitions and recitals. Traces of the old town linger in and around Well Lane and Market Street where the former Guildhall stands. Next door is Foresters Hall, home of the **Museum** and the TIC. The award–winning building has been beautifully restored with a slate-hung front and was opened in 2002 by Prince Charles. The **Pipe Well**, originally late sixteenth century, was restored in the early nineteenth century.

Leave the town by the B3254 Looe road, first stopping in Station Road at the old industrial mill that houses **Merlin Glass**. This is the Pavlova Mill which once made gloves exclusively for Pavlova, the dancer.

Around Liskeard: Looe and Polperro

Beyond Liskeard station follow the sign for St Keyne's Well but turn aside en route and see the **Paul Corin Magnificent Music Machines**. This modern wonder is housed in the family mill deep among lush, narrow lanes beside the River Looe. Spend an hour listening to instruments ranging in size from the musical box which began it all to a 20-foot (6m) high Belgian dance hall organ; an amazing collection to find anywhere but especially in the heart of the Cornish countryside, beside the old Liskeard–Looe Canal.

Two winding ways lead the motorist to Cornwall's most famous well, the longer passing through the hill-high village and church of **St Keyne**. Set below road level where three lanes meet, this beautifully restored well can easily be missed. In the past, newly-married couples always hurried here after their wedding ceremony, believing that the first to drink the water would rule the household.

The lane dips steeply but turn right at Badham's Farm and then take the right fork. There is no signpost here – the map says it leads through Windsor Wood – but visitors who drive along here in spring may be forgiven for thinking that the direction should be 'To Fairyland'. A grass track in the centre of the road tempts cows from their pasture and motorists must wait while they test the quality of the roadway grass, following as the animals make their leisurely way towards the next gate. Ducks, too, use this wooded valley lane and so peaceful is this place that rejoining the B3254 to Duloe seems like finding an unexpected motorway.

In fact, the village of **Duloe** is quiet and attractive, specialising in cottages with country names – fun to list them – but having its own memorable past. The church of St Cuby and St Leonard has a well-preserved thirteenth-century tower and interesting associations. Sign-posted from the main road is a circle of eight stones, 38 feet (12m) in diameter, restored in the nineteenth century.

The B3254 joins the A387 at **Sandplace.** The church of St Wenna at Sandplace, behind a rhododendron screen, is noteworthy for the fine slate memorial to Walter Coode, his wife and their twelve children. The children are represented allegorically as fruits growing out of vines trailing behind their kneeling parents. Also, the walls appear to lean outwards and a tower pinnacle seems to bend out of true. Was the church built like this or was it the scene of devil-worship as portrayed in *Bewnans Meriasek*, one of the Cornish miracle plays? Translated, the lines run:

To my God Jove in his face
I will happily offer a cat:
There can be no better mouser.
I bought it from Morval.

The place where the devil was anointed.

A meal at **Polraen Country House Hotel** would doubtless dispel all witch-craft as would a walk beside the River Looe. Here are birds to watch and old wooden hulks to pass by, left on the mud to rot because ill-luck is believed to come to those who break them up. Looe's golf course is the other side of Morval at Widegates. From there, the B3253 joins the A387 just outside East Looe. The town of **Looe** had a charter as early as 1237 and much of its past is recorded in the **Old Guildhall Museum and Gaol**.

Shark fishing, good sailing and swimming can be enjoyed from the little beach by the banjo pier (so-called because of its shape), which is seen at its best from the cliffs of West Looe. The original bridge was built in 1411, magnificent with thirteen arches and a hermitage chapel, but the present one has only seven arches and was widened in 1960.

Turn left over the bridge, pass the fourteenth-century **St Nicholas church** and go up the steep road that leads to Looe Bay. Beyond the rocks lies St George's Island, once a Celtic monastery. It is possible to walk along the coastal path into Polperro from here, but motorists must return to the church and turn left past the 500-year-old inn, The Jolly Sailor.

This narrow, exciting lane to **Talland Bay**, past the Measured Nautical Mile, cannot be hurried. **St Tallan church** stands proudly at the top of a precipitous hill leading to the beach with its strange pink-grey rocks and grey stony sand. Climb again to **Sclerder Abbey**, a gracious, peaceful Carmelite monastery near the A387, built by the Trelawny family.

Close by is **Trelawne**, an ancient house dating back to before the Conquest and once the home of the famous Royalist Bishop Trelawny who inspired the Reverend R S Hawker of Morwenstow to compose *With a Good Sword and a Trusty Hand*, now almost Cornwall's national song. Trelawne was also the place where one of the first therapeutic cures was effected in the early eighteenth century by Dr Jonathan Couch, grandfather of the author Sir Arthur Quiller-Couch. He advised a neurotic young man staying there after a period abroad to study the habits of the Trelawne rooks daily for a year. The detailed observations he made so absorbed the patient that after 12 months he was completely and permanently cured. The grounds of Trelawne Manor are now the location of a family holiday park.

Much of the coast between Talland Bay and Polperro is National Trust property and fine views tend to offset the rough path. Motorists can enter **Polperro** by the A387, but the roads were made for horses and a large car park outside the village marks the place where you must leave your car and continue the journey on foot or by electric buggy. In the summer horsebus rides are available too, a pleasant mode of travel.

Small though the village is, there is a great deal to see – the unspoiled harbour sheltering behind its sturdy wall, the Three Pilchards Inn where fishermen once had their catch weighed and Couch House where Jonathan Couch was born. But what was Polperro really like before visitors came? The answer is in the **Model Village**, a replica built by local craftsmen and guaranteed to set the imagination working. The history of smuggling in the area is on display at the **Heritage Museum of**

View from the sea of the fishing village of Polperro

Smuggling and Fishing.

Narrow lanes lead to **Lansallos** with its fine church high above Lantivet Bay. Unusual are the 34 carved bench ends, most of them early sixteenth century. Here, too, are some fine slate-carved memorials; and its greatest treasure, Bishop Trelawny's pastoral staff.

To the north, the quiet hamlet of **Lanreath** seems steeped in history – the name recalling a medieval monastery

Right: Safe moorings on the river at Looe
Below: Looe

and the handsome Court Barton, once the Tudor manor home of the Grylls family. Perhaps the famous 400-year-old Punch Bowl Inn holds the village secrets for it has been, in turn, court house, coaching inn and smugglers' distribution house. Artist Augustus John stayed there: the unusual inn-sign outside is a reminder of his visit. It is much sought after by holidaymakers who follow Egon Ronay and Ashley Courtenay recommendations. An added attraction is the fine collection of horse brasses.

On the way back to Liskeard is the **Giant's Hedge**, near to where the Lanreath road joins the B3359 (GR SX178574). This prehistoric earthwork was built by the Devil according to legend. After about 2 miles (3.2km), turn right for **Herodsfoot** – walk across country if preferred – and find the delights of Forestry Commission nature trails in **Deerpark Wood**. In this other world there are holiday cabins deep in the valley overlooking ponds once serving an old gunpowder mill. Sailing, riding and fishing are available for holidaymakers on this self-catering site. To see it at bluebell time is to under-

Selected Car Drive

Lostwithiel – Bodinnick Ferry – Luxulyan – St Austell

The first right turn from Lostwithiel on the A390 towards Liskeard will lead you to St Winnow, the waterside church used in the first filming of the Poldark novels. Look across the Fowey River and remember the story of Tristan and Iseult – it happened round here. Return about one and a half miles (2.4km) then drive right to Lerryn – a place of peace and beauty. The Great Wood where this river joins the Fowey was the inspiration for Kenneth Grahame's The Wind in the Willows. He wrote much of it while staying with his friend Sir Arthur Quiller-Couch at Fowey. Now drive uphill and down dale to St Veep, Lanteglos Highway and down to Bodinnick Ferry. Daphne du Maurier lived beside that ferry for many years. On the other side, the B3269 goes past the Long Stone (which once marked the burial place of Tristan and Iseult) and joins the A3082 and the A390 for St Blazey Church.

Leave St Blazey Church on the A390 and drive about 800 yards (800m) towards Lostwithiel. Take the left turn to Luxulyan and then the right turn which leads to the glory of the Luxulyan Valley. This beauty spot lies under the Treffry viaduct cum aqueduct built by Joseph Treffry. Follow the Luxulyan sign and enjoy that lovely place. Any of the roads from here will take you through the dreamland of Cornwall's china clay country to Roche. A hermit built a chapel on the top of Roche Rock and lived there for many years. The B3274 in the village will take you through Stenalees to the A391 and St Austell.

stand why it won the Civic Trust Award the year after it opened. (☎ 0845 130 8223. www.forestholidays.co.uk)

At nearby **Dobwalls**, on the A38 to Liskeard, the former Dobwalls Adventure Park is being redeveloped as an eco-friendly retreat of woodland lodges, scheduled to open in 2009. Also under development on the site is a major new arts centre, but in the meantime the **Southern Gallery**, famous for its wildlife art, remains open and continues to host a variety of events and exhibitions.

A quite different attraction at Dobwalls is **The Ancient Egyptian Centre** featuring the Edwards and Beilby collection based on the Egyptian tomb finds of the 1930s. Laid out as a 1930s museum, the collection gives visitors an insight into the life of those times.

Lostwithiel & Around

Along the A390 from Liskeard, some 11 miles (17.7km) to the west, is **Lostwithiel**; a quiet, welcoming place, and a good touring centre where picturesque ruins and an old church are daily reminders of its importance in history from 1100 when the Normans built **Restormel Castle**. Today the proud shell is well cared for by English Heritage and visitors may picnic here, high above the Looe valley.

The **Guildhall** in Fore Street was built in 1740 and now houses a free museum displaying linenfold panelling, town insignia and photocopies of the charters. Free parking in the town gives ample opportunity to explore everything – a pottery, antiques, a

good bookshop and restaurants. If your pleasure is fishing, birdwatching, walking or simply enjoying the peace of the country, it is all here. Booklets are available to tell you where Coulson Park is and the best way to reach the Duchy Nurseries and an interesting woodland nature trail.

About 4 miles (6.4km) eastwards along the A390, at West Taphouse, a right-hand turn to **Braddock** dips and climbs to the church, a delight in spring but solitary beside woods where historians remember the Civil War. The Battle of Braddock Downs took place in 1643 when Cornishmen put the Parliamentarians to rout and took 1,200 prisoners. Today members of the Cornish branch of the Sealed Knot re-enact this for their own pleasure and that of many onlookers.

Road and woodland paths, rich in wildlife, pass close to eighteenth-century **Boconnoc**, a house whose 600 years of history include a brawling duellist, Thomas 'Diamond' Pitt (cousin to Britain's youngest Prime Minister), and a modern event, when camera crews filmed part of Winston Graham's *Poldark* series for television. The house and garden are occasionally open to the public on Sundays in April and May. The 'No Thoroughfare' road leads to the church – the key may be borrowed from the nearby estate office. It is small but interesting – more a house chapel, but nevertheless with royal arms, a wall plaque sent to a number of Cornish churches by King Charles II as a token of his thanks for the support of the congregation during the Civil War.

Narrow tree-lined lanes lead to the backwaters of **Couch's Mill** and

Walks

Fowey

10 miles (16km) approx • moderate • 5 hours
Map: OS 1:25,000 Explorer Series 107: St Austell & Liskeard
From Readymoney Cove at Fowey the Coastal Footpath is clearly signed all the way round to Polkerris. It is a very fine walk with views which include Fowey harbour and St Austell Bay. The castle at St Catherine's Point and the outstanding Daymark at Gribbin Head would interest artists and photographers. The way to Polkerris village and refreshment is down through woods. A rest there will enable you to carry on along the upper path which crosses fields to a gate at a road that is part of the Saints' Way back to Fowey. Turn right on that and soon you reach Tregaminion Church, built in 1816 by the Rashleigh family. The Saints' Way is signposted beside the churchyard gate and from there the Cornish symbols should guide you safely back to Readymoney Cove via the Domesday Manor of Trenant.

Hall Walk, Polruan

4 miles (6.4km) • fairly tough going • 3 hours
Map: OS 1:25,000 Explorer Series 107: St Austell & Liskeard
Park in the long stay car park near Caffa Mill Pill in Fowey. Walk to the ferry and cross to Bodinnick. As you disembark from the ferry look up to the right of the slipway where you will see 'Ferryside', the house where Daphne du Maurier once lived. Walk up the road, past the Old Ferry Inn, continue past St John's Church and follow the sign on the right marked 'Hall Walk Polruan'. Continue along the path as it turns east into Pont Pill, cross the cattle grid and follow the path down through the wood. At the bottom turn right, following the sign to Polruan. Descend into the village, turn sharp right down steps, then left at the bottom. The ferry from Polruan Quay runs frequently and will deposit you at Whitehouse Point (Town Quay in winter). Turn back along the Esplanade into Fowey, turn left up Lostwithiel Street and then immediately right along a narrow passage to the church of St Fimbarrus and Place Mansion. Downhill from the church takes you to the water's edge at Town Quay. From here follow the waterside roads back to the car park.

Looe Valley Line

Map: OS 1:25,000 Explorer Series 107: St Austell & Liskeard
This delightful, scenic line from Liskeard to Looe offers the possibility of several fairly gentle walks without the need for a car. There are park and ride facilities at Liskeard station and the tickets offer excellent value. Trains run regularly all year though there are slightly fewer in the winter. A free information pack available from the Discovery Centre at Looe gives details of 10 walks based on the Looe Valley Line. Each station along the line gives access to interesting places such as St Keyne's well and the village of Duloe with its stone circle and church. Finally from Looe there are magnificent walks along the coast in either direction, as far as Polperro to the west or Seaton to the east for the really energetic, with bus services from both places for the return to Looe.

Lerryn, picturesque villages beside the River Lerryn. There are wooded paths on both sides but the one north of Lerryn's sixteenth-century bridge goes to Great Wood and looks seawards along the Fowey. It became the Wild Wood in Kenneth Grahame's *Wind in the Willows*. He discovered it during one of his visits to his friend Sir Arthur Quiller-Couch at Fowey. The path reaches the point jutting into the Fowey and turns upstream to St Winnow, a lovely, lonely churchtown. The church has one of Cornwall's oldest surviving rood screens, Tudor bench ends and fine windows.

From Lerryn, the road, which is very narrow and between high hedges in places, climbs steeply to St Veep church before dipping to Penpoll. Walkers may follow the river and climb to Haye Farm where National Trust land looks across the River Fowey to Golant. **Lanteglos Highway** was rightly named as it runs on the spine of this largely unspoilt parish. Before taking the steep road to the Bodinnick ferry for Fowey, make a detour to **Lantivet Bay**. Park the car and walk to Pencarrow Head, where there are fine views east to Rame and west to the Lizard.

In & around Fowey

Polruan is quaint and very old but has had to give way to Fowey which now claims the first place. In 1066 it was probably the main centre of trade and population at the estuary mouth, but Fowey had a powerful feudal patron to grant and procure necessary privileges and this led, over the centuries,

The bridge in the village of Lerryn

Restormel Castle

The estuary of the River Fowey at Fowey

History of Lostwithiel

The town was granted a charter of rights and port status in 1190, and a timber bridge was built to mark a crossing point which had existed since the Bronze Age. This was replaced in the fifteenth century by one of granite, still in use today. By 1272, the increasing tin trade required an assay point, so Lostwithiel's Duchy Parliament building incorporated the Stannary Court, the Hall of Exchequer and Exchange as well as the prison. The remains are still to be seen – of particular interest is the cobbled way below a fine stone arch on Fore Street, used by pack animals laden with wool or tin from Bodmin en route for the Stannary Court.

In 1337 Edward III proclaimed his seven-year-old son and heir Duke of Cornwall. When he came of age he was a just overlord, much concerned with his domain of Restormel and Lostwithiel, which he administered wisely and well and the town prospered with tin, tanning and wool trading. In 1644 Roundhead forces overcame the loyal inhabitants and desecrated St Bartholomew's church in a manner clearly described by the diarist Symonds:

'In contempt of Christianity, Religion and the Church they brought a horse to the font, and there, with their kind of ceremonies, did, as they called it, christen the horse and called him by the name of Charles in contempt of His Sacred Majesty.'

It is said, however, that when Essex's men later surrendered, the people of Lostwithiel took their revenge.

But this parish church, dedicated to the patron saint of tanners more than 300 years earlier, overcame its indignities. It is still there now for visitors to admire its unusual features, especially the spire of Breton design added at the same time as the font in the fourteenth century.

to Polruan's decline.

On the Fowey side of the river, coasters can be seen loading their cargoes of china clay – a different scene from the days when the Fowey Gallants sailed away to the siege of Calais in 47 men-o'-war.

June is a good time to visit **Fowey**. There is room then to wander at leisure through the narrow streets, which twist and turn till one would think that even a cat might lose its way. Every bend brings the past to life again: the **Town Hall Museum**, probably guild chapel then a prison, displays other treasures, the Ship Inn remembers its days as the Rashleighs' town house (one of the many properties belonging to the family who had been prominent in most Cornish matters for at least 400 years) and even the Fowey Gallants have their name perpetuated by one of the yacht clubs. Fowey seems to offer everything: walks, swimming, sailing, fishing and a wealth of archaeological material close by.

Hall Walk

The 'Q' memorial (a memorial to author Sir Arthur Quiller-Couch, 1892–1944) stands looking downriver at Hall Walk, a National Trust property, covering 40 acres (16 hectares) of cliff. A path leaves the road above the Bodinnick ferry, between the houses. It winds along the side of the hill with splendid views across to Fowey and Polruan. At the 'Q' memorial it turns east up a small creek which is crossed by a footbridge at Pont. Thereafter, the path climbs the hill before continuing to Polruan where the Polruan ferry (for foot passengers only) brings you back to Fowey.

You can park at **Bodinnick ferry** (Fowey side) or you may prefer the larger Fowey car park which is also much closer when you leave the Polruan ferry. This is a delightful walk which should not be missed. The paths are best early in the year when they are bright with a variety of spring flowers. Today Bodinnick ferry carries vehicles but it has been important since the fourteenth century, forming part of the south coast route from Cremyll.

Fowey has literary links with Kenneth Grahame, Leo Walmsley and Sir Arthur Quiller-Couch but probably the most well-known is the author of *Rebecca*. The **Daphne du Maurier Literary Centre** offers an insight into her life and work and has features on other local authors. The Daphne du Maurier Festival of Literature and Art is held in May each year in the village.

The coastal path from the town leads past **St Catherine's Castle** – now ruined, but once one of a chain of south coast forts built by Henry VIII. **Gribbin Head** is memorable with its huge red and white daymark built in 1842, providing an unmistakable warning for shipping. **Menabilly**, set in the woods behind Polridmouth Cove, and formerly the home of the Rashleigh family, was used as the fictional setting for three of Daphne du Maurier's novels including *The King's General* and *Rebecca*. It is not open to the public, but two of the cottages on the estate are available as holiday lets.

Beside the B3269 out of Fowey is the Longstone or the **Tristan Stone**. Its sixth-century inscription reads *Drustanus Fili Cunomorus* which is translated as 'Tristan, Son of Cunomorus' (the name by which King Mark was known). Historians now think that Castle Dore, the earthwork a short way off, was the site of Mark's castle, but facts have not yet verified this and students of Beroul's *Roman de Tristan* continue to puzzle over it.

At Castle Dore, a lane to the right leads to **Golant**, the quiet, sheltered waterside village with more Tristan associations. King Mark and Queen Iseult probably worshipped in the church of St Sampson, as it was near Castle and Lantyan, both connected with them. Today, these names denote farms or similar buildings but the area of **Lantyan Wood** still keeps its secrets of the lovers, silent and watchful beside the River Fowey.

If you park by the riverside to explore

The King of Prussia Inn, Fowey, named after a local man with that nickname

Above: Light shining through a stained-glass window, Fowey

Left: Fowey

Below: The Bodinnick ferry, Fowey. The house to the right was the home of Daphne du Maurier

the village or visit the adjacent pub, remember the river is tidal. Tristan's duel with Morholt possibly took place there, watched, we are told, by Cornish and Irish on opposite banks, looking like 'holmgang' (invading Northmen). Is that perhaps how the Holmbush Inn on the A390 at St Austell came by its name?

St Austell

ECC International, the giant producer of Cornwall's kaolin, has its headquarters at **St Austell** in the heart of the 'mountains'. It is a pleasant place with old buildings, quietly enjoying the life of a medieval village in the churchtown away from the new shopping precinct and rumbling white clay lorries. Modern interests thrive at the **Arts Centre and Theatre**. The B3273

leads to **Pentewan** where stone from Duchy quarries was in great demand for rebuilding churches during the fifteenth century.

William Cookworthy's discovery of china clay at Carloggas in the eighteenth century brought new life to this little port. A harbour was built and wagons took their new loads down to waiting ships until tin-streaming soil and china-clay slurry caused the silting which killed it as a port. Today caravans rest on dunes beside the once prosperous harbour. The latter still contains water despite having no access to the sea these days and is well worth going to see.

Take the Gorran Haven turning on the B3273 to find the **Lost Gardens of Heligan**, a unique collection of gardens within a garden and a joy that no visitor should miss. Formerly the seat

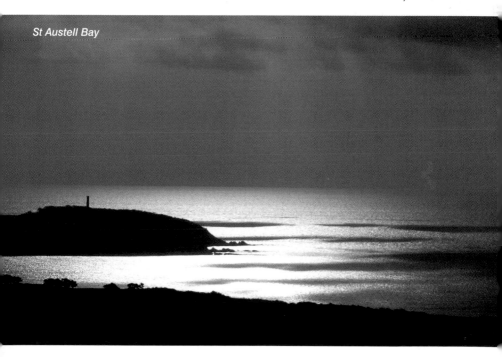
St Austell Bay

Traditional Food

With so much to see and do in Cornwall, healthy appetites are very much the order of the day. What better then, than to sample the many traditional foods that can be found here. Seafood is wonderful from crabs, lobsters and shellfish to mackerel, pilchard and sole. Every harbour and cove will have at least a couple of boats bringing in fresh catches and specialist fish restaurants abound.

According to some people, the only food associated with Cornwall is a pasty. That is certainly not correct but few know that there can be at least ten fillings to this healthy 'convenience food', the traditional one being best steak, potato, onion, salt and pepper. Originally baked for the miners to take to the depths of the mine for their midday meal, the pasty could have a savoury filling at one end and a sweet one at the other. The crimped edge was there for the miner to hold his pasty with his arsenic-stained hands. The crust was then discarded to appease the mine spirits, if you take the romantic view, or to avoid arsenic poisoning if you are a realist. Whichever way you look at it a delicious all-in-one meal was invented that is still enjoyed today.

Others, however, are eager to taste the clotted or scalded creams, made differently from cream produced in Devonshire. Queen Elizabeth I learnt about it from her sailors but probably did not know that it had to be eaten with splits – not scones. Not often met is a teatime delicacy named thunder and lightning: splits spread with golden syrup and topped with clotted cream. The word clotted comes down from 'clout', a thick piece of leather. So the cream served with your tea should be like a thick crust (or leather), not a semi-solid cream.

Dairy produce used to be plentiful in Cornwall and junket was a popular dessert. In traditional households today junket topped with cream is one of the May Day customs still observed. Look too for Cornish cheeses, made on the farm.

According to local tradition saffron cake should only be eaten indoors. Rarely found outside Cornwall, this is a yeast bun delicately flavoured and coloured with saffron, obtained from the stigmas of the crocus flower. Heavy or 'hevva' cake is quite different, made from flour, sugar, butter/lard, currants and cream and scored in a fish-net pattern.

Star-Gazey pie must surely be unique. Pilchards are baked in a pastry crust with the heads projecting from a hole in the centre. Traditionally this pie is eaten on 23 December in Mousehole to celebrate Tom Bawcock's Eve.

Beer drinkers will appreciate Hicks Special Draught, a traditional cask beer from St Austell Brewery. The Brewery was established in 1851 by Walter Hicks and the family name continues to this day in this excellent beer.

Good eating places are everywhere, offering local Cornish produce – new potatoes, fresh vegetables, seafood, strawberries, cream and meat – to give the best of both old and new regional specialities. Make the next visit a food tasting one and add to it by drinking local beer, Cornish mead or wine from one of the vineries.

of the Tremayne family, the estate had been buried for years under unchecked growth of ivy and bramble, laurels and fallen timber. It has largely been revealed and restored in the manner of the great nineteenth-century horticulturists.

A minimum of half a day will be needed to explore all the features and stout footwear is advised if a walk around the 'Lost Valley', the 'Jungle' and the farmland are to be included. There are 80 acres (32 hectares) of pleasure grounds, which include a large collection of rare subtropical shrubs, walled gardens, grotto, kitchen garden (smell the seaweed used as fertiliser) and ravine fernery. Heligan is more than just a lovely garden, however. The aim is to explore man's relationship with the land, the food we eat and the modern environment; to look back at how things were done in the past and look forward to how they may be done in the future.

Farmland adjacent to the gardens has been acquired and there is a herd of cattle and a flock of sheep. Visitors will have the opportunity to learn about the yearly cycle on the farm and taste the results in the restaurant where Heligan beef and lamb are served along with fresh fruit and vegetables from the gardens. A more recent addition is a farm shop in the car park selling local produce. All of this is achieved with consideration for the local wildlife, trees and plants and by managing the land in the most environmentally sustainable way.

Returning towards St Austell, a footpath goes part of the way to Black Head but joins the road where the cliff becomes too sheer for walkers. Views across St Austell Bay to Gribbin Head have a touch of mystery about them for the water shimmers with the constant presence of china clay slurry and the effects are strange and ethereal. Little wonder that Cornwall's famous historian, Dr A L Rowse, chose to live at Trenarren on Gerrans Point.

Charles Rashleigh began to develop the port of **Charlestown** for tin in 1791 and it continued to prosper with the growth of the china clay industry. Then J T Treffry of Fowey constructed the port of Par which rivalled both Pentewan and Charlestown, and it is still the main china clay port for smaller vessels. Today the Charlestown **Shipwreck and Heritage Centre** recreates the heyday of this once thriving port with consummate skill. The little beach is a pleasant place for fishing, bathing and sailing. Only 800 yards (800m) along the cliff path is **Carlyon Bay** the site of a proposed new holiday development called The Beach which has proven hugely controversial.

Excellent recreational facilities are available nearby at the **Polkyth Recreation Centre**, which offers activities from swimming to squash.

There is little of architectural interest in this area, but up the hill past Ralph Allen's birthplace on the A390 is the **Mid-Cornwall Galleries** at **Biscovey**. First-class goods for sale are well displayed and it is also possible to take part in art and craft courses. It is well worth a visit.

At the top of the hill notice the Four Lords Inn – probably a unique name. The sign is attractive, depicting Elizabethan nobles in costume. The build-

First Postal System

Beside the A390, Ralph Allen was born in a cottage on the road towards St Blazey and a small plaque on the wall marks the place. Not many visitors to Cornwall realise that well over a hundred years before Rowland Hill invented the Penny Post, Allen had devised the first real postal system in the country.

ing marks the common meeting point of estates belonging to Edgcumbe, Rasleigh, Carlyon and Treffry – all local landowners and hence the name. Continue down the next hill to **St Blazey**. The church dedicated to St Blaize stands slightly above the Cornish Arms at the bottom of that same hill. St Blaize is not a Cornish saint's name, but in medieval times wool was as important as tin in this area and he is the patron saint of wool-combers in the town that was once a port. Beside the Pack Horse Inn, a short distance away, a solid building standing four square to the

road was the wool market. Now neither tin nor wool finds its way here, and by the traffic lights only the Shell House remains as an interesting reminder of St Blazey's great days as a port.

Par is its replacement perhaps, the port reclaimed from the sea by Joseph Austen who became Joseph Treffry. His finest achievement was the massive viaduct across the Luxulyan Valley, unbelievably beautiful in bluebell time. A left-hand turn before the St Blazey level crossing, then first right, leads to one of Cornwall's loveliest places, with walks through the woods in plenty.

The figurehead at the Rashleigh Arms, Polkerris

Charlestown

The silted-up harbour of Pentewan

Even the viaduct does not detract from Luxulyan's beauty and standing proud still, though unused, this rail, road and water bridge seems almost part of the woodland scene.

The narrow lane winds to **Luxulyan** village, up and up between stone-littered fields: undoubted ploughing hazards but no disturbance to Channel Island cattle happy with the grass rich in minerals from the granite below. Overlooking Tregarden quarry, source of its building stone, Luxulyan's church centres the handsome cottages, all built to endure.

Everywhere beyond are white 'mountains' and at **Roche** (pronounced like 'poach') the scene is unparalleled. In this village the Rock (a rocky outcrop with a ruined chapel) rises like a mute guardian.

Nearby is **St Dennis**, its church set within an Iron Age encampment. The B3274, off the A391 at Stenalees, leads to **Carthew**. Here is the **China Clay Country Park** with its mining and heritage centre. This 26-acre park offers visitors the opportunity to learn about

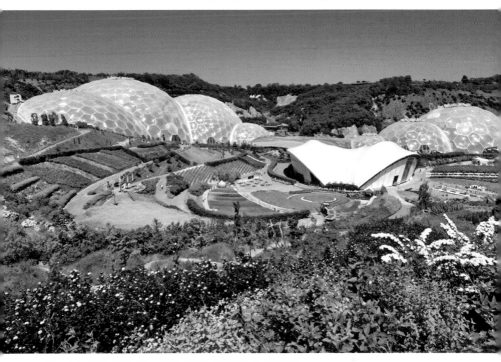

The futuristic biomes of the Eden Project, St Austell

Cornwall's china clay heritage and gives a unique view of a modern clay pit at work. Nature trails, a heritage trail and a children's challenge trail add to the interest with new exhibitions being added all the time. A licensed café and a shop help to ensure there is plenty here to keep the family happy all day.

On the other side of the A391 the road leads to the **Eden Project.** Set in a 37-acre (15 hectare) former china clay pit, 197 ft (60m) deep, this unique 'global garden for the twenty-first century' aims to tell the story of mankind's dependence on plants while demonstrating the opportunities for a sustainable future. Once at the edge of the pit the eyes are immediately drawn to the two huge biomes – greenhouses resembling giant bubbles made of hexagons covered in transparent foil.

The larger of the two, big enough to house the Tower of London, is the humid tropics biome, where plants from the rainforests grow. These huge plants, grouped by region of origin, show man's almost total dependence on plants in many of these areas. Plants provide not just food but shelter and clothing, fuel and tools.

The slightly smaller warm temperate biome illustrates similar principles but in a totally different environment. Here it is cooler and drier and the plants are smaller but the range of uses which man makes of them is just as diverse.

Throughout both biomes there are artworks that complement the scientific information.

A more recent addition is the Education Centre, 'The Core'. An innovative design based on Fibonacci's sequence: 0,1,1,2,3,5,8,13 – where every number is the sum of the previous two – has been brought to life using fully sustainable materials. The ground floor has exhibits which describe how plant energy powers our world and their ecosystems provide essential goods and services. On the upper floors are workshops and lecture rooms for both public and schools, enabling the message of the Eden Project to be brought to an even wider audience.

Outside the themes are continued but with plants that will grow in the Cornish climate. There are useful plants, clever plants, plants for taste, plants for crops and plants for healing and much, much more. This is a place to spend the whole day, taking breaks to absorb what you have seen as you go along. A lot of walking is involved but a land train transports visitors around the site and wheelchairs are available free of charge. Parking is not a problem and buses convey people from car park to visitor centre. There is so much here to learn and to entertain, backed up by friendly staff and excellent facilities all run in as environmentally friendly a way as possible.

Places to Visit

In & Around Liskeard

Liskeard Museum

Pike Street, PL14 3JE
☎ (01579) 346087
Open: 11am–4pm Mon to Fri; 11am–
1.30pm Sat.

 ♿ 👪 ☂

Merlin Glass

Pavlova Mill, Station Road
☎ (01579) 342399
www.merlinglass.co.uk
Gallery shop open Mon to Fri 9.30am–
4.30pm. Sat 9.30am–12.30pm.

Paul Corin Magnificent Music Machines

St Keyne Station, just off B3254
PL14 4SH
☎ (01579) 343108
www.paulcorinmusic.co.uk
Amazing collection of mechanical
musical instruments. Playing daily
10.30am–5pm, Good Friday till end -
Oct. Of special interest to under 12s.

Ⓟ ♿ 👪 <15 ☂

Cornish Orchards

Westnorth Manor Farm, Duloe,
PL14 4PW
☎ (01503) 269007
www.cornishorchards.co.uk
Producer of hand-crafted apple juices
and ciders using traditional varieties of
apples from West Country orchards.
Open: 10am–5pm Mon to Fri, 9.30am–
12.30pm on Sat, Easter to Oct. 10am–
5pm on Wed and 10am–12.30pm on
Sat, Nov to Easter (not open on Sat
in Jan).

Old Guildhall Museum

Higher Market Street, East Looe,
PL13 1BQ
☎ (01503) 263709
Open: 11.30am–4.30pm Sun to Fri,
Easter week and from late May Bank
Holiday to the end of Sep.

👪 <15 ☂

Land of Legend & Model Village

Polperro, Looe, PL13 2RP
☎ (01503) 272378
Miniature replica of old Polperro.
Model railway. Stories of legends and
superstitions from Cornwall's past.
Open: 10am–6pm daily, Apr to Oct;
10am–8.30pm in Jul and Aug.

Polperro Heritage Museum of Smuggling and Fishing

The Warren, PL13 2RB
☎ (01503) 272423
www.polperro.org/museum.html
Brings to life the history of Polperro.
Open: 10.30am–5.30pm daily, Mar to
Oct. Little interest to under 7s.

Ⓟ 👪 <17 ☂

Porfell Animal Land

Trecangate, Nr Lanreath, PL14 4RE
☎ (01503) 220211
www.porfellanimalland.co.uk
Wildlife park and sanctuary for exotic
species, children's farm and tropical
house. Tea room, picnic area, woodland
walks. Open: 10am–6pm daily Apr
to Oct. 11am–4pm Feb half-term and
weekends from then until Apr.

Ⓟ 👪 <13

Places to Visit

The Southern Gallery

Havett Road, Dobwalls, Liskeard,
PL14 6HB
☎ (01579) 320325
www.thesoutherngallery.co.uk
Award-winning gallery specialising
in wildlife paintings. Open: 10.30am–
4.30pm daily (except 24, 25, 26 Dec
and 1 Jan). Free admission. Of little
interest to under 12s.

Ⓟ ♿ ☂

Ancient Egyptian Centre

Junction of the A38 and A390 traffic
lights in Dobwalls, PL14 6JN
☎ (01579) 321811
www.the-ancient-egyptian-centre.com
Museum of 1930s finds from Egyptian
tombs. Open: 10am–4pm except Fri.
Closed Jan to Easter.

Ⓟ ♿ (Call first) ⛹<17 ☂

🐕 (Small/medium dogs only)

Charlestown's historic harbour

In & around Lostwithiel

Restormel Castle

(English Heritage)
1½ miles (2.4km) north of Lostwithiel,
PL22 OEE
☎ (01208) 872687
www.english-heritage.org.uk
Impressive remains of twelfth-century
castle above River Fowey. Has
connections with the Black Prince.
Open: daily, 10am–5pm daily Mar to
Jun, 10am–6pm Jul and Aug, 10am–
5pm Sept, 10am–4pm Oct.

Ⓟ ♿ (GF only for wheelchairs) ⛹<16 🐕

Guildhall Museum

Fore Street, Lostwithiel
Built in 1740, this has linenfold panelling,
town insignia and photocopies of the
charters. Open: 10.30am–12.30pm and
2.30–4.30pm Mon–Sat, Easter Mon to
end-Sept. Free entry.

♿ (Most areas) ⛹ ☂

Boconnoc

North of Couch's Mill, PL22 ORG
Eighteenth-century house and beautiful
gardens. House and gardens only
open to public on occasional Sundays
in April and May.

In & Around Fowey

'Q' Memorial on Hall Walk

Granite monolith facing down River
Fowey, beloved by Sir Arthur Quiller-
Couch.

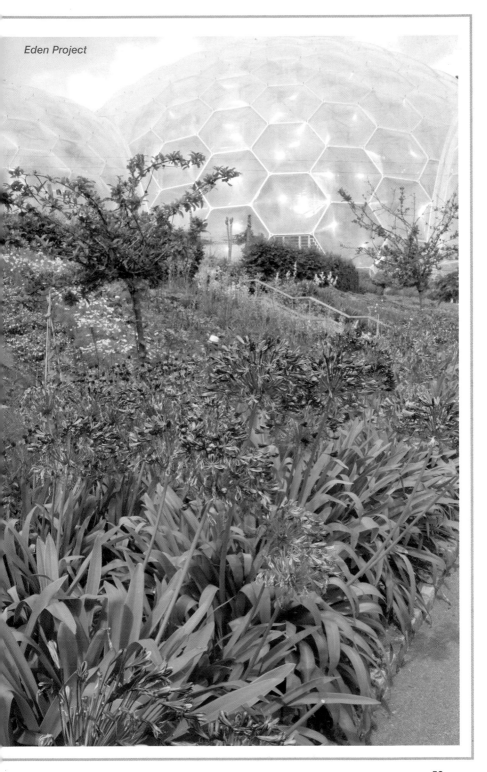

Eden Project

Places to Visit

Daphne du Maurier Literary Centre

South Street, PL23 1AR
☎ (01726) 833616/833619
Displays and videos illustrating Fowey's literary heritage. Book and gift shop. Open: 9.30am–5pm daily. Free admission.

♿ ☔

Town Hall Museum

Trafalgar Square, Fowley
☎ (01726) 833513
Town history exhibits. Possibly guild chapel, later prison. Open: Easter Mon to Oct 10am–5pm Monday to Friday. Poor disabled facilities, 6 steps up to door.

👪<Children Free ☔

St Catherine's Castle

(English Heritage)
Three-quarters of a mile (1.2km) south-west of Fowey towards Gribbin. Remains of Henry VIII's harbour fort. Good views. Free admission.

Ⓟ 🐕

In & Around St Austell

St Austell Brewery Visitor Centre

63 Trevarthian Road, PL25 4BY
☎ (01726) 66022
www.staustellbrewery.co.uk
Guided tours by appointment. Visitor centre and shop. Open 10am–5.30pm Mon–Fri, 11am–4pm Sat and Sun (closed Sun Nov to Mar). Little interest for under 7s.

Ⓟ <13 ☔

The Lost Gardens of Heligan

Pentewan, St Austell, PL26 6EN
☎ (01726) 845100
www.heligan.com
Beautifully restored Victorian gardens. Large areas suitable for disabled visitors. Plant sales. Tea room. Picnic area. Open: 10am–6pm Apr to Sept, 10am–5pm in winter daily. Allow at least half a day for a visit.

Ⓟ ♿ 👪<16 🐕 (Winter only)

Shipwreck and Heritage Centre

Charlestown, PL25 3NJ
☎ (01726) 69897
www.shipwreckcharlestown.com
Recreation of village life, display about shipwrecks including many artefacts recovered from the seabed, hands-on exhibition of lifeboat and rescue equipment and much, much more. Open: 10am–5pm daily, Mar to Oct.

♿ 👪<17 ☔ 🐕

China Clay Country Park Mining and Heritage Centre

Carthew, PL26 8XG
☎ (01726) 850362
www.chinaclaycountry.co.uk
Unique open-air industrial archaeology museum based on restored clay works (dating from about 1880), with waterwheels, etc, demonstrating this important Cornish industry. Access to view modern working china clay pit. All set in country park. Open: 10am–6pm daily, Easter to Oct, 10am–4pm at other times.

Ⓟ 👪<15

Mid-Cornwall Galleries

St. Blazey Gate, Par, PL24 2EG
☎ (01726) 812131
www.midcornwallgalleries.co.uk
Fine collection of craft and painting in skilfully converted school. Open: 10am–5pm Mon to Sat, all year. 10am–4.30 Jan. Free admission.

Ⓟ ♿ (On Request) 🚻 🌧

Eden Project

Bodelva, Nr St Austell, PL24 25G
☎ (01726) 811911
www.edenproject.com
Exploration of man's relationships with plants.
Open: 10am–6pm daily, April to Oct; 10am–4.30pm, Nov to Mar. Closed 24th–25th Dec.

Ⓟ ♿ 🚻 <16 🌧

What to do if it rains

Liskeard

Church of St Martin

Museum

St Keyne

Paul Corin's Magnificent Music Machines

Looe

Old Guildhall Museum

Polperro

Land of Legend and Model Village

Smuggling Museum

Dobwalls

Ancient Egyptian Centre

Southern Art Gallery

Lostwithiel

St Bartholomew's Church

Guildhall Museum

Fowey

Town Museum

Daphne du Maurier Centre

Bodelva

Eden Project

St Austell

Brewery visitor centre

Polkyth Leisure Centre

Biscovey

Mid-Cornwall Galleries

Charlestown

Shipwreck and Heritage Centre

Truro

The exact meaning of the name Truro is uncertain, though of the suggested 'settlement near water', 'three roads' and 'three rivers', possibly the last is the most feasible. The 'three rivers' were the Allen, Kenwyn and a third, long lost under Tregolls Road where the A39 enters the city from the east.

About 2,500 years ago, the first inhabitants settled here on the ridge above the water. Celts then established themselves, but not till 1140 was there any building of importance. This was a Norman castle, but only the name remains, as Castle Hill, the site of the present Crown Court.

The tin trade brought wealth to Truro and it was one of the earliest stannary towns to hold a charter, which was granted by Edward I in 1307. King John built a Coinage Hall in 1200 but this was demolished in the early nineteenth century. The Black Death (1348) halved the population, causing such poverty that the government remitted all taxes. During the Civil War, Prince Charles

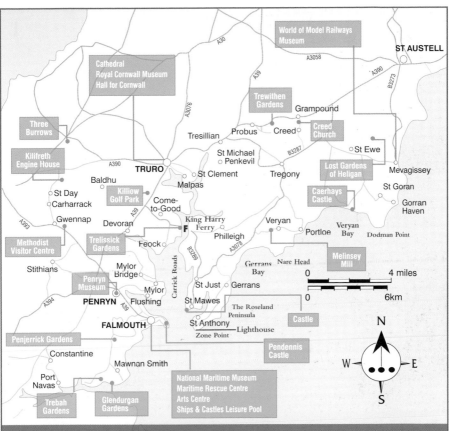

World of Model Railways Museum

ST AUSTELL

Cathedral
Royal Cornwall Museum
Hall for Cornwall

Trewithen Gardens

Grampound

Three Burrows

Tresillian   Probus   Creed   Creed Church

Kilifreth Engine House

TRURO

St Michael Penkevil

St Ewe

Lost Gardens of Heligan   Mevagissey

Baldhu   St Clement   Tregony   St Goran

St Day   Killiow Golf Park   Malpas   Caerhays Castle   Gorran Haven

Carharrack   Come-to-Good

Gwennap   Devoran   King Harry Ferry   Veryan   Veryan Bay   Dodman Point

Methodist Visitor Centre   F   Portloe

Stithians   Trelissick Gardens   Feock   Philleigh   Melinsey Mill

Penryn Museum   Mylor Bridge   Gerrans Bay   Nare Head

PENRYN   Mylor   Flushing   St Just   Gerrans   0   4 miles

FALMOUTH   St Mawes   0   6km

Penjerrick Gardens   St Anthony   The Roseland Peninsula   Castle

Constantine   Zone Point   Lighthouse

Port Navas   Mawnan Smith   Pendennis Castle

Trebah Gardens   Glendurgan Gardens   National Maritime Museum
Maritime Rescue Centre
Arts Centre
Ships & Castles Leisure Pool

N
W — E
S

Truro, Falmouth & The Roseland Peninsula

and Royalist troops were quartered here, and for a while Truro was also the temporary home of the Royal Mint.

In the eighteenth century, the town was as fashionable as Bath, and among the cultural activities were a Philharmonic Society, Library and Book Society.

Many gracious buildings were erected. The **Assembly Rooms** by the cathedral has a fine façade worthy of attention, as does Ralph Allen Daniell's **Mansion House** in Prince's Street. He was nephew to Ralph Allen of St Blazey (see Chapter 2), and wealthy enough to use Bath stone and have the oak specially carved by craftsmen from the local French prisoner of war camp. The date 1792 is engraved on the roof. Merchants like William Lemon built elegant houses on both sides of Lemon Street, named after him, and looking down on them is a monument to Richard Lander. He discovered the source of the River Niger and, in 1830, was the first holder of the Royal Geographical Society's Gold Medal.

The ordinary houses, too, are worth more than a passing glance. Look for strangely shaped roofs, old porticos, decorated façades, narrow, pointed windows and emotive names like Tanyard Court, Tippett's Backlet, Pydar Street and Coombes Lane – recalling the great days of Truro's wool trade. St Nicholas Street may not seem unusual, but here the merchants' houses and warehouses were cheek by jowl with the Guildhall of St Nicholas, probably extending across Boscawen Street down

to Lemon Quay itself. The present car park is where ships anchored while waiting for their cargoes. Today at the Quay, across the A39, pleasure boats berth in the summer and run weekday boat trips down the Fal.

Most Cornish towns have narrow passages between houses. These are 'opes' – pronounced 'ops'. Truro is no exception and Squeeze Guts Alley is perhaps the smallest and most awkward; Cathedral Lane is another 'ope'.

There is much to see in the **Royal Cornwall Museum** (founded in 1818). On display is a wide variety of material connected with life in the region since earliest times; the mineral section is unusually fine. Temporary exhibitions of artworks from the museum's collection and visiting artists are usually on

Truro Cathedral

The Prince of Wales laid the foundation stone on 20 May 1880. It was the first to be built in Britain since St Paul's. Truro, however, had become a city in 1877 when Bishop Benson was enthroned in St Mary's parish church. This was later demolished, except for the south aisle, which was incorporated into the new building.

The three-spired towers are interesting in their dedications. The central one (Victoria) was given in 1901 as a memorial to the Queen's life, and nine years later, another local benefactor gave the two western towers – Edward and Alexandra. Altogether an unusual building, its Gothic style gives the city a continental look. Its Willis organ is famous and interesting features include memorials to 'Q' (Sir Arthur Quiller-Couch the essayist), the missionary Henry Martyn, and the Robartes family. Notice the Bath stone reredos representing Christ's sacrifice, the window showing John Wesley preaching at Gwennap Pit and the painting Cornubia by John Miller.

The first bishop, Edward White Benson, originated the service of Nine Lessons and Carols here in 1880 and after serving in Truro for seven years he was translated to Canterbury. There is also a cathedral bookshop for books and souvenirs and the Chapter House where you can get refreshments.

Walks

Trefusis Point

7 miles (11km) • easy • 3 hours
Map: OS 1:25,000 Explorer Series 105: Falmouth and Mevagissey
Cross to Flushing on the ferry from Falmouth then turn right off the quay. The road runs through a village of picturesque houses built for the nobility and packet captains. Follow it round, bearing left at the next jetty, and carry straight on to the end of the tarmac area. Right here leads to a small, usually quiet beach but walkers carry on left where the path winds round the point, giving fine views of Falmouth Harbour. Nearing Mylor Yacht Harbour and the Ganges Restaurant the views across the Fal are of the Roseland Peninsula. There is a chance to see Mylor Church, quiet and beautiful, before walking up to follow the road down again to Flushing and the ferry.

St Clement

5 miles (8km) • easy • 3 hours
Map: OS 1:25,000 Explorer Series 105: Falmouth and Mevagissey
Leave the Trafalgar roundabout in Truro where the A39 goes up Tregolls Road and take the turning signposted St Clement. Almost at once turn right up Trennick Lane through the grounds of Truro School and continue up the road for about half a mile with the Truro River below, until it reaches a farm called Trennick. Keeping left, take the track straight ahead – it's muddy sometimes! At the valley bottom cross the footbridge and go up the other side. Follow the footpath to St Clement Parish Hall, then turn right down into St Clement hamlet where the church is 'guarded' by picturesque thatched cottages and public toilets are to be found nearby. Go down to the water, enjoy a picnic, wander along beside the river to Tresillian and the ancient Wheel Inn for refreshment before returning to Truro. Alternatively, leave St Clement Church and take the road uphill for Truro.

Place to Portscatho/Gerrans

7½ miles (12km) • easy • 3 hours
Map: OS 1:25,000 Explorer Series 105: Falmouth and Mevagissey
The best way to reach Place is on the ferry across the lovely Percuil River from St Mawes which links with the Falmouth–St Mawes ferry (summer only). At Place Quay the path is signposted to Bohortha. Pass through the hamlet and turn right at the road junction, then almost immediately turn left across the field and left again onto the coast path above Porthbeor beach. Walk along the coast as far as Towan beach and continue along the coast path to Portscatho, an attractive village, then walk up the hill to Gerrans Church and turn left following the signs to the car park. Carry on along the lane passing through Posteague and coming out at Porth. Turn right in Porth, following the path alongside Porth Creek and the Percuil River back to Place.

Truro Cathedral

display. A café is open daily.

The **Hall for Cornwall** is a first-class entertainment venue in Truro offering everything from classical music to pantomime, one-man shows and lectures to plays, opera and popular music plus restaurant and coffee shop. Outdoor entertainment can be found during the summer in Victoria Gardens where there are band concerts, jazz and special children's entertainment.

Both Victoria Gardens and Boscawen Park, along the bank of the river, offer peaceful havens after exploring the city centre.

East of Truro

From the Trafalgar roundabout, a road running past Radio Cornwall, the BBC's first purpose-built local radio station, follows the river to **Malpas** ('Mopus').

At the end of the road there is a footpath to **St Clement**. Photographers love the old church and thatched cottages – the slate-hung upper room over the lychgate provides added interest. From here one of the Duchy's loveliest

creek-side paths leads to Pencalenick, where the A39 is rejoined for **Tresillian**. At the far end of this long village is the uniquely thatched Wheel Inn. Here history was made when the Civil War ended and the Royalist Lord Hopton capitulated to Fairfax after surrendering at the bridge. Fairfax Road beside the water commemorates the occasion.

You will need more than a day to explore the **Veryan** area and to visit some of the interesting places on the way. Follow the road, the A390, out of Tresillian and take the exit to **Probus**, which is now a quiet village but was once an educational centre. Now only its collegiate church and a road name, College Close, are left as reminders. The fine church tower is Cornwall's highest, at 123½ feet (37.6m), lovely with its finely carved granite. Outside the church is an attractive lamp standard erected to celebrate Queen Victoria's Diamond Jubilee.

About 3 miles (5km) beyond lies **Grampound**, quietly at peace beside the rushing traffic, deceptively differ-

Atlantic Crossing

The tannery at Grampound, sadly now closed, is the place which provided skin for the hull and sails of Tim Severin's curragh *St Brendan*, which weathered a force eight gale and crossed the Atlantic safely in 1976. Surely this was ample proof of the theory of the author-historian captain who believed that St Brendan made the same crossing a good thousand years before Columbus – in an identical craft.

ent from the bustling port of Norman times when the sea brought ships there. When silting began, a bridge over the Fal was built at that point and the town was given the name Grandpont – known in 1299 as the Borough of Ponsmur, its Celtic name. Eventually maritime trading ended and the town declined slowly into the present peaceful village.

The entrance to Veryan village

The second turning on the right, up the hill out of Grampound, winds narrowly to **St Ewe**, beautiful and almost unspoilt. The church, enclosed by trees, has old stocks inside – both merit a close look.

After Kestle is **Mevagissey**, one of the Duchy's oldest fishing ports. Its narrow streets and quaint shops, up the hills or by the quays, make it a captivating place. Watch the gulls and the fishing boats or go fishing. If it rains, there are always the **World of Model Railways** and the **Museum** to enjoy. Park on the harbour quays and move for a while into a miniature world. There is

The Lost Gardens of Heligan

Boats in Mevagissey harbour

enjoyment here for the whole family.

The road south to **Portmellon** hugs the cliff before dipping down to the cove famous for Percy Mitchell – the self-taught boat designer. He started his shipyard in 1924 and constructed everything from a 7-foot (2m) dinghy to vessels of over 30 tons. An artist in wood, he built the *Windstar* for Sir Philip Hunloke, Sailing Master to the Queen's father as well as various boats for the Admiralty. Drive out with care along the narrow winding road – summer traffic can be dangerous here.

The coastal path to **Gorran Haven** passes Chapel Point – another place associated with Tristan. He was imprisoned in the chapel but leapt from a window to the safety of a rocky ledge – so the story goes. Views here are reward enough for walkers; even the inland lanes do not compare. Gorran Haven itself is unexpectedly small but opens out into a wide bay. Above, at **Gorran Churchtown**, Anne Treneer was born. Her book, *Schoolhouse in the Wind*, is an excellent autobiography, which breathes the delights of Cornwall in the early 1920s when for her, Falmouth was a distant romantic seaport. She writes of the enchanting bareness of Cornwall and tells how she would walk to Dodman Point and 'look into the sparkling intoxicating space'.

Dodman Point, this 'noblest of Cornish headlands', is a well-preserved Iron Age fort with baulk ditch and rampart. It has been National Trust property since 1919 and this impressive structure can be viewed all round from the circular walk that starts and ends at the Penare car park. At the extreme point is a huge granite cross, erected in 1896 as a mark for seamen by the Vicar of Caerhays. After dedicating the cross he kept a night's vigil beneath it, praying for the souls of shipwrecked mariners. This same promontory fascinated Sir Arthur Quiller-Couch and he used it in his first book, *Dead Man's Rock*.

Hemmick Beach has only a narrow lane beside the water. It is quiet here and there is more than one stretch of sand. Perilous lanes lead to it, so first gear is essential to get to **Porthluney Cove**. There is a large car park here and looking down over the beach is John Nash's Gothic **Caerhays Castle**, built in 1808 for J B Trevanion. A fairytale place, it is scorned by some but loved by all when the rhododendrons are in bloom.

The Grampound road, after climbing past Caerhays church and Tubb's Mill, turns right along more narrow winding lanes to **Creed**. From the Tregony road out of Creed the right-hand turn goes over the Fal to Golden Mill and Manor. This is a privately owned farm but it is possible to drive as far as the main building without trespassing. The great barn on the left still has the fine

William Gregor

He was born not far from Creed in 1761. During his incumbency of the parish, he discovered titanium in black sand sent to him from Manaccan. It has been called manaccanite and gregorite but is now universally accepted as titanium. In the secluded church there is a photograph of a titanium bowl and also a portrait of William Gregor.

windows and sturdy walls of a medieval hall.

In 1577, Francis Tregian and his family lived here and offered shelter to Cuthbert Mayne (canonised in 1974). As they were known recusants their property was searched, Mayne was discovered and executed, while Francis Tregian was condemned to a long period of imprisonment. Somehow he survived it all, went abroad and died there in 1608. There are elegant memorials in **Probus** church to the Tregians and the Wolvedons (Golden is the Cornish mutation of this name).

A different kind of country house is at **Trewithen**, nearby on the A390. It was the eighteenth-century home of the Hawkins family and 20 acres (8 hectares) of its grounds are now internationally famous as **Trewithen Gardens**, which are open to the public in spring and summer, as is the house. Shrubs are always on sale in the nursery here.

The Roseland Peninsula around Veryan

The **Roseland Peninsula** includes the west side of Veryan Bay and Gerrans Bay, involving a long but very lovely drive. Take the A3078 where it turns off the A39 between Tresillian and Probus. It crosses the **Tregony** bridge where the left turn leads up to the now quiet village with its wide central street. This was once a bustling port and had a castle, a medieval market and a thriving wool factory. Even when the river silted up and trade declined,

it was still a society meeting place. In the late nineteenth century, the learned Powder Book Club held meetings there for the improvement of local ladies, but no such excitements now remain.

Little is left of former glories except the fourteenth-century church of **St Cuby** with its slate tower and the handsome seventeenth-century clock tower that was rebuilt in 1895. Tregony is now a place of the past, recalling when ships unloaded ceramics, glass and wine then sailed away with leather, wool and tin.

From Tregony, high-banked, narrow lanes lead to **Portholland**, a harbour of two coves, east and west. There is a fine cliff path to **Portloe** but motorists lose the view temporarily as the road takes the inland route to this tiny port more used to horse and pony transport than motorised traffic. Parking halfway down the steep hill to the beach avoids unpleasant turns, but visitors to the comfortable seventeenth-century Lugger Hotel will find a car park beside it. This village loses the sun very quickly, lying in the shadow of Jacka and Manare Points, but it is a pleasant place in the sunshine.

Veryan is well known but still relatively unspoilt. The reasons for its fame are the unique roundhouses at each end of the village. Some say that a local vicar built them to keep the devil out and away from his daughters. Whatever the reason, the white, thatched cottages have a charm all their own. Pause a while at the New Inn where the food is good and the welcome warm. An interesting **art gallery** at the north end is worth visiting. Inside the church, with its unusual dedication to St Symphorian, lies Admiral Kempe, notable for sailing

Caerhays Castle

Walking opportunities

The National Trust owns land here, as well as a considerable area along the cliff to **Nare Head**, where there is a viewing platform with a ramp for wheelchairs. One of the Trust walks is round the point from Caragloose to Camels Cove. At Kiberick Cove there is a small car park and a footpath to the secluded beach. Another walk from the same parking place is down the valley to Paradoe Cove beyond the Nare, returning via that fine headland – one of the least frequented in Cornwall.

Portmellon

St Just-in-Roseland Churchyard

Gorran Haven

round the world with Cook and scaling Quebec Heights with General Wolfe.

Returning towards the A3078, about half a mile (0.8km) out of Veryan, lies **Melinsey Mill**. This is a sixteenth-century watermill featuring a twelve-foot-high (3.5m), overshot wheel, on the site of a much earlier mill dating from 1210. Last used in 1928 it was discovered derelict but intact and has been fully restored. It is now open as a working museum and tea rooms.

From close by there is a walk down the lovely wooded valley to **Pendower Beach**, another National Trust property. A disused lime-kiln is an interesting feature of this pleasant place. The great tumulus (Cornwall's largest) at nearby **Carne Beacon** is said to be the burial mound of King Geraint who built

Porthluney Cove, a beautiful Cornish beach

Walk to a place of legend

There is a splendid and easy coastal walk round Zone Point to **Place**. Behind the privately owned manor is the church of St Anthony, wrapped in legend. Tradition says that this was once a Celtic monastery whose history is written between the two rows of dog teeth on the south door. A rough translation of it is that Christ visited this peninsula when his uncle, Joseph of Arimathea, came to trade for tin. When they were off St Anthony Head, a storm blew up and they sheltered in the little bay below Place Manor. While making the ship seaworthy again, they camped here, leaving a shrine behind them. Some years afterwards a church was built on that site. Apart from any legend, here is quiet beauty and a good place to picnic looking over to St Mawes.

Dingerein Castle where the Gerrans road leaves the A3078. It is believed that his tribesmen rowed his body, in a golden boat with silver oars, across the bay to be burned and buried at Carne.

The spire of the church at **Gerrans** village is a landmark from both sea and land. From here it is a walk of about 4 miles (6.4km) along the coastpath to St Anthony Head, the eastern arm of Falmouth harbour. This superb route offers unsurpassed panoramic views on every side until reaching Zone Point and the lighthouse. The headland has been fortified since Napoleonic days. It was under military occupation during World War II and then bought by the National Trust in 1959. There is wheelchair access to the viewpoint.

A delightful walk from Bohortha Farm to picturesque **Froe** overlooks the River Percuil and, at the head of Froe inlet, the water almost makes this headland an island. The journey back to Truro along the A3078 and A39 is about 20 miles (32km), but there are views of the Carrick Roads for most of the way, which make the distance worthwhile.

The Roseland Peninsula around St Mawes

The last exploration of the Roseland Peninsula is shorter and could last either an afternoon or a day. From Tresillian on the A390 follow the minor road to **St Michael Penkevil** – a handful of cottages round the church with the great gates of **Tregothnan** proclaiming it as private property, although the garden is very occasionally open to the public and private visits can be arranged. In 1319, the church was an important archpresbytery (a college with four chaplains). An interesting feature is the second altar on the upper floor of the tower, an old tradition in churches dedicated to St Michael. Leaving the churchtown, take the first lane on the right through beautiful **Lamorran Woods** which leads to **Ruan Lanihorne**. This is a haven for birdwatchers and there is also a 4-mile (6.4km) walk beside the river, where ships once sailed to Tregony.

There are walks to **Philleigh** where

St Mawes Castle

The castle, cared for by English Heritage, is a round tower, built by Henry VIII and probably enlarged by his son Edward in 1550. Its name is believed to have come from the hermit, St Mawes, St Mauditus or St Mause who effected cures with the water from a holy well. It is small but interesting with ample parking. The grounds are pleasant – an ideal place to picnic and watch the various activities on the Carrick Roads.

the old Rectory, a fine early Georgian house with an elegant slate-hung façade, is worthy of more than a passing glance. Set nearby in Cornish elms is the church with its unusual dedication to St Filius.

Resist the temptation to drive straight to King Harry Ferry – leave that until later – but watch the last times of sailing! Go on to **St Just-in-Roseland** where the church, in its creekside setting of tropical trees, is possibly unrivalled for beauty of position. At the water's edge of St Just Pool ships' figureheads or specialised work for the *QEII* used to be crafted.

The A3078 eventually reaches St Mawes Castle and drops down into the village to follow the harbour round for the return journey. **St Mawes** is a sheltered place and a yachting paradise, particularly for the wealthy.

Leaving St Mawes follow the B3289 to King Harry Ferry. Just before the ferry take the right turn to Smugglers' Cottage at **Tolverne**. Park where indicated in the lane and walk to the water's edge and the thatched cottage, which is interesting for its history and good for its lunches and cream teas. Contraband was delivered in the past, but today be prepared for a surprise as large ships are anchored here. They are laid up, some full of cargo that could not be sold and some for lack of work, and all seem too large for such a narrow stretch of river. Keep an eye open along the lane to the cottage for plaques that indicate where various parts of the American troop encampment were held in 1944 before embarking for D-Day and the Normandy beaches. A ferry links Tolverne with Falmouth, sailing four times daily during the summer.

Ruined Tolverne chapel was built by Henry VI, who also established the crossing nearby to Trelissick, known as the **King Harry Ferry**. Tales of Henry VIII riding with Anne Boleyn across this reach on their honeymoon may be romantic but they are not true. The latest ferry, launched in 2006, glides smoothly across the Fal to **Trelissick**, another delightful National Trust property. The Trust has made a nature trail round the grounds. The gardens are open to the public but the house is not.

The thatched Punch Bowl and Ladle Inn at **Penelewey** dates from the eleventh century and is probably the only one with such a name. **Cowlands Creek** and **Coombe** are worth a detour to enjoy the birds, the creekside walks and the famous Kea plums.

The lane joins the A39 Falmouth to Truro road at **Calenick**, once the site of Cornwall's chief smelting house. All that remains of it is the handsome clock tower on the slate-hung Bridge House.

West of Truro

The great men of Truro made fortunes in tin during the eighteenth and nineteenth centuries, but it had been 'streamed' in the surrounding districts long before Truro became an important trading centre, so it is interesting to look at those old mining areas. The Truro to Falmouth A39 road, down Arch Hill, goes under the track of a railway before climbing the hill to Playing Place – once the site of a theatre-in-the-round. At the Playing Place roundabout is the entrance to the 18-hole parkland golf course of

St Mawes

St Mawes Castle

Pandora Inn

Across the narrow water from Feock is the thatched Pandora Inn. Originally called The Ship, it was renamed when its captain returned from sailing with Bligh of the *Bounty* to capture the mutineers. On the return voyage, the vessel – the *Pandora* – foundered and though its captain brought home some prisoners he was dismissed from the service. He then bought this inn and named it after his lost ship.

Pendower Beach, Gerrans Bay

Trelissick Gardens

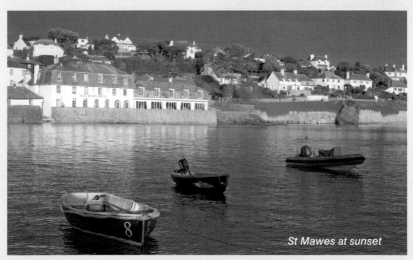

St Mawes at sunset

Killiow which has a floodlit golf driving range.

Carnon Downs looks like a bungalow suburb, but hides much mining history. At the roundabout on the bypass take the left-hand exit for **Come-to-Good**, a misleading name which has quite a different meaning. The thatched Quaker Meeting House of 1710 is called after its location *Cwm-ty-quite* – Cornish for 'the House of the Coombe in the Woods,' appropriate for this attractive building, still in use.

Feock church has an interesting lychgate with a slate-hung upper storey and expensive properties beyond the village straggling down to Restronguet Point beside the Carrick Roads. Before Tudor times a passenger ferry, which functioned to the turn of the twentieth century, took travellers from Truro through Mylor to Penryn and Falmouth.

At **Point**, Restronguet Creek is joined by the Carnon River, a bird sanctuary and a place of beauty. Once it was a prosperous mining port with a smuggling reputation as well. Tin has been streamed in the Carnon River since the days of prehistory, and in the Middle Ages, ore for export from the inland mines was brought here on mules and horses. In 1826 the Redruth and Chacewater Railway opened, the stretch from Devoran to Point still retaining horse-drawn wagons: part of this track can still be seen. Great schooners from Scandinavia anchored there, unloading timber that was taken on barges to Perran Wharf. The Norway Inn is a reminder of those days. There are still bollards and wooden wharves at **Devoran** and the old weighbridge

gate remains at the junction where the Bissoe road leaves the A39.

Beyond the Norway Inn, a road winds away to Perranwell and opposite are the buildings of Perran Foundry (1799), recalling the days when the Fox family established an industrial site there. The machinery was of high quality and many European nations bought it.

Turn right over the railway bridge at **Perranwell** and drive along Grenna Lane. There you will overlook the Carnon Valley and perhaps imagine what it was like when mining was at its peak. Then beyond Perranwell and Frogpool, **Gwennap** village lies in peaceful beech woods, deceptively quiet now, yet once the heart of a region which yielded more copper and tin than any other place in the old world. Gwennap Pit is not in the village, but is near **Busveal**, reached by turning off the A393 Falmouth to Redruth road at the Fox and Hounds, one of the many inns where a service is held and produce auctioned for charity at harvest time.

The road twists and climbs above the derelict expanse of the now silent mines: Crofthandy, Goon Gumpus, Creegbrawse, Tolgullow and others with Celtic names. The men who worked there often died young and left widows with families. Others fell ill and were unable to work. Wesley's message from the Pit and elsewhere brought hope to these people because, as he wrote, 'The more I conversed with the believers in Cornwall, the more I am convinced that they have sustained great loss for want of hearing the doctrine of Christian Perfection clearly and strongly enforced.'

Gwennap Pit was probably formed by the collapse of underground mining excavations. In 1806, circular terraces were cut for seating and since 1807 an annual service has been held there on Whit Mondays. Wesley writes of preaching in a hollow capable of containing many thousands of people. Gwennap Pit is certainly large and was central and ideal for his purpose whether it held hundreds or thousands. A museum of Cornish Methodism was opened near here in 1982 but is now closed pending relocation.

Carharrack is a village of mining memories but **St Day** has a different story to tell. Prosperous mine owners and captains lived there but perhaps its real place in Cornwall's history is its role as one of the resting places for pilgrims en route to St Michael's Mount. Today, living precariously over a honeycomb of mines, it welcomes modern pilgrims to the St Day Walsingham Festival in September.

Killifreth engine house, beside the B3298 St Day–Scorrier road, is undoubtedly one of the most impressive industrial buildings remaining. It is near **Scorrier** where John Williams, the mining entrepreneur, built his fine mansion. At nearby **Chacewater**, formerly Chasewater, there are memories of Cornwall's first true railway. About 2 miles (3km) north-east along the A30 is **Blackwater**, the birthplace of John Passmore Edwards who built reading rooms and institutes for all workers, especially miners. His Reading Room there stands beside the main road; and almost every town in Cornwall owes its library to him. Altogether he was responsible for 53 benefactions from Newlyn to Dundee.

This section of the A30 has three important tumuli beside it, Two Burrows, Three Burrows and Four Burrows, and one of the Midsummer Eve Bonfire ceremonies by members of the Old Cornwall Society usually takes place at the last of these.

From the A390 at Chacewater, minor roads lead to Baldhu (Black Mine) and Wheal Jane Mine, reopened in 1970 as a modern mining complex but now closed. Visit **Baldhu Church** where churchyard memorials tell of the overseas journeys miners undertook to find work and there is a handsome stone commemorating **Billy Bray**. He is buried there but a small chapel nearby was actually built by this preaching miner. The surrounding area is one where mineral enthusiasts can explore ochre pits, arsenic works and similar remains. From here to Truro by way of the winding lanes of Penweathers there are walks and picnic places.

Penryn and Falmouth

Before going to Penryn and Falmouth, turn left from the A39 immediately after the Norway Inn at Perran Wharf. This leads to **Mylor**, a village much sought after by yachtsmen. The steep lane that winds away from the traffic is known locally as 'Craft and Danger', an interesting corruption of *croft an D'Angers* (D'Angers' fields). This must have described it in 1154 when that uncultivated hillside belonged to the Norman from Angers who owned the barton of Crueglew (the enclosed land by the prehistoric barrow).

St Mylor Church

Almost hidden in trees, beside the water at Mylor Churchtown, stands **St Mylor Church**. It is a picturesque building with a separate bell tower and Cornwall's tallest cross, embedded in the ground at the south door. One of the churchyard epitaphs is unusual and visitors are always told to read about **Joseph Crapp**, a shipwright who died 'ye 26th of November 1770, aged 43 years.' His death is graphically described:

Alas friend Joseph

His end was almost sudden

As though a mandate came

Express from heaven

His foot, it slip and he did fall

Help, help he cries, and that was all.

Another gravestone is 'To the Memory of the Warriors, Women and Children, who on their return to England from the coast of Spain unhappily perished in the Wreck of the *Queen Transport*, on Trefusis Point, Jan 14, 1814' just one of the many ships wrecked off the Cornish coast. Inside, the carved wood of the pulpit is believed to have come from Armada wrecks but the choir screen recalls more recent events. It was given in memory of those drowned in 1966 when an overloaded local pleasure boat capsized.

The wealthy mining engineer, William Lemon of Breage, bought the estate in 1749 (then called Carclew) and the house became one of the cultural centres of Cornwall. The Lemons were great benefactors to the people of Mylor: Sir Charles bought the workhouse, converted it into a school and maintained it for years. Fire unfortunately destroyed the manor house but **Carclew Gardens** are occasionally open to the public. The Lemon name died out and became Tremayne, but is perpetuated in the village in the Lemon Arms and Lemon Hill.

Mylor Bridge is at the head of the creek though the original settlement was the churchtown at its mouth one mile (1.6km) away. In the mid-nineteenth century the buildings by the pier were known as HMS *Ganges*, at that time the Royal Navy's only shore-based training centre and hospital. The ship, however, was anchored at St Just Pool across the Carrick Roads. Today it is a yachting centre but the restaurant there still bears the old name.

The writer Howard Spring found this creek so enchanting that he moved here in 1939 and used it as the background for his bestselling novel *All the Day Long*. The walk round Trefusis

Falmouth harbour

Point has views of Falmouth Bay, which some say is the finest natural harbour in the world.

The walk ends at **Flushing**, meeting the road from Mylor. Its Celtic name was Nankersey, but when Dutch engineers arrived to build Falmouth's quays, they settled here and changed the name as a reminder of their homeland. The cottages cling to the waterside, the village is reputed to have the mildest climate in the country and flowers bloom all the year round as if endorsing that claim. In the nineteenth century, the great days of packet ships, it was a fashionable place to live. Lord Exmouth was born here and Lord Buckingham dined and wined with other society notables. Today sailors are there for pleasure, not national business, as were those men of former days.

There is a bus service from here to Falmouth and Truro but the ferry across to Falmouth is the quickest way out of

The National Maritime Museum Cornwall

Richard Trevithick (1771–1833)

The son of a mining engineer, he followed his own ways even while he was at school, paying little attention to lessons because he was absorbed in his own diagrams and calculations. He would not even learn to spell yet could produce the correct answer to any mathematical problem six times faster than any adult. When he left school officially, Trevithick refused to have anything to do with the mine administration affairs in his father's office and wandered about the underground workings, examining and studying everything. The miners appreciated his knowledge of the machinery and his skill as a wrestler made him a popular figure.

His invention – the high-pressure engine – so impressed the wealthy Cornishman, Davies Gilbert (later President of The Royal Society) that they grew to be close friends. On Christmas Eve 1801 Trevithick frightened the local people with his 'puffing devil', which carried ten or more passengers even uphill (the model he made in 1797 is now in the Science Museum in London). Two years later he took a similar engine to London but had to bring it home because of financial difficulties.

There is no room here to tell more about the extraordinary career of this great man except to say that his high-pressure locomotive pre-dated Stephenson's *Rocket* by 12 years. Among his other inventions were the blast pipe, a ship propeller, screw propeller and central heating, yet the government flatly refused him any remuneration for his brilliant work. In desperation he turned to the New World but there met similar ups and downs of fortune.

Eventually he went to London and died while working at Dartford in Kent. Because of his penniless state he was buried in an unmarked grave but there is a tablet to his memory in the parish church, and windows in Westminster Abbey record his main achievements. His statue outside Camborne Library faces the street where he first put his theories into practice.

the village. At the head of the river is **Penryn**, reached either by a waterside path or inland road. These ways meet at the bottom of the steep hill beside St Gluvias, the parish church of Penryn. A place to visit is the **Town Hall Museum**. It was once the gaol but now houses a variety of interesting items connected with Penryn's history.

The town, in fact, grew from a settlement on the hill across the river. It has an interesting history, part splendid, part sad, but cherishes hopes for the future. Founded as a borough in 1216, it was granted a charter in 1236 and saw the rise and fall of Glasney collegiate church from 1265 to 1549. This establishment was a centre for religious instruction (renowned throughout Europe), growing in importance as Penryn's trade increased.

The closure of Glasney at the Dissolution, however, followed by the unexpected rise of Falmouth at the mouth of the river, led to a decline from which Penryn has never really recovered. But in 1977 its unique medieval character was recognised as rare, and government grants were given to save old buildings, so bringing a conservation programme into being. As a result, the town, whose granite is to be seen in buildings as different as London's Thames Embankment, Singapore harbour and Fastnet Lighthouse, has become a tourist attraction.

In Tudor times, the Fal River saw more shipping than any other port in the kingdom and Henry VIII, concerned about possible Spanish attacks, had **Pendennis Castle** built. It commands **Falmouth**'s best views: on one side, the holiday beaches; on the other, the docks and the town.

In the coaching days, the **Greenbank Hotel** was important. In the early years of last century, Kenneth Grahame began his *Wind in the Willows* here – proof of this is framed in the lobby – while Florence Nightingale's signature can be found in the old register. Down High Street – much changed since a disastrous fire in the nineteenth century – and to the left, is the Prince of Wales Pier where the Flushing ferry disembarks its passengers. It is also the berth for numerous pleasure boats.

The Moor lies above Market Strand and deceives most people with its name. From the bottom of Jacob's Ladder – 111 steps – boatmen used to ferry people over and moor outside the Seven Stars. This small building (dated 1610) is where generations of innkeepers have drawn beer from the wood, a

Founders of Falmouth

Opposite **Arwenack House** is the waterside granite obelisk erected in 1738 by Martin Lister Killigrew as a memorial to his wife's family. They had lived at Arwenack and founded Falmouth, which evolved from Sir Walter Raleigh's plan to develop the harbour. He had stayed at Arwenack with the Killigrews and urged them to press forward with the project. By 1613, in spite of objections from Penryn, the town's identity had been formed and Falmouth was born.

tradition carried on today.

The granite obelisk in the centre of the Moor in Falmouth is a memorial to men of the packet service when 'Falmouth for Orders' was the command obeyed by all captains of these ships. For over 250 years, the packets carried mail, cargoes and passengers to many parts of the world. In 1833 a wagon loaded with bullion from a packet ship left Killigrew Street on Monday and was in London by Saturday.

Walking through the town is a casual affair; traffic usually gives priority to pedestrians. In Church Street is the **Falmouth Arts Centre**, where in 1833 the Fox family of Quakers established the Polytechnic Society and reading rooms, setting a trend later followed throughout the country. At the far end of the town is the Georgian **Custom House**, handsome with its Greek Doric columns and fine façade. Beside and below is the **King's Pipe** – a chimney where contraband tobacco was burnt – an interesting reminder of the manner in which contraband tobacco used to

Above & below: Pendennis Castle, Falmouth

The Old Barracks, Pendennis Castle

be destroyed.

Dominating the harbourside is the **National Maritime Museum Cornwall**, opened in 2002. This innovatively designed building, using granite, slate and green oak boarding, holds a fascinating collection of boats. Through unique and interactive displays visitors learn how boats are shaped by the part they play in people's lives. Entering the first gallery, three storeys high, visitors experience audio-visual displays of life on and by the sea while viewing boats suspended in this great space. Smaller galleries tell of Cornwall's maritime heritage and of the ways that people use boats for work and pleasure.

The top of the lookout tower gives wonderful views over the harbour and of the boats moored on the pontoon outside. At the base of the tower visitors are five metres (16 feet) below high tide level and can see passing fish or the rise and fall of the tide. Move on through another tall gallery of famous craft to see boatbuilders at work, learn about navigation and meteorology and finally put all that information into practice by sailing a radio-controlled boat in the large indoor pool designed for the purpose. A café and shop complete an unmissable day out for the whole family, even the irredeemable landlubber. It is even possible to arrive by boat as a park and float system has been set up. Park just outside Falmouth and take the special ferry to the Museum.

The view over the docks from **Castle Drive** is one no visitor should miss. With the background of Trefusis Point and the Roseland Peninsula, this busy area is probably unique and there are hopes for a prosperous future as business people appreciate its potential.

Pendennis Castle is a well-preserved defence built by Henry VIII in 1539–43, shortly after the Little Dennis blockhouse below it. Later Elizabeth I had it enlarged but it was besieged successfully by Fairfax during the Civil War. Now owned and cared for by English Heritage, its exhibitions and displays are well worth a visit. Nearby is the modern **Ships and Castles Leisure Pool**, offering water fun for all the family.

Pendennis Point is ideal for a coast-guard station and the **Maritime Rescue Co-ordination Centre** was opened in 1981 by Prince Charles. In 1982 it was the first centre in the eastern Atlantic to answer calls on the Marisat satellite system. Here officials co-ordinate search and rescue round the coastline of Great Britain and Northern Ireland. In early 2009 the Centre was temporarily put out of action after being struck by lightning.

Round the headland, the road leads to Castle Beach, Gyllyngvase and beyond to Swanpool and Maenporth. These are beautiful beaches with sands and rock pools to keep children happy for the whole holiday. Swanpool – as its name implies – is something else as well; rowing boats and canoes often share the waters with a variety of birds.

Take the road out of Falmouth that leads past the hospital to **Budock**, its church and the village of **Budock Water**. The church was the mother church of Falmouth and had its origins as the centre of a religious community in the sixth century. An alternative route out of Falmouth leads to **Mabe** with its church high above the Argal and

College Reservoirs. Look down from the Penryn–Constantine road and pause to walk or fish.

The way to **Mawnan Smith** passes **Penjerrick Gardens**, a Fox property now opened to the public. Springtime is best for a visit here – then the flowering shrubs are a mass of colour. From the beaches the coast path goes to Rosemullion Head but motorists are restricted to the road, which ends at Mawnan church. It was built on an Iron Age site, the tower warning seamen that they were near the dreaded Manacle Rocks. Over the lychgate an inscription in Cornish reads: *Da thym ythyn nesse the Thu,* which means 'It is good for me to draw nigh unto the Lord'. Inside is a wide variety of colourful tapestry kneelers; those of the choir are patterned with medieval runes.

Round the headland lies **Durgan**, a tiny village reached either by cliff path or road by way of Mawnan Smith. It consists of a handful of cottages, just beside the small beach. There is no sand here, but safe bathing and an ideal place for windsurfing. This area, together with **Glendurgan**, is National Trust property. Although the house is occupied by members of the Fox family and is not open to the public, the valley garden may be visited. It is a garden of great beauty with fine trees and shrubs, walled and water gardens; a wooded valley runs down to Durgan on the Helford River.

Nearby is another place of delight beside the Helford River. **Trebah Gardens** are dramatic, uniquely beautiful and a friendly paradise for children and families. They are open all the year round and dogs are allowed provided they are kept on their leads.

Porth Navas and **Polwheveral Creeks**, between here and Constantine, are rivals in beauty but the former has an added interest, being the site of the Royal Duchy Oyster Farm. There are no cliff walks here but tracks lead to the Merthen earthworks. **Constantine** church, high in the village, has seen continuous worship since the fifth century and is worth visiting for its brasses and 200 embroidered kneelers. It may be locked but the key is at a nearby cottage.

On the right of the lanes to **Stithians** is the Rosemanowes Quarry where successful hot dry rock experiments have been carried out by the Camborne School of Mines. This village hides its church behind a screen of trees.

From here a secondary road climbs to overlook the village of **Ponsanooth** and Kennal Vale where at one time gunpowder was manufactured at Kennal Mills. Gunpowder was an important part of industrial mining. Woollen mills were here, too, forming the basis of carpet manufacture and cloth exports. Sadly, now the river has all but dried up and could not possibly support the 39 waterwheels it did when Magdalen ('Maudlin') Mine and the Perran Foundry were at peak production. These mine workings are hidden beneath undergrowth by the viaduct over the lane leaving Ponsanooth at the school and dropping to the A39 at Stickenbridge. A public footpath passes close by but there is little to show the world the tinworks that were old in Tudor times.

The A39 is at the bottom of Magdalen Lane, named after a Tudor chapel. To the right lies Falmouth; to the left, Carnon Downs and Truro.

Selected Car Drives

Truro to Porthluney Cove and Caerhays Castle

Leave Truro on the A39 for St Austell but after Tresillian at the roundabout take the turn for Tregony. Through the village, after admiring the clock tower, you will be on the B3287. About 3 miles (4.8km) on there is a right turn to St Ewe and so on through High Lanes to Porthluney Cove. This has a car park and a wonderful view of Caerhays Castle where the gardens are open in springtime. A steep hill leads up to Tubbs Mill and eventually across the B3287 to Creed and Grampound, which is on the A390 for your return to Truro.

Truro to Gwennap and Trelissick

On the A390 west out of Truro is a lane that falls away on the left to Penweathers, a twist of countryside which you can follow to Baldhu Church, built for miners who soon were forced to emigrate to find work. Beyond there is Billy Bray's Chapel, a place of great interest. The lanes lead to the little villages of Chacewater, St Day and Carharrack with its Methodist Museum. Gwennap Pit is at nearby Busveal, from where you should take the lanes through Frogpool and Perranarworthal to find the A39 Falmouth to Truro road. The valley of trees is beautiful at all times of the year as you drive towards Truro. Before taking the hill road across the Carnon River causeway at the end of the valley turn right and wander beside the Carnon River to Point and out of Penpol to join the B3289 where a right turn leads to Trelissick with its Barn Restaurant, shop and gardens. You may be tempted to cross the Fal on the King Harry Ferry for St Just and Veryan's round houses but another alternative is to drive to Playing Place and join the A39 to Truro. If you still have time to spare turn right at the bottom of the hill. That lane will take you to Calenick and Coombe. In season there are Kea plums in plenty at Coombe and tranquillity at any time. The drive back to Truro means retracing the road but these lanes are so lovely that it will be a pleasure.

Feast Day

St Stythian's Feast and Agricultural Show are held in the second week in July. Second only to the Royal Cornwall Show, it was first held in 1834 to stimulate competition between local farmers at a time when agriculture was at a very low ebb.

Places to Visit

Truro

Truro Cathedral

Truro, TR1 2AF
☎ (01872) 276782
www.trurocathedral.org.uk
Designed in Gothic style by J L Pearson, constructed 1880–1910, cleverly incorporating part of the former parish church. Monuments to 'Q' and missionary Henry Martyn, and a stained glass window of John Wesley at Gwennap. West porch niches facing High Cross have figures of kings and bishops. Look out for the beautifully carved memorial to one of the Robartes family of Lanhydrock who died in the Great War. Open: 7.30am–6pm Mon to Sat, 9am–7pm Sun (open 9.30am on bank holidays).

The Royal Cornwall Museum

River Street, TR1 2SJ
☎ (01872) 272205
www.royalcornwallmuseum.org.uk
Founded 1818, this museum exhibits Cornish history, has a library of Cornish books for members and an interesting art gallery. Seasonal displays of special interest. Open: 10am–4.45pm except Sun and Bank Holidays. Free admission.

Hall for Cornwall

Back Quay, Truro, TR1 2LL
☎ (01872) 262466
www.hallforcornwall.co.uk
Spectacular arts and entertainment centre offering something for everyone. Occasional antiques fairs and flea markets during the daytime. 'Stars Restaurant' and coffee bar.

Boat Trips to Falmouth

Town Quay, Truro
Enterprise Boats
☎ (01326) 374241 or 313234
www.enterprise-boats.co.uk
Take a one-hour trip from the centre of Truro to Falmouth, sailing the full length of the Fal river. When tides do not permit sailing from Truro departure will be from Malpas, a short way down the river. A bus connection from Truro to Malpas is included in the ticket price.

East Of Truro

World of Model Railways

Meadow St, Mevagissey, PL26 6UL
☎ (01726) 842457
www.model-railway.co.uk
An unusual attraction offering a miniature world of nearly 50 trains. Additional 'backgarden' layout indoors which can be operated by visitors. Collection of model locomotives and rolling stock. Children's layout at floor level. Model shop. Open: 10am–5pm daily, Easter to Oct. Winter, weekends only and occasional school holidays 10am–4pm. Telephone for details.

♿ 👫 <15 ☔

Mevagissey Museum

East Wharf
☎ (01726) 843568/843570
Open Easter to Oct, daily 11am–5pm.

Dodman Point

Given to National Trust in 1919; a well-preserved Iron Age fort with baulk, ditch and rampart, crosses the neck of the headland. Granite cross, erected as mark for seamen.

Caerhays Castle and Gardens

Caerhays, PL26 6LY
☎ (01872) 501310 or 501144
www.caerhays.co.uk
A picturesque mansion built by John Nash for J B Trevanion (1808). Early spring displays of shrubs are fine, especially camellias, magnolias and rhododendrons. Open: Gardens 10am–5pm daily, mid-Feb to end-May. Castle 12noon–4pm, Mon to Fri, mid-Mar to end of May. Visitors view the house on a conducted tour. These take place every 90 mins from 12 noon.

Ⓟ (On Beach, summer charge) ♿

👪 <16 🐕 (Gardens & Beach only)

Creed Church

1 mile (1.6km) from Grampound
Rebuilt in 1734 and retaining some of its wagon roof. Portrait of William Gregor and photograph of a titanium bowl near organ.

Trewithen House and Gardens

Grampound Road, nr Truro, TR2 4DD
☎ (01726) 883647 or 882764
www.trewithengardens.co.uk
Privately owned, 30 acres (12 hectares), internationally famous for rare shrubs such as camellias and rhododendrons of special species. Plants for sale on summer afternoons. Eighteenth-century house with splendid interiors. Open: Gardens 10am–4.30pm Mon to Sat, 1 Mar to 30 Sep. Sun in Mar, Apr and May only. House 2–4pm Mon, Tue and Aug Bank Holiday Mon, Apr to Jul. Tours every 20 mins in groups of 8, lasting 40 minutes.

Ⓟ (Nearby) ♿ (Ground Floor Only) 🐕

West of Truro

Gwennap Pit and Methodist Visitor Centre

2 miles south-east of Redruth
☎ (01209) 820013
On Whit Monday, Methodists come here for a celebratory service. Open: Pit open daily. Visitor Centre 10am–12.30am and 2–4.30pm, Mon to Fri, and 10am–12.30pm on Sat, Spring Bank Holiday to Sep.

Cornish Methodist Museum

In process of relocation. Contact Ian Haile ☎ 01872 223755

Killifreth Engine House

Beside the B3298 St Day–Scorrier road. Impressive industrial building.

Two, Three & Four Burrows

Important prehistoric tumuli. Beside the narrow road south of B3277; beside A30 at junction of A30 and A390; beside A30 about 2 miles (3.2km) east of above.

On & around the Roseland Peninsula

Melinsey Mill

Nr Veryan, TR2 5PX
☎ (01872) 501049
Working museum and tea rooms in a restored watermill. Open: 10am–5.30pm, Apr to end-Oct, Tue to Sun, Mar–May plus Oct. Free admission.

Ⓟ (At Quarry Mill) 👪

St Mawes Castle

(English Heritage)
TR2 5DE
☎ (01326) 270526
Described as Henry VIII's most decorative fort. Colourful gardens and lawns to the sea. Unusual clover-leaf plan produced by a central tower with three semi circular bastions. English Heritage special events during summer. Open: 10am–5pm Easter to Sep, Sun to Fri, open until 6pm in Jul and Aug.

10am–4pm daily in Oct. 10am–4pm Fri to Mon, Nov to Mar.

Ⓟ ♿ (Ground Floor Only) 👫

🐕 (Grounds only)

Smugglers Cottage and Ferry to Falmouth

Tolverne, TR2 5NG
☎ (01872) 580309
www.thesmugglerscottage.co.uk
Riverside restaurant serving lunches, cream teas and pasty suppers. Open: 10.30am–5.30am (8.30pm in high season), daily, Apr to end-Sept. History and artefacts of American departure for D-Day on view. During summer, departure point for ferry to Falmouth.

Ⓟ 👫 🐕

Trelissick

(National Trust)
Feock, nr Truro, TR3 6QL
☎ (01872) 862090
Gardens only but they have fine shrubs and nature trails. Shop, gallery and barn restaurant. Open: daily, mid-Feb to Nov 10am–5.30pm, 11am–4pm winter, 11am–4pm Wed Sun 27 Dec to 1 Jan. Parkland and estate open all year, daily.

Ⓟ ♿ 👫 (Family Ticket)

🐕 (Limited)

Penryn & Falmouth

Penryn Town Hall & Museum

☎ (01326) 372158
Standing centrally on Penryn's spine road, it houses offices and a museum of local history. Open: 10am–4pm, Mon to Fri all year. Opening times may vary as staffed by volunteers; check with Town Hall. ☎ (01326) 373086.

Falmouth Art Gallery

Municipal Buildings, The Moor, Falmouth, TR11 2RT
☎ (01326) 313863
www.falmouthartgallery.com
Permanent collection includes nineteenth and early twentieth-century paintings, prints and drawings. Regular temporary exhibitions. Shop area, access for disabled. Open: All year, Mon to Sat 10am–5pm, free admission. Guardian Family Friendly Museum of the year.

Ⓟ ♿ 👫

National Maritime Museum Cornwall

Discovery Quay, TR11 3QY
☎ 01326 313388
www.nmmc.co.uk
How boats and people interact for work and leisure; stunning displays; interactive exhibits; café and shop. Open: 10am–5pm daily, all year (not Christmas). Family ticket available.

Ⓟ(Charge) ♿ 👫 <5 Free <17

Pendennis Castle

(English Heritage)
Falmouth, TR11 4LP
☎ (01326) 316594
Museum, discovery centre, displays of coastal defence armaments and access to former secret installations. Regular special events from Apr to Oct. Open: 10am–5pm daily Easter to Sep (open until 6pm Jul and Aug), 10am–4pm daily, Oct to Easter. Castle closes at 4pm on Sat from Easter to Sep.

Ⓟ ♿ 👫 🐕

Ships and Castles Leisure Pool

Castle Drive, Pendennis Headland, TR11 4NG
☎ (01326) 212129
www.shipsandcastles.co.uk
Modern leisure pool with wave machine, 230-foot (70m) flume, river run, water geysers, spa pools, fitness suite, solariums, café.

Ⓟ ♿ ♟<16

Penjerrick Gardens

1 mile (1.6km) S of Budock Water, Falmouth, TR11 5ED
☎ (01872) 870105
www.penjerrickgarden.co.uk
Large garden created by the Fox family featuring rhododendrons, camellias, bamboos, tree ferns and magnificent trees. Open: 1.30–4.30pm, Mar to Sep, Wed, Fri and Sun.

Ⓟ ♟<16

Glendurgan Gardens

(National Trust)
Mawnan Smith, nr Falmouth, TR11 5JZ
☎ (01326) 250906
Valley gardens of great beauty – best seen in spring for flowering shrubs. Ferry runs to Durgan village on Helford River. Open: 10.30am–5.30pm, mid-Feb to Oct. Closed on Sun & Mon, Good Fri.

Ⓟ ♿ ♟

Argal and College Reservoirs

Penryn–Constantine Road
Pleasant recreational areas, ideal for walking.

Trebah Gardens

Mawnan Smith, Falmouth, TR11 5JZ
☎ (01326) 250448 or 252200
www.trebah-garden.co.uk
Magnificent 25-acre (10 hectare) garden cascades down a wooded ravine to a private beach (open to visitors to the garden). Special events programme including children's activities, plant sales, coffee shop. Open: 10.30am–5.30pm, daily all year. Motorised buggies available. Dogs are welcome in the garden and on the beach, water bowls are available outside the visitor centre and poop scoops given to dog owners on arrival.

Ⓟ ♿ ♟<15 <5 Free 🐕

What to do if it rains

Truro
Cathedral
Royal Cornwall Museum

Mevagissey
World of Model Railways Museum

Veryan
Melinsey Mill
Veryan Gallery

St Mawes
Castle

Trelissick
Shop and art and craft exhibitions

Penryn
Museum

Falmouth
Pendennis Castle
National Maritime Museum Cornwall
Falmouth Art Gallery
Ships and Castles Leisure Pool

About halfway between Truro and Penzance is historic Helston where on 8 May each year the past takes over as old houses and twisting streets echo with Flora Day celebrations – once a pagan welcome to spring.

Legend links Flora Day with St Michael and the devil, who tore the lid off hell in a final effort to defeat the saint. An inaccurate aim sent the stone away and till 1783 it was to be seen embedded in the courtyard of The Angel Hotel. This is an attractive building with parts dating from the sixteenth century. At the end of the seventeenth century it was the town house of Cornwall's great statesman, Sidney Godolphin, and later it became the Excise House. This included the Assembly Rooms with a minstrels' gallery. Great celebrations followed and the townsfolk adopted the saint as their patron. Whatever the truth, this annual event is worth seeing, particularly the noon dance, when couples in morning dress pick up the words of the song played by a local band and dance literally 'in and out of the houses'.

Helston

Helston's 1305 charter ruled that tinners should bring their mineral

Opposite page: Cadgwith fishing village and port

Left: Trevarno Gardens

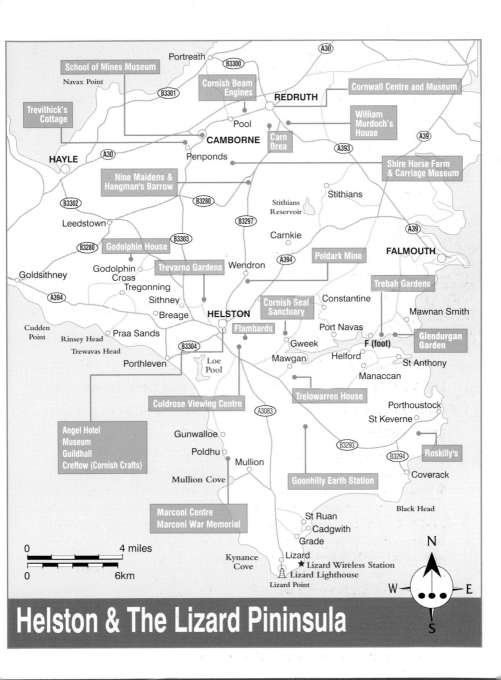

School of Mines Museum

Portreath   B3300   A30

Navax Point   B3301   Cornish Beam Engines   REDRUTH   Cornwall Centre and Museum

Trevithick's Cottage   Pool   William Murdoch's House

CAMBORNE   Carn Brea   A39

HAYLE   A30   Penponds   A393   Shire Horse Farm & Carriage Museum

Nine Maidens & Hangman's Barrow

Stithians   Stithians Reservoir

B3302   B3280   B3297   Carnkie   A39

Leedstown   Godolphin House   B3303   Wendron   A394   Poldark Mine   FALMOUTH

B3280   Godolphin Cross   Trevarno Gardens   Trebah Gardens

Goldsithney   Tregonning   Constantine   Mawnan Smith

A394   Sithney   Cornish Seal Sanctuary   Port Navas   Glendurgan Garden

Breage   HELSTON   F (foot)

Cudden Point   Praa Sands   Flambards   Gweek   Helford   St Anthony

Rinsey Head   B3304   Mawgan   Manaccan

Trewavas Head   Porthleven   Loe Pool

Culdrose Viewing Centre   Trelowarren House   Porthoustock

A3083   St Keverne

Angel Hotel Museum Guildhall Creftow (Cornish Crafts)   Gunwalloe   B3293   Roskilly's

Poldhu   B3294   Coverack

Mullion

Mullion Cove   Goonhilly Earth Station

Black Head

Marconi Centre Marconi War Memorial   St Ruan

Cadgwith   N

Grade

Kynance Cove   Lizard   Lizard Wireless Station

Lizard Lighthouse   W   E

Lizard Point   S

0 ———— 4 miles
0 ———— 6km

Helston & The Lizard Pininsula

Walks

Helford River/Gillan Creek

5 miles (8km) • easy • 2½ hours

Map: OS 1:25,000 Explorer Series 103: The Lizard, Falmouth and Helston

This walk starts at the picturesque village of Helford which can be reached by road (parking available near the church) or by ferry (foot passenger service available from Helford Passage from Easter to the end of October). It extends for 5 miles (8km) along the edge of the Helford, through the tiny waterside hamlet of St Anthony in Meneage to Dennis Head. Your return journey takes you along Gillan Creek to Manaccan. In Manaccan, go through the churchyard (a 200-year-old fig tree grows from the church wall), turn past the school and follow the footpath marked to Helford where you will find refreshments.

NB Dogs are not allowed on the section of the path that runs through the Bosahan Estate. This section is a permissive path by courtesy of the Bosahan Estate.

Lizard to Mullion

9 miles (15km) • strenuous in places • 4 hours

Map: OS 1:25,000 Explorer Series 103: The Lizard, Falmouth and Helston

A spectacularly beautiful walk, well worth the effort and offering stunning coastline views and a wealth of wildlife interest. The walk passes through lowland Britain's largest National Nature Reserve. Public transport can be combined with your walk, allowing you not only to leave your car behind but to avoid retracing your footsteps.

At Mullion, park in the car park to the north of the church. From here you can catch the bus to Lizard village green. Walk down to the Most Southerly Point and follow the coast path west in front of the Wave Crest Café. The path takes you past beautiful Kynance Cove to the Rill from which point spectacular views of the coast are afforded. It was from here that the first sighting of the Spanish Armada heading for Britain occurred in 1588. When you reach Mullion Cove, follow the road uphill back into the village. Do not forget to visit the fifteenth-century church, with some of the finest carving in Cornwall.

here for coinage or testing. Below the old Grammar School, where Charles Kingsley was educated, Coinagehall Street is an echo of medieval days. The church at the back of the town is behind the **Guildhall** and the **Folk Museum**. Neither of these should be missed, particularly the latter with its emphasis on the former crafts and industries which flourished in and around Helston during the nineteenth and early twentieth centuries. It has a good display of folk history, which includes Henry Trengrouse's life-saving rocket – invented after the *Anson* shipwreck on Loe Bar. Modern crafts are found opposite the museum in the **Creftow Gallery**, where the artists and craftspeople of modern-day West Cornwall display their products. Fresh fish and craft shops in Meneage Street are of above average quality.

In contrast to the bustle of Helston's streets a 3-mile (5km) drive northwards along the B3302 will take you to the turning for **Trevarno Estate and Gardens**. Here is an oasis of peace and tranquillity combining mature woodland landscapes with formal gardens. The history of the estate dates back to 1296, when it acquired its name from Randolphus de Trevarno, and it has been developed continuously over the intervening 700 years. Restoration is still being carried on today with something new to delight frequent visitors on each occasion including the **National Museum of Gardening**.

To the west of Helston

Porthleven is the birthplace of Guy Gibson, 'Dambusters' hero, and a road bears his name. It is a good place for tea after wandering through its narrow streets and visiting Breageside by the harbour. This was once the heart of a thriving port – note the picturesque store built originally to hold some 7,000 tons of china clay.

Off the A394 to Penzance, running almost parallel with the coast, several lanes lead to headlands and byways. **Trewavas Head** (Joseph Trewavas received Cornwall's first VC in 1856) and nearby **Rinsey Head** are ideal for picnics. Part of the area and the car park belong to the National Trust, who have partly restored the engine house and chimney of a disused copper mine, Wheal Prosper.

Praa ('Pray') **Sands**, a caravanners' haven, has a silver mile of dunes and safe beaches. Motorists can drive on to the privately-owned Acton Castle where the violinist Sandor Vegh began his Masterclasses. This unusual place was built at the end of the eighteenth century for John Stackhouse, who originated seaweed studies here. There are footpaths only for **Cudden Point** with its unusual view of St Michael's Mount. Walkers will enjoy Prussia Cove and Betsy's Cove, both haunts of John Carter, eighteenth-century smuggler and self-styled 'King of Prussia'.

The great inland mining area is reached via **Goldsithney**, a busy place in coaching days, now a quiet village. St Hilary Church, Goldsithney dates from 1854 but the tower dates from the thirteenth century, while an inscribed stone in the churchyard is probably sixth century. The unusual pictures on the inside walls are reminders of

Annual Events & Festivals

Throughout Cornwall there is a busy programme of events and festivals all year, some ancient and traditional, some of more modern origin but all providing fun and entertainment for visitors and local residents alike. Surfing festivals and championships are held regularly at Newquay and other watersports events at many of the beaches and harbours in the area. Art exhibitions are held in the various galleries in the region while agricultural shows are a constant feature of the summer calendar, as are flower festivals in spring and summer. Music, drama, literature, traditional ceremonies, sailing, windsurfing, carnivals and air displays; all are catered for. Details can be found in the local press and in the Tourist Information Centres. The following are a few to look out for:

February
Hurling, Columb Major, traditional street ball game

March
St Piran's Day (5th) Cornwall's patron saint
Festival of Spring Gardens (to end of May)

April
Trevithick Day, Camborne

May
Obby Oss procession, Padstow (1st)
Flora Day, Helston (8th)
Gwennap Feast, Methodist service at Gwennap Pit
Minack Theatre season (until September)
Daphne du Maurier Festival of Arts and Literature, Fowey and St Austell
Wesley Day, Wesley's Cottage, Trewint

June
Murdoch Weekend, Redruth
Golowan Festival, Penzance includes Mazey Eve and Mazey Day
Royal Cornwall Show, Wadebridge
Midsummer Eve bonfires throughout Cornwall starting at Chapel Carn Brea near Land's End
Truro Jazz Festival

July
RNAS Culdrose Air Day
Camborne Show
Bodmin Riding and Heritage Day

August
Bude Jazz Festival
Falmouth Regatta
Newlyn Fish Festival
Fowey Regatta

September
Cornish Gorsedd, various venues
Crying the Neck – several places
St Ives Festival of Music and the Arts
Helston Harvest Fair

October
Falmouth Oyster and Fresh Seafood Festival
Lowender Peran, Perranporth – Celtic dance and music

November
Camborne Music Festival

December
Tom Bawcock's Eve, Mousehole

The holiday resort town of Porthleven

the despoliation of the church in the 1930s when violent protests were made against the vicar, Fr Bernard Walke, who had introduced Anglo-Catholic services. It was originally whitewashed and served as a landmark for ships in St Ives and Mounts Bay. Its broached spire is one of the few in Cornwall.

Off the B3280, a turn to the village of **Godolphin Cross** comes after the hamlets of **Relubbus** and **Bosence**, both busy, lively places in Roman times. Relubbus had the tide at its feet and Roman remains at Bosence prove its trading capabilities. Deep in woodland lies **Godolphin**, a house that deserves a book to itself. This fifteenth-century mansion was built with wealth from nearby mines. Sir Sidney Godolphin, Elizabeth I's great High Treasurer, and the famed Godolphin Arab stallion are only part of the history associated with this property. The Godolphin estate is now cared for by the National Trust,

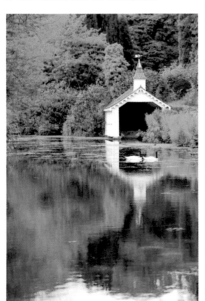

Left: Trevarno Gardens
Below: Kynance Cove

Loe Pool

The B3304 passes the boating pool on the Porthleven Road but walkers and ornithologists will want to explore the grounds of seventeenth-century Penrose beside **Loe Pool**, Cornwall's largest lake. Owned by the Rogers family since 1770, it is the main feature of their gift to the National Trust in 1974 – some 1,600 acres (648 hectares) altogether, the largest from Cornwall. A condition of this gift, that it be kept as a place of quiet beauty, makes it excellent for birdwatching. The house itself is not open. There is easy parking at the two entrances and the 6-mile (9.6km) walk taking in Loe Bar Sands will probably mean a rambling day and a picnic. The Loe is a long shingle bank dividing the freshwater lake from the sea.

with a programme of restoration work to outbuildings beginning in 2009.

The whole area of Godolphin and Tregonning is ideal for walks and picnics are made more pleasant by easy roadside parking. Chief Conin's dwelling, **Tregonning**, is a hill of ancient settlements and of more recent interest for William Cookworthy's discovery of china clay there in 1746. His subsequent findings at Carloggas near St Austell eventually led to the formation of Cornwall's china clay industry. The white 'signal' house was used to send messages to the ships defending Britain against Napoleon.

Before returning to Helston, stop at **Breage** (pronounced like 'vague') church. It has Margaret Godolphin's coffin plate, a Roman milestone and some fine murals among its other features.

North to Camborne & Redruth

Three miles (5km) north of Helston, along the B3297, is **Wendron** and the **Poldark Mine**. Here you can go safely underground and experience for yourself something of the past. Tin lodes, working machinery, and even dripping water help to recreate the mining age, with some of Richard Trevithick's instruments on display. Ample picnic space inside or out is available and there are entertainments for the children. Allow plenty of time here.

North once more, the bleak **Carnmenellis Moor** emphasises the mining atmosphere and a short climb to Hangman's Barrow and the Nine Maidens stone circle adds still more. This, too, is a place of many walks. Nearby, **Stithians Reservoir** is a must for ornithologists and yachtsmen but they should first obtain permission from South West Water.

The village of **Carnkie**'s disused engine houses have a melancholy beauty best viewed from the centre of the village and then in panorama from **Carn Brea**. Here is another place to visit whether you are artist, historian, birdlover or gourmet. Come when gorse and heather are out, explore the top of the Brea, where you can sit and relax and, while admiring the view, perhaps wonder about the Neolithic families who once lived here. The 90-foot (27m) granite monolith is a memorial to Francis, Lord de Dunstanville and Basset of Tehidy, erected in 1837. Then find the path downhill to **St Euny**, Redruth churchtown.

Nearby Reswythen Bridge was made unstable in 1301 by the mining operations of Ralph Wenna and John de Treveyngy and their goods were confiscated to pay for the damage. In **Redruth** itself, in Cross Street, William Murdoch used his invention of gaslight for the first time in 1792. **Murdoch House** has been restored as a memorial to him and is a centre for the Cornish Global Migration Programme. It is possible to see the house though there are no Murdoch artefacts on view. Redruth has a number of interesting old buildings, which can be seen by following the three town trails.

In the Old Post Office building on Alma Place is the **Cornwall Centre.** This houses the Cornish Studies Library and a well-stocked visitor centre. Through the building and down the stairs that connect with Market Way are the 58 panels of the Tregellas Tapestry, each beautifully embroidered with a different aspect of Cornish history.

Pool has the fine **Carn Brea Leisure Centre** and it is a good place to spend a day enjoying sport or relaxing – sometimes plays are performed here, too. The leisure centre almost closed in 2000 but was rescued by an enormous community effort. It is now run by a charitable trust.

Beside the main road at Pool are the **Cornish Mines and Engines.** On the south side of the road is a huge, restored Cornish beam engine, while just north of this is the **Industrial Discovery Centre** and another great beam engine

---

Sir Richard Tangye

Sir Richard Tangye (1833–1905), born at nearby **Illogan**, became a national benefactor and a brilliant engineer. He instituted the Saturday half-holiday and also built machinery to raise Cleopatra's Needle on the London Embankment. He was inspired by a fellow-countryman, the neglected genius, Richard Trevithick (1771–1833).

---

which has recently been restored. The engines raised copper ore and men to the surface, and pumped water out of the workings. These two engines are now in the care of the National Trust.

It is worth pausing for a while in **Camborne** to explore the town trail and see the fine architecture of many of the old municipal buildings there. Just off the B3303 at **Penponds** is the cottage – now managed by the Trevithick Trust – where Trevithick lived for a great part of his life and perfected most of his inventions. **Barriper** (from Beau Repaire) road was once part of the pilgrims' route to St Michael's Mount and the whole area is so peaceful that it is difficult to imagine it as a prosperous industrial locality. The un-Cornish name of **Leedstown** is a reminder of the time in 1740 when the youngest daughter of mining magnate Sir Francis Godolphin married the Duke of Leeds.

William Oliver lived at Truthall, a fine privately-owned manor in **Sithney** parish. He later moved to Bath and made famous the biscuits that bear his name and portrait, Bath Olivers. The church has a fine collection of glass medallions believed to be from the thirteenth century.

Above: Porthleven

Above Right: The monument on Carn Brea, above Redruth

Right: Cadgwith

Below: Cadgwith harbour and bay

The Lizard Peninsula

From Helston take the A394 Falmouth road to Trewennack where you will see a right-hand turn to Gweek. These lanes wander down to that little village at the head of the Helford River and you could pause there to visit the Seal Sanctuary. At the end of the village turn sharp left by a thatched cottage and follow the wooded lanes through Mawgan to Garras by Trelowarren on the B3293. Turn off immediately after the lodge entrance to that estate on your left and wander at leisure to Newtown, St Martin and Manaccan. Consult your map and watch for Helford village with the old Shipwright's Arms and you will see Frenchman's Creek signposted on the way. A short drive from here is St Anthony and Dennis Head beside Gillan Harbour. The lane from this peaceful place is very steep but beyond the cove of Porthallow is St Keverne, attractive and historical as you will see on the plaque on the church wall. The B3293 from here will take you past Goonhilly Satellite Earth Station back to Helston. As you approach Culdrose watch for a lane on the left to Gunwalloe. Driving down the lane into the village look out for the thatched cottage on the right where a plaque notes the time that Compton Mackenzie spent here in 1908–9, another Cornish literary connection. Pause in the village with its very ancient church and Halzephron Inn before returning to the A3083 and so to Helston.

Helston – Tregonning – Godolphin

Leave Helston on the A394 towards Penzance and follow it to Ashton, turning right for Breage church before reaching Ashton. In the centre of Ashton a right turn to Balwest will take you below the little-known Tregonning Hill. A drive or walk to the top will give you wonderful views over Mount's Bay and place you in history because Cookworthy discovered china clay on this hill. A short distance ahead is Godolphin Cross, and the Manor which is not far from Townshend on the B3280. A right turn here goes to Leedstown and Praze-an-Beeble with its right turn to Nancegollan on the B3303 to Helston. It is also possible to wander round the narrower lanes within this small rectangle of B roads and still not get lost.

Right: St Keverne Church

The Lizard Peninsula, Eastern Side

From Helston, the **Lizard Peninsula** can be explored by turning off the A394 Falmouth road past Trewennack to **Gweek**. Pleasant high-hedged lanes lead to Boskenwyn Downs and open on to a straight road probably constructed by the Romans to take tin from Grumbla to the port. Gweek's unusual name comes from the Latin 'Vicus' which confirms the Roman presence. Since very early times the valleys all round have been streamed for tin, and careful observers may still discover ancient tin moulds built into the quay walls. In 1201 Gweek was important enough to warrant a merchant guild as well as burgess privileges.

The creek is now silted up but beside it is the **National Seal Sanctuary**. It was established in 1958 and is the largest in Europe. Over the years the objectives of this conservation centre have been expanded and it now cares for all marine animals. It also shows how everyone can help.

The B3293 to St Keverne runs between a thatched tollhouse and the water – a pretty road affording occasional glimpses of the creek and walks through the woods. But a narrower primrose-clad lane on the far side of the house offers rewards for brave motorists. It is narrow and steep, winding up past an ancient earthwork, dipping through beech and elm woods before crossing the B3293 to wander up and down into the valley where **Mawgan-in-Meneage** lies. The whole parish of Monks (Meneage or Menaig seems to come from Cornish *managh* or monk)

is full of beauty and history – its church provides something of both. Look for the seventeenth-century sundial, a dog door and an unusual brass memorial to the unknown Hannibal Basset with the words 'Shall we all die'.

Keep to the Manaccan road through wooded lanes until a signpost to Kestle is reached. This lane leads to the unbelievably beautiful haven of **Frenchman's Creek**, which Daphne du Maurier saw, loved and made famous in her book of the same name. It has rightly been described as a place of 'distinct, eerie charm', and access to it is close by the farm. Over 35 acres (14 hectares) along the south bank are National Trust property and footpaths go to Tremayne Quay and Helford.

Motorists should return to the Manaccan road for **Helford** to see its thatched beauty. Stop at the old Shipwrights Arms and cross the river at Helford Passage to the Ferryboat Inn. Cars, other than exempted vehicles, are not allowed in Helford village between mid-March and the end of October, during the hours of 10am to 6pm. There is a car park above the village on the Manaccan side but it is quite a steep descent to the village.

The road to **Manaccan** is a delight. So is the village, perched saucily on a hillside. The centuries-old New Inn provides a wide variety of good food – beside a log fire. Geologists will remember that William Gregor discovered titanium from here and all should note that ill luck befalls those who pick figs from the tree in the church wall. Few, however, may know that Bligh of the *Bounty* came here to survey for the Admiralty, was mistaken for a French spy and promptly arrested.

St Anthony church on the beach at **Gillan** harbour is as beautiful as its surroundings. This was a busy port in medieval times, with ships sailing to Southampton loaded with fish, fish oil, hides, slate and tin. Today, the charm of this quiet corner of the Lizard lies in its remoteness and not in trade. The lonely village across the water is protected by a difficult access road so walkers may follow the coastal path, as motorists have to turn inland again.

St Keverne lies a little south of Manaccan and its church, about 1 mile (1.5km) inland from Manacle Point, has reminders of shipwrecks and has rightly been called the 'church of heartbreak'. A plaque on the churchyard wall is in memory of Michael Josef an Gof, the blacksmith who led the Cornish army to Blackheath with Thomas Flamank of Bodmin. This was the first rebellion of 1497 and he paid for this fight with his life. However, before his grim death at London's Tyburn, he told the crowd that both his name and fame would not be forgotten. His words came true for his memory and deed live still in the hearts of all Cornishmen.

Just outside St Keverne is the Tudor farmstead of Tregellast Barton, a small traditional Cornish dairy farm. Here the famous **Roskilly's** ice cream is made and the farm is open to visitors. As far as possible everything offered in the restaurant is made on the premises and Cornish produce, much of it from the farm, is sold in the shop. See the cows being milked in the late afternoon and take a walk around the farm to visit the wildlife habitats that have been created.

At this point some may wish to return to Helston, wandering quietly through the narrow lanes. If so, look for **Trelowarren**, between the villages of **St Martin's** and **Garras**. For 500 years it has been home to the Vyvyan family and the handsome house is now used for conferences and retreats. Some of the most secluded self-catering accomodation in Cornwall takes up a small part of the extensive grounds and a cluster of former barns and outhouses have their own attractions. A craft centre and an excellent restaurant will tempt most people while others may like to buy Trelowarren herb plants or visit one of the variety of craft exhibitions held throughout the summer.

The Lizard Peninsula, Western Side

There is even more to see and enjoy on the western side of the Lizard so allow plenty of time for this. Immediately outside Helston, along the A3083, is the Royal Naval Air Station at **Culdrose**. It is one of Europe's largest helicopter bases, established shortly after World War II. Good views of air traffic may be obtained from its public viewing area and subject to operational commitments, visitors can enjoy guided tours of the base.

A very different kind of entertainment is to be found just off that same road in **The Flambards Experience**. All-weather family amusements are set out here and include a life-size layout model of the London blitz, a re-creation of a Victorian Village and an aviation museum.

The B3293 from here will lead you

The National Seal Sanctuary, the largest in Europe

to **Goonhilly Downs** and the startling sight of a group of futuristic-looking dishes. This is the **Goonhilly Satellite Earth Station**, where the enormous aerials turn to the sky like creatures of science fiction. They were sited in this particular area because only the depth of granite found here was strong enough to bear the weight of these impressive structures. The station began operations in 1962. The first commercially funded satellite was known as Telstar. There is a very fine centre for visitors. Here you can study working models of both dishes and satellites, enjoy the well-presented audio-visual explanation of the mystery of modern telecommunications and try the interactive exhibits of the very latest technology; even send an email into outer space. The latest attraction, **Future World @ Goonhilly**, gives visitors the chance to decide what life will be like in the next hundred years – and beyond.

About 4 miles (6.4km) further along the B3293 is **Coverack**, a picturesque village, still mainly Cornish in character, with an appeal for those who enjoy sea views and a safe beach. The local lifeboat station is a particular place of interest.

There are numerous cliff walks in this

Lizard Point from the coastal path

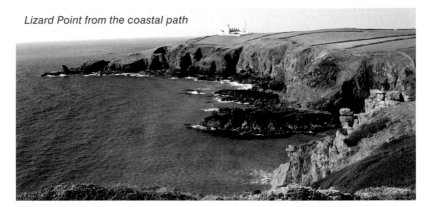

History of the Lizard Light

The first guiding light on this headland was built in 1619 by Sir John Killigrew of Falmouth, who needed money and planned to collect the dues from passing ships. So many vessels passed by without paying, however, that he was forced to give up his scheme as it was too expensive to maintain. In the mid-eighteenth century, two towers were built here to house a coal-fired warning light, but that produced so many problems that the idea was abandoned until oil lamps were installed in 1812. 1840 saw the first fog signals, and in 1878, a steam-driven generator powered two electric arc lamps, which gave good service until 1903 when they were replaced by a single 12 million candlepower beam. The light that shines from the Lizard today is one of the most powerful in the world.

Rare flowers and plants

From July to October the barren downs that surround the Goonhilly Earth Station are brilliant with white-pink and deep lilac Cornish heather which is only found on the Lizard Peninsula. A walk round the adjoining **National Nature Reserve** affords the chance to see some of the Lizard's unique flora. However, do not be fooled by the colourful succulent growing over many of the walls and cliffs at the Lizard point. This is the hottentot fig and is not native but an introduced plant that has taken over. The National Trust is trying to eliminate it to restore the natural flora in that area.

area; the one leading to **Kennack Sands** ends in a safe beach for swimming in fine weather. The motorist, however, must return to the B3293 and turn left at Traboe Cross in order to reach the National Trust **Poltesco Cove**. It is reached by scrambling down beside a trout stream, but is well worth the effort, and for energetic walkers there are nature trails to follow.

Cadgwith is a very 'picture-postcard' village, which is a little sad because it has lost most of its former fishing activities, although it still attracts artists and photographers. Serpentine can be found around these parts, and inland

Goonhilly Downs Earth Station

Kennack Sands

from Cadgwith, great blocks of it can be seen in the church towers of **St Ruan** and **Grade** – the latter to be found at the end of a cart track.

Marconi conducted some of his pioneering wireless experiments for the **Lizard Wireless Station** at Bass Point overlooking Housel Bay. It was here that on 23 January 1901 he received a communication from the Isle of Wight, which proved that wireless signals could travel well over the horizon. Replicas of the original equipment are now on view here. In earlier times the Lloyd's signal station was based here. Ships would semaphore details of their cargo to the shore and these could then be relayed to the ship's master well before the ship itself reached the Port of London.

All the cliff walks round here offer spectacular views of **Lizard Point** but the motorist has to go inland a short way from Landewednack and Grade to reach **Lizard village** which is little more than a cluster of souvenir shops with serpentine goods in great variety. At the end of the road is a lifeboat station, open for viewing when not in service, and Britain's most southerly beacon with interesting historical points to note. It was from here, about 400 years ago, in the summer of 1588, that the ships of the Spanish Armada were first sighted.

The **lighthouse** is now automatically controlled but with the aid of a Heritage Lottery grant, its buildings are being converted into a **Lighthouse Heritage Centre**, scheduled to open in spring 2009. A youth hostel is established in the buildings next door.

Cliff walkers will have no problem in finding the lovely places along the western coast of the Lizard Peninsula – **Kynance**, **Mullion** and **Gunwalloe** – before the return to Helston. Perhaps this is one of Cornwall's finest cliff walks because, not only are there attractive villages to see en route, but all the time there is a view of St Michael's Mount, topped by its fairytale castle and looking different at every turn.

Motorists will need to look out for signpost directions along the Lizard–Helston A3083, watching particularly for the turn to Cury and Poldhu where Guglielmo Marconi's Memorial stands on the cliffs of **Poldhu Cove.** This is near the site from where, on 12 December 1901, the first wireless communication was sent across the Atlantic to Marconi in Newfoundland, just eleven months after the earlier Isle of Wight transmission. Exactly 100 years later the **Marconi Centre** was opened at this spot to celebrate the event, exploring Marconi's place in history. So wireless telegraphy was born here and, in time, played a vital part in World War I. It is also interesting to note that the coaxial cable, which is an integral feature of every home television installation, was devised in the course of research done at Poldhu.

So, although the Lizard Peninsula may seem small in relation to the rest of Cornwall it has been, and will continue to be, responsible for events that make vital contributions to the progress of world science. A thought to remember on the return to Helston.

Places to Visit

In & Around Helston

Creftow (Cornish Crafts)

Helston, TR13 8TG
☎ (01326) 572848
www.creftow.com
Open: 10am–5pm Mon to Sat, Easter to Christmas. Closed on Wed between Christmas and the following Easter.

Guildhall

Coinagehall Street
In 1576 a market house was built here and it incorporated the Town Hall. The classical structure seen today, when erected in 1837–8, also had a corn market in part of the building, so carrying on the purpose of the original.

Helston Folk Museum

In the former Market House in Church Street. TR13 8TH
☎ (01326) 564027
It was built in 1837–8 and was composed of two buildings, one selling butter and eggs, the other meat. Open: 10am–1pm, Mon to Sat; open till 4pm school hols and Dec. Free admission.

Ⓟ ♿ (Ground Floor Only) 👫 ☂

Trevarno Estate and Gardens

Off B3302 north from Helston,
TR13 0RU
☎ (01326) 574274
www.trevarno.co.uk
Beautiful formal Victorian and Georgian gardens with collections of rare shrubs and trees. Woodland walks, a gardening museum, fountain garden conservatory, hand-made soap workshop, pottery and bee

centre. Refreshments available. Open: 10.30am–5pm, daily, all year.

Ⓟ ♿ 👫 <14 ☂ 🐕

Poldark Mine

Wendron, Helston, TR13 0ES
☎ (01326) 573173
www.poldark-mine.co.uk
A real mine to explore. Another world of tunnels, chambers and caves where old machinery is at work. Also museum of mining ephemera, picnic areas and undercover amusements for children. Open 10am–5.30pm Sun to Fri, Easter to Oct, open Sat in high season. Evening ghost tours and family ticket available.

Ⓟ ♿ 👫 <15 ☂

West of Helston

Loe Pool

(National Trust)
2 miles (3.2km) S of Helston
☎ (01326) 561407
This freshwater lake is an unusual example of the 'drowned valleys' occurring in Devon and Cornwall. The Loe Bar, formed by accumulated shingle from the Atlantic, has dammed the former estuary, which made the port of Helston. A 6-mile (9.6km) footpath runs round it. Small car parks at various points make it ideal for a day's outing.

St Hilary Church

Near Goldsithney
On an ancient Celtic site. Despoiled in 1932 but it remains open for those who want to see its treasures.

Places to Visit

Godolphin House

(National Trust)
Godolphin Cross, TR13 9RE
☎ (01736) 763194
Fifteenth-century mansion, standing 3 miles (4.8km) from Mount's Bay on the lower slopes of Godolphin Hill. Tin mines provided the family fortune. House open: end-Apr to Sept, 11am–5pm, daily. Garden open: Mar to Nov, 10am–5pm, Sat to Wed.

 (Estate Only)

Tregonning Hill

Ashton
A place of prehistory with Bronze Age barrows and fortified 'rounds'. The site of St Breaca's Celtic settlement, later the church at Breage. Today a good picnic place with walks and wide views to St Michael's Mount and beyond.

In & Around Redruth

Nine Maidens/Hangman's Barrow

Near junction of B3297 Wendron road and B3280 Praze-an-Beeble to Redruth road. Megalithic standing stones.

Stithians Reservoir

A centre for birdwatching, water sports and natural trout fishing. For permits apply to the SWWA (see FactFile).

Shire Horse Centre and Carriage Museum

Treskillard, TR16 6LA
☎ (01209) 713606
Open: 10am–6pm Mon–Fri, Easter to Oct. In Oct – Tue and Thu only.

William Murdoch's House

☎ (01209) 215736
Not far from the Buller's Arms this renowned house is tucked away in a Redruth back street. House only, no museum. Open: 9.30am–12noon on Fri or by request Mon–Thu.

Cornwall Centre (Kresenn Kernow)

Alma Place, Redruth, TR15 2AT
Cornish Studies Library, visitor information, Tregellas Tapestry.
☎ (01209) 216760
Open: 10am–6pm, Mon to Fri; 10am–4pm Sat.

Cornish Mines and Engines

(National Trust)
Agar Road, Pool, TR15 3NP
☎ (01209) 315027
www.nationaltrust.org.uk
Cornwall Industrial Discovery Centre at Taylor's Shaft with exhibition and nearby fully restored pumping engine house with its enormous 90-inch (2.3m) cylinder. Across the road is Mitchell's winder, a splendid working winding engine built in 1887. Open: Discovery Centre, 11am–5pm Sun, Mon, Wed, Thur, Fri, Apr to End-Oct.

Ⓟ (Morrisons Car Park) 🚻 👫<16

Carn Brea Leisure Centre

Station Road, Pool
☎ (01209) 714766
www.cblc.co.uk
Swimming pool, sports, sauna, indoor surf training.

Richard Trevithick's Cottage

(National Trust)
Lower Penponds, Camborne
☎ (01209) 612154
Residence of Richard Trevithick the Cornish Engineer. Trevithick Room full of memorabilia. Open: 2–5pm Wed from Apr to end of Oct by courtesy of the occupiers.

Crowan Reservoirs

Beside the B3280 Redruth–Hayle road.

Cows grazing at Roskilly's

Places to Visit

The Lizard Peninsula

National Seal Sanctuary

Gweek, TR12 6UG
☎ (01326) 221361
www.sealsanctuary.co.uk
Started in 1958, now devoted to seal rescue and care. Baby seals are in the hospital from Sep to Mar, but others are always on view. Two safari trains are available for transport from the car park to the main points beside the lovely Gweek River. Open: 10am–5pm daily except Christmas Day (10am–4pm in winter).

Roskilly's

Tregellast Barton, St Keverne, TR12 6NX
☎ (01326) 280479
www.roskillys.co.uk
Working farm plus woodland walk, farm shop and restaurant. Open: 10am–8pm daily during the summer, 11am–3pm weekends only in the winter. Free entry.

Trelowarren

Mawgan-in-Meneage, TR12 6AF
☎ (01326) 222105
www.trelowarren.co.uk
Woodland walks open 10am–6pm daily, April to end-Oct. The chapel may be open during daylight hours if not in use by the Trelowarren Christian Fellowship. Plant nursery and courtyard open all year. Restaurant Free admission.
Restaurant open: all year, every day except Mon for coffee and lunch; every day except Sun and Mon for evening meals. ☎ (01326) 221595

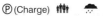
Ⓟ(Charge)

Cornwall Crafts Association

Trelowarren, TR12 6AF
☎ (01326) 221567
www.cornwallcrafts.co.uk
Temporary exhibitions, local crafts on sale. Open: 10.30am–5pm daily, Mar to Nov. Free admission.

Royal Naval Air Station

Culdrose
☎ (01326) 565085
This is beside the A3083 Helston–Lizard road. It is one of Europe's largest stations and machines are always on standby. Public viewing enclosure is close to the B3291, tours available. Open: 9.15am–5pm, Mon to Fri, Apr to Oct.

The Flambards Experience

Clodgey Lane, TR13 OQA, nr Helston
☎ (01326) 573404
www.flambards.co.uk
Aeroplanes, life-size Victorian village. Also 'Britain in the Blitz' – recreation of a wartime street. Children's attractions and rides. Open: 10am–5pm Apr to Oct, daily in high season, closed Mon and Fri at other times. Contact for winter opening times.

Ⓟ 🚹 ♿ 👫<11 ☂

FutureWorld@Goonhilly

Helston, TR12 6LQ
Beside the B3293
☎ (0800) 679593
www.goonhilly.bt.com
There is a public viewing enclosure and a visitor centre with unique multimedia visitor experience and interactive displays. Open: 10am–5pm (6pm in high season) daily, mid-Feb to Nov.

11am–4pm in low season. Closed on Mon Feb and Mar.

 <16

Lizard Lighthouse Heritage Centre

TR12 7NT
Signposted from Lizard village on the A3083 from Helston
☎ (01326) 290967 or 572607
www.lizardlighthouse.co.uk
Please see the website or call 01255 245011 for details of opening hours.

Ⓟ 𝗶𝘁𝗶 <16

Marconi sites:

Lizard Wireless Station

Bass Point (National Trust)
☎ (01326) 290384
Email: dbarlow@lizardwireless.org
www.lizardwireless.org
Open: regularly throughout the year, normally 12noon–3pm. Telephone or email for details. Opening is weather-dependent – when there are gales, fog, persistent rain or waterlogged paths the station is not opened

The Marconi Centre

Poldhu Cove, Mullion, TR12 7JB
☎ (01326) 241656
www.gb2gm.org.uk
Open: all year Sun 1.30–4.30pm, Tue–Fri 7pm–9pm; May, Jun & Sept Sun and Wed 1.30–4.30pm; July and Aug Sun, Wed and Thur 1.30–4.30pm and Summer Bank Holidays 1.30–4.30pm. Telephone for details. Free admission, but donations welcome as run by volunteers.

Marconi Memorial

Poldhu
The first radio signals across the Atlantic were sent from here by Guglielmo Marconi. Spot marked by a small Art Deco obelisk just south of Poldhu Bay, behind the Poldhu residential home.

What to do if it rains

Camborne
Richard Trevithick's Cottage

Helston
Folk Museum
Creftow, craft centre
Flambards Village Theme Park
FutureWorld@Goonhilly
Godolphin House, early Tudor manor
Trevarno Estate, museum and pottery

Mawgan-in-Meneage
Trelowarren Craft Centre

Pool
Carn Brae Leisure Centre
Cornish beam engines and Cornish Industrial Heritage Centre

Redruth
Shire Horse Centre and Carriage Museum
Cornwall Centre

Wendron
Poldark Mine

Travellers have always thought of Penzance as the place of journey's end. It is certainly the rail terminus in the west but the locals say that it is in fact where Cornwall begins. Before exploring the area of West Penwith (**Penwyth** is the Cornish for extremity) to discover the truth of this statement, there is much to enjoy in the town of Penzance itself, for it is a place of surprises.

Penzance

Beautiful still, with its high, stone-stepped pavement is Market Jew Street, the main thoroughfare that greets pedestrians, motorists and rail travellers who have left the station at the bottom of the hill. The long road leads to the handsome granite Town Hall, before which stands the statue of Sir Humphry Davy.

The road behind the former town hall, now the Market Hall, turns left towards the harbour and the Barbican

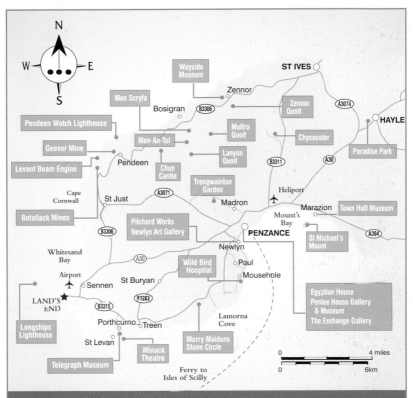

West Penwith, Penzance & Land's End

Sir Humphry Davy

He was born in a house near to his statue and there, too, began the experiments which eventually brought him fame. He was knighted in 1812 for his contributions to science and was later created baronet for his invention of the miner's safety lamp. It is perhaps not surprising that Davy, one of the foremost European chemists of the nineteenth century, was the one who realised and encouraged the talents of Michael Faraday. Davy's wide range of interests also touched on poetry, as well as the natural sciences. President of The Royal Society at 41, founder of the Athenaeum Club and the London Zoo, this man of Penzance was worthy to be called a genius.

complex down Chapel Street. This once bustled with mule trains laden with their copper ore for ships' cargoes. Now it is a backwater of memories, many of them lingering in the **Union Hotel** where the Battle of Trafalgar victory was first announced from the minstrels' gallery. Local fishermen had learnt it from the ship racing up-channel to Falmouth with the news. Such was local pride in this 'first' that Penzance men made the Nelson banner (now in Madron church) which has ever since been carried in procession on the Sunday nearest to Trafalgar Day. At the back of this historic building there is the shell of a Georgian theatre, opened in 1789. Here miners sought relaxation in the performances of Edmund Keen, Grossmith and other well-known actors.

Number 25 Chapel Street claims different honours. It was the **home of Maria Branwell** who married in Yorkshire and became mother to Charlotte, Emily, Anne and Branwell Brontë. She never lost her love for Cornwall, remembering it even on her deathbed when she begged the nurse to raise her up so that she could watch her clear the grate because 'she did it as it was done in Cornwall.' The house is not open to the public.

The Landmark Trust's **Egyptian House** with its flamboyant façade, also in Chapel Street, is of unusual interest. There are many side ways and shop-lined lanes to explore in this most western of Cornish towns and each has something to offer.

Not far away is the **Penlee House Art Gallery and Museum** in Morrab Road – a place of many treasures which houses a permanent collection of paint-

ings by artists of the 'Newlyn School'. It stands in subtropical gardens where camellias bloom at Christmas above the long promenade stretching from Newlyn to the memorial at the end of Chapel Street.

Another gallery has recently opened on the site of the old telephone exchange in the centre of Penzance. **The Exchange** is a sister venue to the long-established Newlyn Art Gallery, and hosts a changing programme of exhibitions, as well as housing a café and shop.

Madron village is very close to Penzance on the former B3312, now unclassified. It is high over the port and has a huddle of cottages pleasantly grouped near the church, which is named after a sixth-century holy man from Brittany, Maddern. It is the mother church of Penzance and, acknowledged to be one of Cornwall's finest, is well worth a visit. The pew ends are unusually fine, there is the Nelson banner (mentioned earlier) and the great bell from the famous Ding-Dong Mine, whose ruined engine house is silhouetted starkly on the high land ridge behind the village.

The lovely **Trengwainton Garden**, a National Trust property, lies beside the A3071 below Madron. There has been a house here since the sixteenth century, but it is now privately owned. In 1814, Rose Price, the son of a rich West Indian sugar planter, bought the house and estate and began to develop it along the lines seen today. He enlarged the original house, gave it a granite façade, built the lodge, planned the walled gardens and planted the magnificent woods of beech and sycamore which are so greatly admired today.

Walks

St Just-in-Penwith

3–4 miles (5–6km) • fairly strenuous • 1½ to 2 hours
Map: OS 1:25,000 Explorer Series 102: Land's End, Penzance and St Ives

Start at St Just at the large car park. Take the footpath beside the churchyard gate across the town square. On reaching the road at Nancherrow Farm, follow the narrow path on the left that runs down the narrow Nancherrow or Kenidjack Valley to the sea. Notice the huge waterwheel pit at the seaward end. Follow the coastal footpath signposted up to the right and enjoy dramatic cliff scenery and some of the most famous ruined mine engine houses in the world, Botallack and Levant. From the latter place a narrow road almost 1 mile (1.5km) long leads inland to Trewellard village where you can get refreshments and catch a bus back to St Just.

St Michael's Way

12 miles (19km) • easy • 5 hours
Map: OS 1:25,000 Explorer Series 102: Land's End, Penzance and St Ives

Part of the European network of ways followed by pilgrims travelling to the shrine of St James of Compostela, this leaves the church of St Uny at Lelant, near Hayle on the north coast, and carries on across the narrow 'waist' of land to St Michael's Mount. It is signposted all the way, marked with a stylistic shell based on the Council of Europe's sign for pilgrim ways.

Lamorna

12–15 miles (19 24km) • some strenuous • all day
Map: OS 1:25,000 Explorer Series 102: Land's End, Penzance and St Ives.

The magnificent scenery in this part of Cornwall can be enjoyed by those who like cliffs and the sea. The South West Coastal Footpath is clearly marked by Acorn signposts. Start at Mousehole and follow the route to Lamorna where there is rest and refreshment. On to the National Trust's Penberth Cove and round to the Logan Rock from where the lovely sights of Porthcurno can be viewed – the beach, the strangely blue sea and the unique Minack Theatre, as well as the fascinating Telegraph Museum. Footpaths inland lead to Treen, Tresidder and St Buryan where doubtless a bus will take the weary walker to Penzance.

The Landmark Trust's Eqyptian House in Penzance

Penlee House

East to St Michael's Mount

From Penzance, the road follows the vast, magnificent sweep of Mount's Bay past the Heliport (for the Isles of Scilly) and Long Rock to **Marazion**. This place is a delight, with its view of St Michael's Mount (acknowledged to be the earliest identifiable place in Britain). Its golden sands and safe bathing are ideal for children while the marshes nearby attract birdwatchers. Marazion was a thriving port as long ago as the Bronze Age as it was on one of the main overland routes for merchants taking Irish gold to Brittany. You can learn more about its history in the small but fascinating **Marazion Museum** in the town hall.

Wishing Well

A short distance from the village of Madron is its famous wishing well. Those who care to walk about half a mile (800m) down a damp ferny lane will probably see rags hanging from the surrounding bushes – offerings still made to St Maddern, possibly for happiness in love or simply to placate the invisible spirits and hope for their protection.

Trengwainton Gardens

Meaning of a name

Marazion is usually interpreted as meaning 'Little Market' but probably 'Small Sea' is a better meaning of the interesting name: 'mara' meaning sea and 'zion' coming from *vyghan* or small. The latter describes perfectly the narrow strip of water between the village and the Mount, which can perhaps be seen to better advantage from the higher villages inland.

St Michael's Mount

Ordnance Survey maps mark **Long Rock** just offshore and the houses along the main road take their name from it. Legend relates that St Michael appeared to some hermits, supposedly on a large rock, which has ever since been known as St Michael's Chair, while history tells us that it was Edward the Confessor who established a Benedictine chapel on **St Michael's Mount**. The monks' domestic buildings are now incorporated in the fourteenth-century castle on the rock summit but the abbot's kitchen is well preserved and stands apart.

Even grey skies cannot dim the magical quality of the Mount, which was given by Lord St Levan to the National Trust in 1954 although the St Aubyn family still live in the castle. Visitors reach it by foot across a causeway or ferry from Marazion. Apart from the situation of this spectacular retreat, there is interest here for all. The harbour and village may always be visited, but

St Michael's Mount

Historic past

It would be easy to spend a whole day on St Michael's Mount thinking of the past: perhaps of 1497 when Perkin Warbeck left his wife on the Mount to make an abortive claim for England's throne, or of 1549 when the owners of the castle were involved in the Prayer Book Rebellion. Later in 1642–3 the future King Charles II was given sanctuary en route for the Isles of Scilly – a plaque proclaiming this is on the wall of a house in Marazion.

the castle is normally closed between November and March and does not open on Saturdays.

West to Land's End

Brenda Wootton, who was a popular cornish folk singer, had a song called *My Yesterday Town*. It is about **Newlyn** where she was born and looks back sadly to former times when it was an important fishing harbour before artists and visitors poured in to intrude on the intimacy of its community life. Then it was a village with five bridges, five pubs, one church and cottages tip-tilting down the hill to the sea: their livelihood, their joy and their sorrow.

Memories of sadness are still retained in the name **Mount Misery**, high above the bay. This was where anxious wives and sweethearts watched during storms, fearful that their men might not return. The fisherman's world is no

longer the same, but the charm of the old cottages remains and there is still the fine quality of clear light which later on attracted Stanhope Forbes and other artists who exhibited in the **Newlyn Art Gallery** donated by Passmore Edwards. Eden Phillpotts, the prolific novelist, began his career while staying in this area.

The name **Penlee** reverberated round the land like the tolling of a funeral bell at the end of 1981 when storms off this coast caused a lifeboat tragedy. Penlee Point is on the coast road to **Mousehole** ('Mouzel'), the prettiest fishing village according to many visitors, and which, with Penzance and Newlyn, was burned by the Spaniards in July 1595 and almost destroyed. Its delightful cluster of cottages hugging the harbour appeals to artists, photographers and most holidaymakers. Others enjoy visiting the **Bird Hospital** on Raginnis Hill, founded by the Yglesias sisters, now a registered charity.

The village of **Paul** clusters round its church, another guide for shipping. The church is high above Mousehole and on the churchyard wall is a memorial to Dolly Pentreath, whom some consider to have been the last traditional speaker of Cornish. She was buried there under her married name of Jeffery in 1777.

Only 2 miles (3.2km) along the cliff path, but further by road past the Roman encampment of Castallack, lies the fertile and lovely **Lamorna Valley**. A bubbling trout stream and colourful gardens tempt visitors down to the little harbour or cove, justly known as one of Cornwall's loveliest, enticing them to linger. The artist Samuel John Birch could not leave, added Lamorna to his name, and gained fame as S J Lamorna Birch RA. The 10-mile (16km) cliff walk from here to Land's End is one that should not be hurried as there are flowers, birds and views sufficient to satisfy everyone.

Above Lamorna Cove, past Trewoofe ('Troove') is **Boleigh**, site of the last battle between the Cornish and the English, which took place in AD935. To celebrate his victory, King Athelstan gave a charter to found a collegiate church at **St Buryan**. The two immense megaliths known as 'the Pipers' are believed to have been erected by the king as peace stones to seal the treaty.

St Buryan is a handsome church of the late fifteenth century with a fine rood screen and a 92-foot (28m) granite tower. Further along the B3283 lies the village of **Treen**, once the heart of a busy tin-streaming area, now only a cluster of houses in the beautiful

Selected Car Drives

Newlyn, Mousehole, Porthcurno and Land's End

Leave Penzance station and follow the road along the coast, round Cornwall's only promenade into Newlyn and on to Mousehole. A steep hill up to Raginnis and a right turn at the next junction will take you to the B3315. A little over 2 miles (3km) further on a minor road on the left is signed to Lamorna. That romantic steep lane is worth the climb down. Returning to the B3315 notice the Merry Maidens standing stones. After a short distance take the minor road to St Buryan, enjoy the village and join the B3283 and B3315 on to Porthcurno where everything is lovely: a magical blue sea and the Minack open-air theatre which has to be seen to be believed. The Telegraph Museum is also well worth a visit. Return up the same steep hill out of Porthcurno but turn left at the top to Land's End, joining the A30 before stopping at the complex there. This road returns to Penzance.

St Just and the north Penwith coast

Leave Penzance on the A30 towards Land's End but at Castle Horneck take a right turn onto the A3071. It opens out to ancient moorland where the small fields remain as they were in ancient times. The little granite village of St Just sits solidly against the storms but leave it for the B3306 and detour to Botallack for a glimpse of majestic old engine houses clinging to the cliff edge. The B3306 follows the coast all the way round to St Ives where the A3074 will lead you to the A30 and Penzance again. On the coast road is the isolated Zennor Wayside Museum and a church with tales of a mermaid. Numerous lanes lead inland to the moors and it is worthwhile driving along them to see Chun Castle, Men Scryfa and Lanyon Quoit, knowing that you can return to the safety of the B3306 at any time.

Marconi's romance

Few people know the story of how the famous Marconi met and fell in love with Betty Paynter on the Lamorna cliffs. She was then the fifteen-year-old daughter of Colonel Paynter of nearby Boskenna House, but the vast difference in age did not stop the engineer. He installed a radio receiver in her schoolroom at home, sent diamond bracelets to her at school and sailed his yacht into Bournemouth almost every weekend in the hope of a meeting; a story in the best romantic tradition, but one that did not end according to the Cinderella pattern. After three years of fun and friendship, the schoolgirl, then grown up, realised that the love was all on his side and refused him for the last time.

Fort consists of 36 acres (14.5 hectares) and incorporates a complex of defensive ditches dating from the Iron Age. Here is the famous **Logan Rock**, once moved ill-advisedly by Oliver Goldsmith's nephew for a prank. It weighs 66 tons and the overenthusiastic young man had to replace it at his own expense. Space is limited on this headland so visitors must leave their cars above the bridge over the stream and walk the last quarter of a mile (400m).

Motorists who leave the B3315 to drive to **Porthcurno Beach** and on to the Minack Theatre must be prepared for narrow and winding lanes. The road passes the former Cable and Wireless Training School before the car

wooded valley leading to the National Trust properties of Penberth Cove and part of Treryn Dinas. The cove is a reminder, perhaps, of the way of life once common in many Cornish fishing communities where wives and children grew violets and narcissi for the London market – now you can buy wines there. The old trade developed considerably after the opening of Brunel's Royal Albert Bridge in 1859. The valley, cove and headland passed to the National Trust in 1957, many of the small gardens are still cultivated and inshore fishermen are as active as their forefathers were.

The fine jagged headland of **Treryn** ('Treen') **Dinas** forms one side of **Porthcurno**, a bay of startling blues and greens with the **Minack Open-air Theatre** on its other side. **Treryn**

Waves breaking on Porthcurno beach

Above & Right: Minack Theatre

Land's End

The Old Lookout on the cliffs above Sennen Cove

Newlyn Harbour

park nearest to the beach. The building is now the **Porthcurno Telegraph Museum**, housed in a series of tunnels built in 1941 to protect the telegraph station during World War II.

Theatregoers have to drive up the steep road beyond to reach their destination, but the **Minack Theatre** is a place not to be missed. It is unique. In 1932, Miss Rowena Cade and her gardener began the task of creating an amphitheatre out of the natural rock on the cliff edge for a performance of *The Tempest*. Stone seats now replace the original grassy ledges, sound and lighting and dressing-room accommodation are of the best, but the original magic remains. The theatre is open all day for visitors (except during matinee performances) but those who are fortunate enough to attend a play see it at its very best. No matter what the play or the players, the setting makes every performance one of individual delight – the sight of the moon rising over the backcloth of ocean is a never-to-be-forgotten experience.

The church of **St Levan** and its holy well lies beyond the Minack, and there the road stops, so motorists must return to the B3315 for Land's End. The walk along the coast from here would take most people about two and a half hours.

On a fine day the views are unrivalled. Here is another place for a whole day's exploration; photographers, botanists, poets and holidaymakers of all ages will find something here to please them. Longships Lighthouse lies due west of the last group of rocks while 7 or 8 miles (11 or 12km) beyond is Wolf Rock. This was the place used by Trinity House for their experiments in airlifting supplies to lighthouse crews. The results were completely successful.

Also at **Land's End** is one of Cornwall's most varied family attractions with exhibitions, visitor centre, discovery trail, RSPB hide, shops and restaurants. It takes a day to see them all.

North of Land's End

About a mile (1.5km) to the north lies **Sennen**, near the Mayon and Trevescan Cliffs, both National Trust properties. Mayon Cliff is topped with a good example of a Cornish cliff castle (Mayon meaning *maen* or stone) with sheer drops to the sea and a view of basking sharks cruising off the rocks in summer. Above Sennen Cove, which continues on to Whitesand Bay, is

---

Prayer for sunshine

Today at Chapel Carn Brea (not to be confused with Carn Brea at Redruth) members of St Just Old Cornwall Society light the first in the chain of forty bonfires which illuminate Cornwall on Midsummer Eve from Land's End to the Tamar. This is a particularly festive occasion. Songs and prayers (usually in Cornish) accompany the 'sacrifice' of herbs and flowers thrown into the flames by the Lady of the Flowers to propitiate the sun god; a plea, shared by all visitors, for summer sunshine.

the ancient church of St Sennen, the westernmost church in Britain. It is small and low, as befits its site, and was reconsecrated in 1440.

Before the village of **Crows-an-wra** (Witch's Cross) several paths leave the main road and climb to **Chapel Carn Brea**, which also belongs to the National Trust. It is the first and last hill in Britain and is reputed to have the widest sea view from the mainland of the British Isles. Two Bronze Age barrows and the remains of a medieval chapel dedicated to St Michael may be seen after a gentle climb to the top, where in 1907 one of Cornwall's largest Bronze Age urns was found (it is now in the Royal Cornwall Museum in Truro).

The whole area is good for picnics and walks and for exploring the many antiquities in the locality. Nearby **Sancreed** church is worth looking at. There is a good rood screen, original barrel roofing and five crosses in the churchyard. One, which has lilies on it, is said to be noteworthy. Half-hidden in trees in a field close by is the Sancreed holy well and baptistry possessing an exceptional air of mystery and sanctity.

The road from Sancreed runs past Drift Reservoir to join the A30. It is a pleasant place for walks and picnics as old mingles with new here, for **Drift** village is mentioned in Cornwall's best-known folk tale – John of Chyannor. He left Treen when mining was at a low ebb and went to look for work in the east. That to him was not land overseas, but a farm a few miles east of Marazion. This particular story is especially interesting as it names all the places John visited in his wanderings, something which does not often occur in folk tales.

Deep in the valley of **Buryas Bridge** there is a cross inscribed with symbols of the Cretan mysteries – another link with the strange past of West Penwith. These insignia appear to relate to the famous Cretan labyrinth where the Minotaur lurked, but no one has yet provided a real explanation for the designs.

The Penwith Coast

To see the best of the northern part of this peninsula follow the A3071 out of Penzance. It passes **Castle Horneck** shortly after leaving the edge of the town, a splendid place for a youth hostel and once the home of the Levelis or Lovell family. They owned much of the land in this area in early medieval times and were greatly involved in the Crusades. A well-known Cornish Christmas song, *The Mistletoe Bough*, is based on a tragic incident in the Lovell family. A young bride hid from her husband in an old oak chest and was entombed there, trapped by an unseen spring lock.

The countryside around **St Just** is almost other-worldly; its small fields and drystone walls bringing to mind the first men who ever settled here many centuries ago. The tower of the church, though low, can be seen from quite a distance as it has stood in granite solidity since the fifteenth century. Near the clock tower a grassy arena is used today for the ceremony of choosing St Just's Carnival Queen. It is, in fact, a *plen-an-gwary* (Cornish for 'playing place'), where medieval mystery plays were performed.

From St Just explore the Penwith coast starting from Cape Cornwall

Top: Lamorna Cove

Middle: Trewellard, Levant Steam Engine

Bottom: Botallack Mine

now has a different character, and is very popular with local swimmers.

Beyond Land's End is the Longships Lighthouse while in the other direction are the picturesque cliff-edge ruins of the Three Crowns Mine at **Botallack**. The coastal path, like the road, goes towards **Trewellard**, an old mining village with a unique church. The Reverend Robert Aitken designed it himself and by 1851 it was finished, built entirely by the local miners. Some may think little of the plain, bleak place of worship but no one can deny that it suits the surroundings and reflects the comfortless life which was the lot of most people who lived at Trewellard in those days.

Street which leads from the Square to **Cape Cornwall**, now a National Trust property. Many people find it pleasant to spend a day here, taking advantage of the numerous walks, picnic places and advantageous locations for bird-watching. The towering nineteenth-century chimney at the summit of Cape Cornwall, known as the Sentinel, is a reminder of the many mines once busy in this district. There is an extensive view from this height although Priest's Cove to the south is probably hidden. It was once a medieval landing beach but

Land's End

Three Crowns Mine

In 1865, the Prince and Princess of Wales (later King Edward VII and Queen Alexandra) came here and descended the mine. This profitable mine caught the imagination because it produced riches from beneath the very seabed itself. Tunnels 7ft by 4ft (2m by 1m) were cut into a rich copper lode and men worked there each day at a depth of 1,360 feet (415m) below sea level and half a mile (800m) from shore. When the quarterly accounts were produced, owners and mine managers would celebrate their gains with a feast at the Count House.

Pendeen Manor, an attractive sixteenth-century farmhouse, was the birthplace of Dr Borlase, the father of Cornish archaeology. In the yard there is a fogou or underground passage which runs for 23 feet (7m) in one direction and 33 feet (10m) in another. At the angle of these is another chamber. There has been much speculation as to the original use of these constructions – Cornwall has several of them. Archaeologists have not yet been able to agree on a satisfactory reason for their existence so no one can say whether the fogous were built for storage, defence or even primitive housing. One recent thought on the subject is that they might have been designed for worship.

Past the manor, the road leads to **Pendeen Watch lighthouse**. Perched on a cliff edge, it is surrounded by open land where there are birds and flowers in plenty. Also at **Pendeen** is the spectacularly situated **Geevor Mine**, which once yielded both tin and copper. It was registered as a limited company in 1911 and incorporated the old mines of Wheal Stennack and the ill-fated Levant. Tragedy struck in the latter in 1919 when the man-engine, carrying its full complement of men and boys to the surface, broke, crashed in ruins to the bottom of the shaft and killed 31 miners. The deeper workings were then abandoned, work ceased altogether from 1930 and the sea took possession of them.

Fortunately the Cornish Engine Preservation Society (now the Trevithick Society) saved the beam engine in 1935 and in 1967 handed it to the National Trust. They then restored both engine and engine house, a fascinating reminder of the prosperous times of 1870 when the area supported about 20 mines. The **Levant Steam Engine** is now open to the public for most of the year and volunteers from the Trevithick Society run the engine in steam regularly.

Geevor, a working mine until 1990, is now a preserved mining site offering underground tours and a museum to tell the tale of how local people fought to win the minerals from hundreds of feet underground and out under the sea. For many other mines only their ruins remain, picturesque and sad, along the cliffs, slowly but surely weathering away.

From here to Zennor, the coast road is particularly interesting, especially at **Bosigran** beyond Morvah on the

Penwith Antiquities

Penwith is an area full of ancient sites and many legends exist which have been told from generation to generation. Ludgvan (Lugian) is a quiet churchtown set well above Mount's Bay amidst narrow, twisting lanes. Dr William Borlase, born at Pendeen in 1695, was village rector for 52 years and published several books including *The Natural History of Cornwall* in 1758, 31 years before Gilbert White's well-known *Natural History of Selborne*. This energetic clergyman was the first archaeologist to detail the heritage of Beaker Age monuments and his work in this field is still unsurpassed.

From the steep B3309 below the church towards Crowlas, just east of Penzance, the second lane on the left leads to the exciting Penwith countryside, studied by Borlase. A lane curves round the foot of **Trencrom Hill** (SW 518362), a hill fort with fine views over the narrowest part of Cornwall and forming part of the granite backbone of West Penwith with well-preserved Iron Age remains at the summit. The soil here is good and Channel Island herds thrive in the area. The site was given to the National Trust by Colonel G L Tyringham of Lelant in memory of the men and women of Cornwall who gave their lives in the two World Wars. It consists of 64 acres (26 hectares) of gorse-covered hill, overlooking an expanse of both land and sea, that is ideal for views, walks and picnics.

Here are numerous well-preserved antiquities – an Iron Age stone-walled hill fort enclosing several hut circles. Legend says that Giant Trecobben used to throw 'pebbles' at his brother Cormorran who lived on the Mount: the gigantic Bowl Rock beside the Lelant to Towednack road to the north, given to the Trust in 1962, has the notice 'thrown by a giant'!

Further along that same road is **Trink** – once reputed to be the home of another giant but now a delightful place for holidaymakers. North-east from here, a turning off the B3311 leads to lonely **Towednack** church. A strange story lingers in its history which is remembered on 28 April when the Towednack Cuckoo Feast used to be celebrated. The event recalls the time when a local farmer caught a cuckoo which flew from a log he was burning during a party. Perhaps the villagers hoped to hold and preserve the spirit of spring in this way. (Most Cornish churches hold their feasts to commemorate the arrival of their patron saint.)

The way to **Castle-an-Dinas** and **Chysauster** is down the Nancledra valley where tin has been streamed since earliest times. The former is one of the chain of hill forts across the country, the latter (along a pleasant lane off the B3311, 2½ miles/4km NW of Gulval) probably one of the best-preserved beehive hut circles in Great Britain. It was an Iron Age village from about the second century BC to the third century AD and consists now of a series of stone houses, each containing a number of rooms. Partial excavations have been made here and the walls of the buildings are still clearly visible.

Chysauster is an English Heritage site with set opening times and a charge for entry. Open: 10am–5pm (6pm July and August, 4pm October or dusk daily March to October); ☎ (07831) 757934

Not far away at the head of the Trevaylor valley, towering over the Penwith Peninsula is **Mulfra Quoit**. This close group of standing stones on the site of an ancient settlement at Mulfra Hill gives substantial evidence to the theory of ancient ley lines. Three of the four original uprights still stand and support a partially displaced capstone. Traces of a circular barrow about 40 feet (12m) in diameter, the original covering of the chamber, can be seen.

Also in the same area is the **Men-an-Tol**, a fascinating monument with numerous legends. In 1749 Dr Borlase learnt that local people still crept through the hole to cure their rheumatism, while children who suffered from rickets were passed through it at certain times of the year. Sir Norman Lockyer wrote that this megalith was an astronomical instrument for the observation of certain sunrises and sunsets.

Close by are the **Men Scryfa** (3 miles/4.8km NW of Madron), an 8 foot- (2.4m) tall inscribed stone, and the **Nine Maidens Stone Circle**. Were these stones really girls who had danced on the Sabbath and had been turned to stone for their sin? That is what the legend says. The Men Scryfa, however, is thought to be closer to reality. *Rialobranus Cunovali Fili* is the Roman inscription and could be translated as 'Son of Chief Royal Raven'. Some think it was the grave of a giant warrior, others consider it another ley marker and there are those who think it could be the gravestone of the noble Rialobran (Royal Raven) who lived between the fifth and sixth centuries BC on nearby Carn Galver.

Beside the lonely secondary road which runs from Morvah to Madron about 4 miles (6.4km) North-west of Penzance stands **Lanyon Quoit** – probably Cornwall's most famous monument and the only known example of the remains of a long barrow. A huge granite capstone (18 x 9ft - 6 x 3m) on three upright stones, it was originally 90 feet (27m) long, its capstone so high that Dr Borlase rode his horse under it. It was re-erected by public subscription in 1824 after a violent storm (1815) broke one of its four stone supports and this accounts for the present lower height.

Another group of stones – the **Merry Maidens** – stand alongside the B3315 Newlyn to Treen road. This is the best-known stone circle and consists of nineteen stones, the whole being about 75 feet (23m) in diameter, and is one of the places where the Cornish Gorsedd is sometimes held. This gathering is an annual event at which new bards are admitted to the Gorsedd, or College of Bards, an organisation unique to Celtic communities enshrining their common cultural heritage.

Carn Euny near Sancreed, 4 miles (6.4km) west of Penzance, is an ancient Iron Age village now cared for by English Heritage. The remains are said to rival those of Chysauster and there is the added attraction of a fine 60 foot- (18m) long fogou or underground chamber. The Blind Fiddler Stone – source of many legends – stands beside the A30, and down a farm lane opposite is Boscawen-un, an isolated stone circle with a central heel stone or altar. Henry Jenner, who revived the Cornish Gorsedd in 1928, chose this place for its first assembly.

Each of these sites, created by the ancient Cornish people, will reward visitors with a special atmosphere and sense of history.

National Trust cliffs. These are wild and exposed but man has learnt how to survive here from prehistoric times, sheltering his crops and animals in tiny fields surrounded by their stone hedges which remain from the Iron Age. The adventurous will probably enjoy the circular walk westwards from Porthmeor Cove to the Iron Age ruins of Bosigran Castle, along the spur path and back to Porthmeor Cove along the main road.

The village of **Porthmeor** is missed by most people who, not unnaturally, are eager to reach Zennor. It is, however, worth asking at **Bosporthennis** for permission to cross the private land and look at the Iron Age village court-yard house here. It is similar in many respects to Chysauster but in addition has its own fortification and gatehouse and is one of the best of the numerous ancient monuments scattered on the downs above the B3306.

Today, **Zennor** is a picturesque min-iature village lying in the slight shelter of Trewey Hill. It has, however, a long

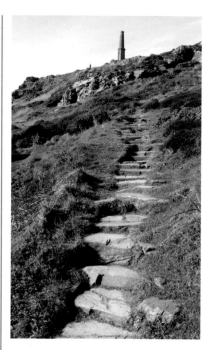

The path to Sentinel Chimney, erected in 1875, Cape Cornwall

and interesting history. Isolated as it was by the natural features of land and sea, Zennor remained almost inaccessible for centuries, which is why the presence of the past is still so strong in and around it. The small fields of middle and late Bronze Age settlements are still to be seen at Trewey and Wicca. Some tools and farm implements used for agricultural work down the years are among the exhibits in the small **Wayside Museum**, close to the car park. Whether mining is quite as old as farming here no one knows, but it is said that tin-streaming has thoroughly worked almost every area of the Foage valley. Tools used for this are another feature of the museum.

Both these industries were quite local but Zennor's stone-workers were once famous far beyond their homes.

Climbing connections

Adjoining Bosigran is more National Trust property with a rather special history. Here, during World War II, commandos trained (the western side of the valley is, in fact, named 'Commando Ridge'). Here, too, Lord John Hunt and Sherpa Tensing climbed together to celebrate the tenth anniversary of the ascent of Everest. Never before had Tensing seen the sea and it was his first experience of cliff climbing. Cars can be parked by the road here and access to the coast is by the spur path past the Climbers' Club hut.

Pendeen Watch

Tradition tells that the granite for St Ives' church was brought by sea from here, boats sometimes having to wait for weeks in order to take advantage of a spell of rare fine weather. Great cubes of Zennor rock were also used in the construction of Falmouth harbour and some also went to London for pavement edging.

The square church tower is not high but stands as a clear marker of the centre of Zennor life. On the outside wall of the church just inside the gate is John Davey's memorial stone. He was a man of history who died in 1891 and was said to have been the last one to speak the traditional Cornish language – more than a century later than Dolly Pentreath, mentioned earlier. There are only two old bench ends in the church but one of them is especially interesting. It portrays a finely carved mermaid and recalls the story of the beautiful sea-creature whose charms were the downfall of Matthew Trewhella. Opposite is the Tinner's Arms, so old that its origins are unknown.

Behind the inn the path, which runs parallel to a trout stream flowing into Pendour (Mermaid) Cove, leads down to Zennor Head. This is part of the 84 acres (34 hectares) owned by the National Trust along the cliff, enabling walkers to enjoy the delights of thyme-scented springy turf all the way to Wicca Pool, an Anglo-Saxon name, so out of place in this essentially Cornish area.

There is a great deal to see in this little valley: another Logan Stone, Zennor Quoit, Giant's Rock and the very fine views from the gorse-covered slopes. Little wonder that D H Lawrence loved it here and that Virginia Woolf, who spent childhood summers in St Ives, wrote that Cornwall's cliffs and seas had endowed her with riches beyond price.

The quickest way back to Penzance by car is up Trewey Hill, climbing away from Zennor and onto moorland that tempts many to a last walk and picnic above the magnificent cliffs of Penwith's north coast.

Zennor Head in Penwith

The Tinners' Way

This ancient trackway – in Cornish, *Forth an Stenoryon* – runs from St Just to St Ives. Only quite recently has the Tinners' Way been brought to the notice of the public, the person responsible being a past Grand Bard, Hugh Miners (a Grand Bard is the elected titular head of the College of Bards in each of the Celtic countries). For the experience of a lifetime join a night group at the full moon nearest to Midsummer Day and you will always remember your walk in the steps of the tin traders.

No one knows the exact age of this moorland path but it was certainly used by tinners more than 2,000 years ago while ornaments and ingots made by Bronze Age goldsmiths found close to the trackway go back another 1,500 years. Stone axes, which had been quarried from the Kenidjack cliff, have been discovered throughout southern Britain and such discoveries lead to the logical conclusion that West Penwith's Tinners' Way was originally part of a nationwide network for trade in Neolithic times.

To explore the area yourself, take an Ordnance Survey map and walk the route on your own. Although it consists mainly of rough tracks and paths, no part of it is particularly difficult and when you reach the harbour at St Ives you will have the satisfaction of knowing that you have travelled over many centuries of history. Begin by walking down the church path away from St Just until Nancherrow Bridge where the way turns up towards Carn Kenidjack. This is often called the 'Hooting Carn' and is associated with many tales of haunting but as you climb, the colourful moorland surroundings of barrows, holed stones and chamber tombs will more than hold your attention. The B3318 crosses the path now but the ancient route carries on, skirting Woon Gumpus Common towards **Chun Quoit** and **Chun Castle**. The latter is the remains of an exceptionally large and strongly built Iron Age fortress with 12ft (3.6m) thick walls, which until a century ago were still 12ft (3.6m) high.

Before reaching Bosullow Common note that the map shows the site of a settlement. This was, in fact, the Iron Age village of Bosullow Trehyllys where its inhabitants were comparatively secure with Chun Castle in the vicinity. Beyond this, a modern road again crosses the trackway that rises to Watch Croft, Penwith's highest hill (827ft/252m). From here it is possible to make a slight detour and wander to look at **Men Scryfa** and the famous **Men-an-Tol**. Many people are sceptical about the tales told of cures at the latter site but they are said to still happen today. The ruined engine house of **Ding-Dong Mine** is easily visible from here. Tradition says that the famous tin mine was worked in Roman times. It re-started in 1814 but finally closed in 1928.

It is peaceful and lovely along here where the track runs high and almost parallel to the coast road to Zennor and St Ives, crossing the minor road from Treen to Newmill. Try Valley is marked on the map but not Try Round, said by tradition to have been a corral for mules. Further on, near Lady Downs a branch track goes off along the hill above Chysauster, passes the Castle-an-Dinas hill fort and eventually reaches Mount's Bay. Historians believe this to be the route referred to by Pytheas, the Greek geographer, who wrote that the people of West Penwith took their melted tin in wagons to export it from Iktis (St Michael's Mount).

For a short distance a metalled road now overlays the ancient track at Embla and Amalveor, names which go far back in history. They only occur elsewhere in Cornwall, north of Wadebridge at Chapel Amble. As with so many Cornish place names, these have been distorted over the centuries but their origins can still be recognised. *Amal* is Cornish for slope, boundary or ledge, and its plural *emlow* is Embla today; and walkers who reach this area will be well able to confirm the existence of numerous slopes in the proximity.

After Coldharbour Moor, the track passes that now lonely church of Towednack, which was mentioned earlier. Its closeness to the Tinners' Way probably indicates that it is a place where the Celtic holy man or 'saint' who lived there would welcome weary travellers with rest and refreshment.

Road and pathway now run together down Rosewall Hill with the ivy-clad ruin of an engine-house reminding the world of the presence of tin. The ancient route ends at St Ives, through the part called Stennack (*sten* is Cornish for tin).

Lanyon Quoit, situated just off the Tinners' Way, with Ding-Dong Mine on the horizon

Places to Visit

Penzance

Chapel Street

www.iriss.co.uk/Chapel_Street
Many of the buildings have tales to tell in this historic street.

Penlee House Art Gallery and Museum

Morrab Road, TR18 4HE
☎ (01736) 363625
www.penleehouse.org.uk
Entirely local display reflecting the history and environment of Penzance. Unrivalled collection of work by the Victorian Newlyn School of Painting. Open: 10.30am–4.30pm Mon to Sat all year,10am–5pm Easter to Sep. Free admission on Saturdays.

Ⓟ(Charge) ♿ ♟<17 Free ☂

Trengwainton Garden

(National Trust)
Madron, TR20 8RZ
☎ (01736) 363148
www.nationaltrust.org.uk
Unique garden with many exotic shrubs and trees. Wonderful views of Mount's Bay and the Lizard. Tea room, shop and plant sales. Open: 10.30am–5pm Sun to Thu, mid-Feb to end-Oct.

Ⓟ ♿ (Most Areas) ♟<16 🐕

The Exchange Gallery

Princes Street, TR18 2NL
☎ (01736) 363715
www.newlynartgallery.co.uk
A new exhibition space in an eye-catching building on the site of the former telephone exchange. Open: Mon to Sat 10am–5pm, Tue to Sat in winter. Free admission.

♿ ♟ ☂

Trip to the Isles of Scilly

Three modes of travel are available for day trips to the Isles of Scilly: helicopter, plane or boat. Helicopters depart from just outside Penzance on Mount's Bay for the 20-minute flight. Shuttle bus available from Penzance. ☎ (01736) 363871 for details. Flights operate from Land's End with a shuttle bus available from Penzance. Boats sail from Penzance quay. ☎ (0845) 7105555 for details of both these services. See also chapter 9 and www.scillyonline. co.uk or www.simplyscilly.co.uk.

Around Penzance

Marazion Town Museum

Town Hall, Marazion
Exhibition about historic Marazion including reconstructed jail cell. Open: every day during the summer season.

♿ (Mostly) ♟<10 ☂

St Michael's Mount

(National Trust)
Marazion, TR17 0EF
☎ (01736) 710507 or 710265
www.stmichaelsmount.co.uk
When the approach causeway is covered there is a ferry service from Marazion. Owing to the quick tidal movement visitors will probably walk back so return tickets should not be taken. The small chapel is

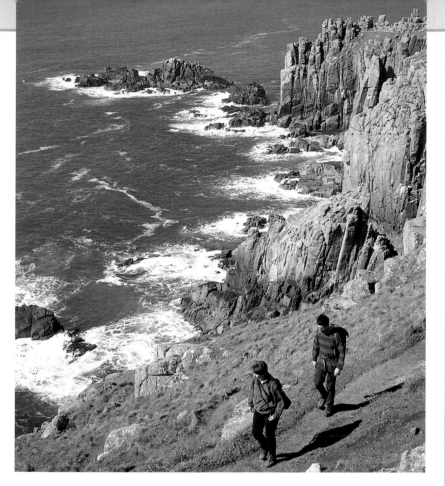

Above & below: Land's End

Left: Geevor tin mine

Places to Visit

unusual in size and location. It is open on Sundays from June to September at 10.30am for Divine Service which begins at 11.00am. Café and National Trust shop. Please note there are no facilities for dogs on the island. Paths are unsuitable for wheelchairs, prams and pushchairs. Sensible shoes are advisable. Open: 10.30am–5pm Sun to Fri, Apr to end-Oct. Nov to the end of Mar – please telephone for details. Private garden (not NT): open weekdays May and Jun; Thu and Fri only Jul to Oct. All visits are dependent upon weather and sea conditions. Please call to check conditions prior to your visit.

Ⓟ (Nearby) ♿ (Limited) 👪

Newlyn Art Gallery

Newlyn Green, New Road, TR18 5PZ
☎ (01736) 363715
www.newlynartgallery.co.uk
Donated to artists and the community in 1895 by Passmore Edwards. Open: Mon to Sat 10am–5pm, Tue to Sat in winter. Free admission.

♿ 👪

Mousehole Bird Hospital

Raginnis Hill, nr Penzance, TR19 6SR
☎ (01736) 731386
www.mouseholebirdhospital.org.uk
Opened as a bird sanctuary by the Yglesias sisters (1928) when they cared for an injured jackdaw found in a drainpipe. Open: daily, admission free.

North Penwith Coast

Geevor Mine

Pendeen, TR19 7EW
☎ (01736) 788662
www.geevor.com
Ruins of famous tin and copper mine. Underground tours and museum. Open: 9am–5pm Apr to Oct daily except Sat, 10am–4pm, Nov to Mar.

Ⓟ ♿ (Limited) 👪 (Family Ticket) 🌧

Wayside Museum

Zennor, TR26 3DA
☎ (01736) 796945
On the St Ives to Land's End coastal road the exhibits include tools and implements connected with the mining, agricultural, quarrying and domestic life of Zennor. Bridge House gift shop. Open: 10.30am–5.30pm Sun to Fri May to Sep, 11am–5pm Sun to Fri, Apr and Oct.

Ⓟ (Nearby) 👪 <16 🌧

Levant Steam Engine

(National Trust and Trevithick Society)
Trewellard, nr St Just, TR19 7SX
Engine steaming days: Apr to Oct when open.
☎ (01736) 786156
Open: 11am–5pm Mar to Oct including bank holidays, 11am–4pm Nov to Feb. Always open on Fri; additional days between Mar and Oct including bank holidays. In steam except between Nov and Feb.

Ⓟ ♿ 👪 🌧 🐕

Land's End Peninsula

Land's End Holiday Complex

Land's End, TR19 7AA

☎ (0870) 4580099

www.landsend-landmark.co.uk

Range of family attractions and exhibitions at the Visitor Centre. Family restaurants and bar.

Open: 10am daily except Christmas Eve and Christmas Day. Closing times vary by season.

Ⓟ ♚ <15 ☔

Telegraph Museum

Porthcurno, TR19 6JX

☎ (01736) 810966

www.porthcurno.org.uk

Cornwall's secret wartime underground communications centre and cable links around the world.

Open: 10am–5pm daily, Easter to Oct; 10am–5pm Sun and Mon, Nov to Mar.

Ⓟ (Nearby) ♿ ♚ <16 ☔

Minack Open-air Theatre

Porthcurno, TR19 6JU

☎ (01736) 810471 or 810471

www.minack.com

A unique open-air theatre fashioned from a natural rock amphitheatre and the Rowena Cade Exhibition Centre with photographs, models and audio-visual displays. Coffee shop. Theatre performances are held from end of May to the middle of Sep.

Open: 10am–5pm daily from Easter to Nov; 10am–4pm daily Oct to Mar. Auditorium closed from noon to 4.45pm when there is a matinee. Shows only cancelled in extreme weather conditions at which point customers are refunded the full cost of their ticket. Shows continue in light rain & showers.

♿ ♚ <17 🐕 (Day visitors only)

What to do if it rains

Penzance

Penlee House Museum and Art Gallery

The Exchange Gallery

Porthcurno

Minack Theatre and Rowena Cade Exhibition Centre

Telegraph Museum

Land's End

Family entertainment complex

Pendeen

Geevor Tin Mine

Levant Steam Engine

Pendeen Lighthouse

Zennor

Wayside Museum

Newlyn

Newlyn Art Gallery

Marazion

Town Hall Museum

6. The North Coast

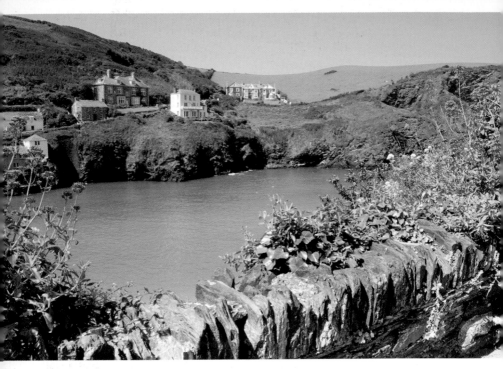

Legends cannot be avoided when telling the story of Cornwall, but the one particularly associated with St Ives is usually shrugged off in disbelief, for it is said that the holy St Ia, who was the first to come to this part of the coast, sailed across the water on a leaf!

The idea is very picturesque but seems too extreme to be at all possible – that is, until one remembers the comparatively recent cross–Atlantic voyage that successfully re-enacted the journey undertaken by St Brendan many centuries ago. A replica of the saint's small craft was made, a mere wooden framework covered with hide and surely as close as could be to the 'leaf' of St Ia.

ST IVES

Apparently St Ia eventually established a settlement here and it later became the attractive fishing port of **St Ives**, but as miraculous leaves are in short supply today, people who want to see the town in comfort should leave their cars at Lelant Saltings if they are only

Opposite page: Port Isaac

Left: Newquay

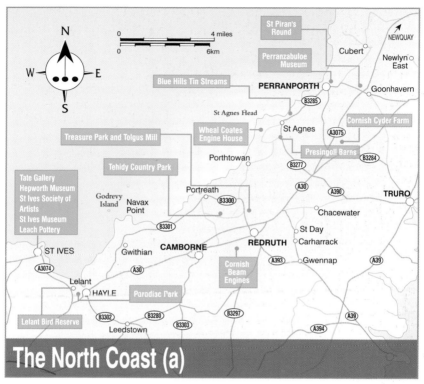

The North Coast (a)

See page 150 for north-east of Newquay

staying a few hours. This avoids parking problems and adds another pleasure for, if the weather is fine, there can be few railway journeys more delightful than the small local train, which runs from St Erth to St Ives and collects passengers on the way. There is ample parking space at Lelant and the ride takes a little over 10 minutes, which most people say is all too short.

From the Saltings, with its interesting estuary scenery, the friendly train takes its passengers along the cliffside to give a clear view of the famous 5-mile (8km) stretch of the golden sands which edge the coast from St Ives to Godrevy Point. Vehicular access to the town is restricted during the season, though buses are available from Trenwith car park on the outskirts, so it is both wiser and more pleasant to arrive on the local train. The steep, winding cobbled streets of this 'picturesque seaside town par excellence', as it has been called, do much to retain its Cornishness. Looking over the water at Westcott's Quay where the Warren turns into Pednolva Walk, it is easy to understand why the St Ives Art Club decided to hold meetings in that wharfside fishing cellar – the view from there is so characteristic of the whole place. Turner was probably the first artist to come here and paint scenes of the town. That was in 1811, but it was Whistler and Sickert who, in 1884, actually established the art colony here. Today the **St Ives Society of Artists** exhibit their work in their gallery at Norway Square.

In the first half of the twentieth century people like Sir Alfred Munnings, Lamorna Birch, Barbara Hepworth and Bernard Leach were active in St Ives. Leach, a potter, designed the tiled stone round the grave of Alfred Wallis, the self-taught primitive painter who is buried in Barnoon cemetery beside the car park. In 1920, Leach established a workshop at Higher Stennack on the B3306; **The Leach Pottery** is still there. Following a recent restoration programme, the pottery has recommenced production and a new exhibition space has been created, in which examples of his work are always on display. Stennack comes from *sten* (Cornish for tin) and the whole valley was once a profitable mining area. The most notable of the workings was prob-

ably Wheal Trenwith as it produced not only tin but also copper, pitchblende and the radium used by Madame Curie in her experiments.

Barbara Hepworth lived and worked near the harbour just behind the parish church. Many of her sculptures and paintings are on exhibition permanently since the Tate Gallery bought her studio and garden and now administers the **Barbara Hepworth Museum and Sculpture Garden**.

After World War II, other artists came to St Ives and produced work that greatly influenced the development of painting in Britain. As a result, **The Tate Gallery St Ives** was opened in 1993. Managed by the Tate Gallery, it displays both local and international artists' work.

Earlier times can be recalled in a visit to the nearby **St Ives Museum**, a building with a history that is interesting on its own account. This site was originally Wheal Dream copper mine but it was unsuccessful like many others, so it was used as a store to cure and pack pilchards for exporting to Italy in the mid-nineteenth century. Afterwards the

Fishing traditions

On the island beside St Nicholas' chapel in St Ives, a huer's hut looks down on the harbour and Smeaton's Pier. In former days, the lookout posted there would watch for pilchards and then cry 'Hevva!' to the waiting fishermen. After a good catch the toast in the town would be to 'Fish, Tin and Copper'. Today, Cornish cooks remember the heyday of Cornwall's fishing industry when they make their 'heavy cake'. When the men were on the beach waiting anxiously for the shout that would send them out to their nets, their wives stood beside them. Then when the welcome call announced the approach of a shoal, the women ran home to bake something good for their husbands to eat after toiling with their heavy nets. And it was the 'heavy' – or 'hevva' – cake that took just the right time to prepare and cook, being ready, with its criss-cross net pattern on the top, to eat with a piping hot 'dish o' tay' when the weary fisherman returned home.

Bible Christian sect took it over, then it became a laundry and later a cinema. The first floor, however, continued to have a maritime connection when a British Sailors Society Mission used it to house shipwrecked mariners who were waiting to be repatriated.

It is strange to see animal traps on show but one could trap three mice inside at once and this is a strong clue to the reason for the local preference for cats. St Ives is known for two types of cat. One is short-backed and stubby-legged, the other a large, contented animal resembling Alice in Wonderland's Cheshire Cat. It was no doubt the local interest in cats that accounted for the nursery rhyme that helps many youngsters learn to count, 'As I was going to St Ives'.

Between 1925 and 1941 there was a silk factory on 'The Island', just behind the museum. A unique form of hand block printing on silk was practised here, known as Cryséde, and good examples of this can be found in the museum.

Five splendid sandy beaches, which can accommodate many people, form a golden crescent round the town. On one of them – or perhaps all –Virginia Woolf played when she was on holiday at Talland House and later brought these early memories of Godrevy into *To The Lighthouse*. Today St Ives, with its cliff walks, windsurfing, fishing and sailing, still welcomes visitors to the essential Cornish atmosphere which people so enjoy.

The train returns from a small station above Porthminster Beach and as it moves away, Tregenna Castle Hotel, one of Cornwall's finest, with its castellated turrets, may be glimpsed high above on the cliff top. The next stop is Carbis Bay, which has such fine, smooth sands that it is perhaps the most popular of all the local beaches. This is in sharp contrast to the appearance it had in the nineteenth century when it was used as a dump for mining waste.

The Hayle Estuary

Lelant is an unexpected place with a quiet individuality that has to be searched for. This probably stems from the knowledge that it was a thriving seaport in the Middle Ages, long before

John Knill

A large part of the main room of St Ives Museum is devoted to exhibits connected with John Knill (1733–1811), perhaps the most memorable of all St Ives' citizens. Customs officer, mayor, lawyer and lovable wealthy eccentric, Knill was at one time private secretary to the Earl of Buckingham and a trustee of his estate. Rumour has it that he was also a privateer, and he did have plenty of opportunity for this. On his instructions John Smeaton built the harbour pier which provided such necessary shelter for shipping and Knill built the Steeple monument just outside the town. He intended this to be his final resting place but he was buried in London. In his will he laid down that every five years there was to be a ceremony held on 25 July when ten girls and two widows should dance round the Steeple. A strange request but one that has kept his memory alive. The next ceremony is scheduled for 2011.

Tate St Ives

St Ives achieved popularity.

The church lies behind the Salt-ings in a village of old world charm. It is dedicated to St Uny and was the parish church for St Ives as well until 1826. Inside are interesting memorials to members of the Praed family from Trevethoe, the mansion at the foot of Trencrom Hill. William Praed (1620) and his family are remembered in a slate carving, with kneeling figures, flowers, sand–glass and skull. His famous descen-dants are Mackworth (whose portrait is in the St Ives Museum) and William. The former was the eminent engineer

A corner of the harbour, St Ives

who planned England's canal system, the latter the banker after whom Lon-don's Praed Street is named. Another building of the past is the abbey in Lower Lelant, a long, low sixteenth-century construction, and L-shaped as

Porthmeor Beach, St Ives

Porthmeor Beach at St Ives

befits the period. Neither Trevethoe nor the abbey is open to the public.

The St Ives branch line ends at **St Erth**, which is another example of a once proud and busy place. The Star Inn was there in the seventeenth century when the Trewinnards startled everyone by introducing the first private coach to Cornwall. The Royal Cornwall Museum now has that same vehicle in its safe keeping.

Most drivers hurry through **Hayle**, glad when they are beyond it, but its present dullness does, in fact, hide one of Cornwall's oldest ports. This particular estuary has been important since Bronze Age times when copper and gold were sent from Ireland to Brittany via St Michael's Mount.

Centuries later, when the Industrial Revolution demanded the best in engineering, this part of the world provided it. The old wharves, still visible near the railway bridge, were once part of the great foundry and engineering business belonging to Harvey's – known throughout the world simply as 'Harvey's of Hayle'. They provided the world's largest-diameter steam engine (12 feet/3.5m) to Holland for draining the Harlem Meer, where Schiphol Airport is now situated. Known as the De Cruquius Engine it survives near Vijfhuizen on the N201.

Beside the B3302, which leads out of the square and up Foundry Hill, are some remains of this once extensive complex – the hammer mill and the old millpond can still be found. Those who designed the town's modern purpose-built library were (fortunately) determined that Hayle's great past should not entirely be forgotten and now for all to see on its gable are three original wood patterns for gear wheels for mining machines made in Harvey's foundry in the late 1880s.

Today that secondary road makes its way to a more modern concept – **Paradise Park**. Here is a fine collection of the world's rarest and most beautiful birds, including flamingoes, toucans and free-flying parrots. Within the grounds there is also the Cornish otter sanctuary, an ambitious conservation scheme to help restore the otter to the local countryside.

Another project, probably even closer to Cornish hearts, is 'Operation Chough', a study into the possibility of re-establishing the chough in selected locations on the coast. This rare bird which, with its red beak and legs, was once a familiar sight on Cornwall's rugged cliffs, is associated with King Arthur and so synonymous with Cornwall that it appears on the County Council's coat of arms.

Detailed research has been done in other parts of Britain and results show that the chough's decline is closely linked to the disappearance of the Large Blue butterfly. However, in 2001, before any birds were released into the wild, three wild choughs appeared on the coast. Two of them bred successfully in 2002 and 2003 so later in 2003 some of the captive-bred birds were released in the hope that they would mate with the wild ones and form the basis of a colony for the future. In 2006 it was announced that a second nest had been successfully established. All sightings of choughs in Cornwall should be reported to Paradise Park. In 2005, the JungleBarn indoor play centre was opened at Paradise Park to offer facilities for younger children, whatever the weather.

Copperhouse, now an extension of Hayle, has only the Copperhouse Inn sign and, by the old quay, walls built of dark green copper slag blocks, to serve as a reminder of its former importance as a copper-smelting site. Across the Hayle Canal, the romantically named church at **Phillack** (St Felicitas) overlooks the water and nearby is Riviere House where Compton Mackenzie and his sister, the actress, Fay Compton, spent many happy childhood holidays.

Elizabeth Arden

It would be wrong to leave Hayle without remembering a person who was born in the town and whose name is as internationally famous today as Harvey's was in the last century. She was Florence Nightingale Graham, born in 1884, one of the three children of a chemist who encouraged her experiments with cosmetics. The Graham family anticipated the collapse of Cornish mining and in 1908 emigrated to Canada. Young Florence soon moved to New York, became a partner in a beauty salon business but, before long, opened her own beauty parlour on Fifth Avenue. She took the name of Elizabeth Arden from the novels *Elizabeth and her German Garden* and *Enoch Arden*. In 1915 she introduced mascara and eye-shadow and eventually extended her business to thirty-five countries. She also achieved another first when she opened her health farms. In 1966 she died but the company she founded continues to thrive.

Selected Car Drives

A circuit around Newquay

Leave Newquay on the A3075 to Goonhavern. Turn right onto the B3285 and drive slowly for just over 1 mile (1.5km) so that you do not miss the entrance on the right to Piran Round, Cornwall's largest open-air theatre during medieval times – used for 3-day cycles of miracle plays. Follow the road to a junction and leaving the B3285 turn right above the sand dunes to Gear and Cubert. Watch for a T-junction with a right turn to Newlyn East. This little village is delightful and narrow lanes will take you to Trerice and the Lappa Valley Railway, not adjacent but close. Kestle Mill is on the A3058; follow the road to Quintrell Downs and there wander along the A392 but take a left-hand turn towards St Columb Major. You will not get lost. More lanes from there, when you have left the handsome church, will take you to Castle-an-Dinas – a magnificent Iron Age fort. Sir Arthur Quiller-Couch wrote an intriguing novel involving this fort and Fowey. He called it *Castle D'Or*. It is fascinating detective work in history. You are about 4 miles (6.4km) from Tregonetha on the B3274, a road which will take you to a T-junction at the A39. Between 1 and 2 miles (1.5–3km) along there in the St Columb Major direction take the first right for St Mawgan and the delights of the Lanherne Valley. Follow the Trenance direction and you will come to Mawgan Porth and the B3276 which will take you back to Newquay.

Wadebridge to Padstow and back to Wadebridge via the coast

Leave Wadebridge on the A389 road to Padstow and enjoy the villages of St Issey and Little Petherick – especially the churches. Into and out of Padstow on the B3276, where after the village of Treator the second right will take you to Harlyn Bay and semicircle out to the B3276 again. Drive along it to Porthcothan, small but delightful. About 2 miles (3km) along here you will find Bedruthan Steps, an impressive National Trust section of the coast. Return towards Porthcothan and the first lane on the right will, if you watch the signs, take you to the almost hidden church of St Ervan. Turn right through nearby Rumford and you are on the B3274. Cross the A39 at Winnard's Perch and head for St Breock Downs and narrow lanes which will lead you down to St Breock on the edge of Wadebridge.

The huge stretch of towans (sand dunes) which forms part of St Ives Bay is ideal for holidaymakers to walk, swim, or laze, although all lifeguards' warnings must be observed. **Connor Downs** is a sprawling development beside the A30 above Gwithian and many historians think it possible that the ancient city of Connor (Irish for 'haven') lies there beneath the dunes.

The Coast around St Agnes

Gwithian is a small village with a low-towered fifteenth-century church. The unusual sight of thatch here makes it an artist's delight: animal lovers, however, take pleasure in watching the seals which are sometimes seen at Navax Point (belonging to the National Trust) beyond Godrevy Lighthouse. The cliffs all round here are turfy and good for walking but bathers will find that the water is often stained by the Red River, which collects tin waste on its way to the sea.

In July and early August, the cliffs of **Reskajeage Down**, between the B3301 and the sea, are brilliant with gorse and heather. Once past the fearful Hell's Mouth, however, the coastal footpath is easier and safer. The views along the coast towards St Agnes Head and St Agnes Beacon are really spectacular on a bright day; the colours sometimes appear almost too brilliant to be real.

Most of the land between Carvannel Downs and the A30 was once the vast **Tehidy** estate and belonged to the Basset family until about 1921. In 1983 the local council bought the estate's 250 acres (101 hectares) of woodland and

Royalist shipwreck

In 1649, Godrevy Island was the scene of a notable shipwreck. After the execution of King Charles I, many loyal subjects tried to save some of his lace-trimmed garments and other possessions and sent them abroad for safe keeping. Unfortunately the ship carrying them was wrecked and only a few of the royal clothes were washed ashore – together with the only survivors, a man, a boy and a dog.

restoration work has been in hand ever since. The whole area has been used to encourage the public in matters of environmental conservation as well as offering them a variety of recreational facilities. An events programme is published each year and includes bird watches, bird survey opportunities, etc. The **Tehidy Country Park** was officially opened in 1987. Quite near the western end of the Park is Magor Farm and it was here that the remains of a Roman villa were discovered, something very unusual in Cornwall.

From these roads, and for some distance around, can be seen the **Carn Brea monument** at Carnkie, Redruth, which was erected to the memory of Francis Basset de Dunstanville, a great local benefactor. His main concern was to improve the lot of the numerous poor, especially those who risked their lives gathering the succulent herb that grew in dangerous places on Samphire Island. He built **Portreath Harbour** in 1760 and this not only afforded protection to the ships, but also facilitated the loading and unloading of copper ore. Before that, the ships had to be loaded from the beach, a very irksome task. By 1840, when mining was at its peak, the population of this area was about 30,000 with people at work in mining as well as all the ancillary industries connected with it.

Slightly further inland, on the B3300 towards Redruth, **Treasure Park** is a celebration of Cornwall's gold and jewel country, with a range of attractions and exhibits based on these precious commodities. It is also the home of **Tolgus Mill**, an original and authentic tin-streaming mill which was preserved with the help of the Trevithick Trust and Madame Tussauds, while the **Redruth Old Cornwall Society Museum** has also recently moved here from its former home in the town.

Pleasant minor roads afford a quiet drive towards either Portreath or St Agnes while the section of the north coast path between Portreath and St Agnes has been described as the finest walk in Cornwall. **Porth Towan** and **Chapel Porth** have fine sandy beaches, but the undertow of currents and lifeguards' warnings must always be heeded. All round the National Trust's land at Chapel Porth and inland for some way, there are derelict mine buildings in profusion. The heathery slopes of the cliffs still only partly cover the great heaps of arsenic waste that have been there for so long. In the mid and late nineteenth century, **St Agnes** parish was one of Cornwall's most active mining areas and those who worked here boasted that *Sten Sen Agnes an gwella yn Kernow* ('St Agnes' tin is the best in Cornwall'.) All

Towanroath Shaft at Wheal Coates, west of St Agnes on the coastal path

Walks

St Piran

4 miles (6.4km) approx • easy • 2 hours
Map: OS 1:25,000 Explorer Series 104: Redruth and St Agnes
Park your car beside the minor road that leads north-east from the B3285 road about 1 mile (1.5km) east of Perranporth. The path you need starts opposite the lane from Rose. Go through the gate and follow the well-walked path marked with white stones. Bear slightly right following the acorn marker posts of the Coastal Path and aim for the stone cross on the skyline. Placed there about AD900, this Celtic cross marks the site of the Norman church built as a successor to St Piran's Oratory. Then head downhill towards the sea and on through the dunes until you reach the mound covering St Piran's Oratory, topped with a rough granite block marked 'St Piran'. Your way continues towards the sea, well below with extensive views right and left. Follow the left path, cross a concrete road and continue on the cliffs. Perranporth is soon within view and the way is gently sloping to the beach. Cross the sands, keeping left to meet the river, and follow the track beside it out to the road. Turn left here then left again at a waymarker, up steep steps. Stay to the left of the clubhouse and cross the road to a stile. Continue diagonally up a field towards a goal post then another stile takes you over the road to an enclosed path leading to a lane and after a right turn you will find your car.

Part of the Saints' Way

7 miles (11.2km) • quite strenuous • 3 to 4 hours approx
Map: OS 1:25,000 Explorer Series 106: Newquay and Padstow
At the start of the Saints' Way leave the lychgate of Padstow's church and walk along wooded Hill Street. Then cross New Street, continue along Dennis Lane, past the boating lake and turn left at a footpath sign, then follow Saints' Way

these little porths or landing places have been used since very early times and foundations of the chapel traditionally dedicated to St Agnes can still be seen in the cliffs at Chapel Porth.

Driving along the B3277 notice the **Presingoll Barns** complex on the right-hand side. Entrance is free and there is plenty of parking space for vehicles while visitors wander round to

see potters at work and candles being made. For a small charge they can try their hands at the potter's wheel and candle dipping. Delicious teas, fudges, jams and chutneys are available. Take a picnic there or enjoy the refreshments in the Rafters Café. Further inland, **Healey's Cornish Cyder Farm** on the A3075 at Penhallow is not only an opportunity to enjoy a refreshing glass

signs for about 3 miles (4.8km). After Little Petherick Church, the Saints' Way lies a few hundred yards along the main road before turning right up the valley to Mellingey. Leave the Saints' Way here, follow yellow arrows then after a stile, stepping stones and a footbridge, the path leads to St Issey Church which you leave by the north gate. Cross the main road, follow the yellow arrow to the right, go left after the stile then over a footbridge staying with the path through a right-hand gate and keep the hedge on your right. At the road go right, then left and after about 400 yards (365m) take the right-hand signed path. This continues over a grassy bridge up the left of a long field to a gate at another road. Carry on with this, signposted Old Town Creek, and you will reach the River Camel. Leave the Halwyn car park, go up the steps to the old railway line – now the Camel Trail – and turn left into Padstow.

Crantock

4 miles (6.4km) approx • easy • 2 hours
Map: OS 1:25,000 Explorer Series 104: Redruth and St Agnes
Leave Newquay along Crantock Street, cross Tower Road, along Atlantic Road and descend Trethellan Hill signposted to the Gannel. Cross the plank bridge and at the field by Penpol Creek follow the path left to a gate into a wood. Through this is another gate into a sloping field; walk up to a gate on the left of Penpol House, finding a lane to Crantock. The village is very ancient and a lane below the church leads to Crantock Beach and sand dunes. To complete the circuit, leave the village by Beach Road, take the path indicated right through a gate and follow it through bushes and fields for it will take you to the steps down to the pedestrian bridge back to Newquay.

of cider but has been voted the nation's favourite farm visit.

On the edge of St Agnes you will find the **Parish Museum**. The handsome **Miners' and Mechanics' Institute** in the centre of the village is a different reminder of the past. Built in 1893, it was one of the first of many gifts from the Cornish philanthropist, Passmore Edwards, who was anxious to help the men educate themselves. It is now a social club, but inside there are some interesting old mining records. The fine old church lies low beneath the road beyond the Institute. Carrying on down the hill go slowly and notice the picturesque miners' cottages at **Stippy Stappy** along the left side which overlook the area of Peterville.

The north coast route continues

Watergate Bay

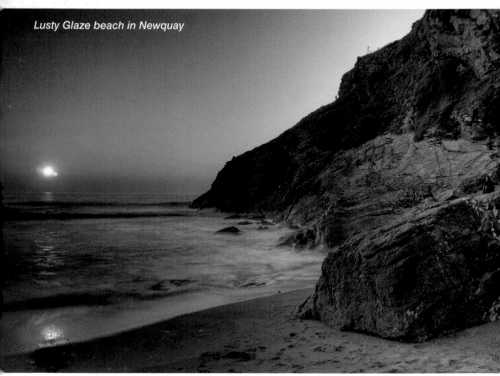

Lusty Glaze beach in Newquay

along the B3285 towards Perranporth but it is worthwhile making a detour down the first lane on the right after Barkla Shop. This is narrow and steep and motorists need to travel slowly so that they do not miss the thatched cottage called '**Harmony Cot**', birthplace of the famous painter, John Opie, who is buried in St Paul's Cathedral. Beyond the ford over the Silver River, so named because of its trout, the lane climbs towards the B3284.

An alternative detour on the left-hand side of the road goes to **Blue Hills Tin Streams.** Here the Wills family has been producing tin for 30 years and the process can be followed on site. Custom-designed giftware and jewellery can be purchased.

Leave the car here and walk the short distance along a narrow lane to Trevaunance Cove, which is possibly the real heart of St Agnes and once a busy port from which ships sailed with their cargoes of tin and copper. A glance at the cliffs would make anyone wonder how an important harbour could ever have been built in such a place, but success was only achieved after several efforts. The final attempt of 1793 resulted in completion in 1797 but then stagings had to be constructed on the cliffs so that cargoes could be transferred by means of a horse-whim – a satisfactory arrangement which made Trevaunance Cove the scene of a very lucrative trade.

On the coastal side of the B3285 are the headquarters of the Cornish Gliding and Flying Club, just beyond **Cligga Head,** an ideal place for birdwatching. Views from these cliffs rival the Mediterranean in the varied colours of the sea, sand and rock formation.

Halfway along Perranporth's short main street is a turning to the left. It can easily be missed but to do so would mean losing the opportunity of seeing the **Perranzabuloe Museum**. Housed in a handsome Victorian building, this small but fascinating collection of exhibits includes material that depicts life in the parish from prehistoric times.

Beyond the village on the north side is a stretch of sand dunes, once visited by pilgrims from many lands. They came to pay homage to St Piran, patron saint of tinners whose chapel, as old as that of Iona, is now protected by concrete because inroads by the sea had despoiled

Rocky shore in Newquay

most of the ancient building. The coast path at the extreme end of Perran Beach is in an area now used by the military so wait for the sentry to give the go-ahead if the red flag is flying.

The B3285 climbs out of Perranporth, passing **St Piran's Round**, an impressive Iron Age fortification, adapted in the Middle Ages as a *plen-an-gwary* (playing place) where religious instruction was given in the form of miracle plays. This open-air theatre has an amphitheatre that is 50 yards (46m) across with circular terraces for the audience. In 1969 and 1973 productions of the Cornish medieval plays were performed here – the first time for many centuries. Although the theatre subsequently closed, the Round was cleared once more in the mid-1980s, and the Gorsedd of the Bards of Cornwall was held here in 1985 and again in 1992.

In and around Newquay

About 5 miles (8km) along the A3075 is **Newquay** – a lively town with something for everyone in all weathers and voted first among Cornwall's holiday resorts for its magnificent beaches. At low tide these become one bay but each has a different character when the tide comes in.

Newquay existed as a port in the mid-fifteenth century and the export of pilchards to the Mediterranean was extremely profitable during the seventeenth and eighteenth centuries when the huer's hut below the Atlantic Hotel came into its own. In 1838, Joseph Treffry of Fowey decided to use the shelter of this harbour for his china clay exports so he built a new quay. For 40 years cargoes came and went until Par was developed and usurped Newquay's usefulness.

The list of attractions here covers everything holidaymakers expect at a popular resort. Some may surprise visitors – particularly the pleasantly situated **zoo and leisure park** set in 8 acres (3.2 hectares) of landscaped gardens, 5 minutes away from the town centre. One or two days could well be spent here during a Newquay holiday.

Today Newquay is renowned for surfing and offers great facilities for devotees of this exciting sport but there is much more besides for those who prefer safer pastimes. **Trenance Park** has gardens, a toboggan run, miniature golf and the indoor delights of **Water-world** with its tropical fun pool and flumes. In the big, pink building on St Michael's Road is **Tunnels Through Time**, a mix of fact and fiction that brings alive the history and legends of Cornwall. Further on, at Towan Beach the **Blue Reef Aquarium** takes visitors on an undersea safari to see the life of the oceans.

Towan Head, which stretches out to sea past the huer's hut and the golf course, boasts a small castellated tower and private chapel belonging to the Molesworth family and from here Cornwall offers another fine two-way expanse of distant coastline. **Pentire Point East** at the opposite arm of Fistral Bay has good views and the vantage point was also appreciated by prehistoric man: tumuli remains have been found to prove this.

There are numerous places of interest near Newquay, including **Porth Reservoir** off the A3059 to St Columb Major. Along the coast road there are prehistoric round barrows on **Trevelgue Head**, which lies beyond the bay of Porth on the B3276.

On high ground behind Watergate Bay lies **RAF St Mawgan**, formally affiliated to the parish of St Columb Major, the first local authority to be so linked. It now shares its runway with Newquay airport.

Further north, the smallness of **Mawgan Porth** is delightful with the tranquil Lanherne valley leading inland, little known though very lovely. Halfway up the valley and in the shelter of long-established trees **St Mawgan** village hides its charms. The church has Cornwall's best collection of brasses, mainly of the Arundells whose former home was **Lanherne**, the nearby manor house. It become a Carmelite monastery in 1794 and the small chapel is open to the public.

The creeper-clad inn opposite seems to have an out-of-place name: The Falcon. Nevertheless it is particularly apt as during the persecution of Roman Catholics in Reformation days priests celebrated Mass in secret and the signal to the faithful that it was about to begin would be the freeing of that particular bird.

The road climbs through leafy lanes to another village that has been important in the past – **St Columb Major**. Once considered a possible site for Cornwall's cathedral it is best known now perhaps for the Shrove Tuesday Hurling Contest when a ball of silver-coated applewood is used in the Town versus Country game. This custom was once a feature of most village feast days and is believed to have originated as a pagan festival in honour of spring.

The handsome church dominates the houses around and, proud of its fourteenth-century foundation, plays host to a popular annual music festival. The Ring o' Bells inn across the road is a secular reminder of the fine tradition of bell-ringing associated with this church. And a mere few hundred yards away is the Red Lion, proud of a former landlord, James Polkinghorne, also Cornwall's most famous wrestler. An unusual memorial on the roadside wall depicts him in action. A short way along the A39 towards Wadebridge is the **Cornish Birds of Prey Centre** where flying displays take place three times a day and visitors also have the opportunity for coarse fishing or quiet walks.

A new development near St Columb Major reflects Cornwall's status as Europe's surfing capital. **Retallack Surfside**, due to open in 2010, is based on Britain's first surfing wave pool, and will also include holiday cottages and an artificial sandy beach.

Over the roundabout at the beginning of the bypass there is a sign to **Castle-an-Dinas**, about 2 miles (3km) along the road. There is only pedestrian access across private land but it is worth the climb for the panoramic view beyond Goss Moor to the china clay country. These remains of a massive Iron Age fort are some 700 feet (213m) above sea level and composed of three concentric rings, hedges and ditches. The single entrance emphasises the wisdom of prehistoric builders.

See page 135 for south-west of Newquay

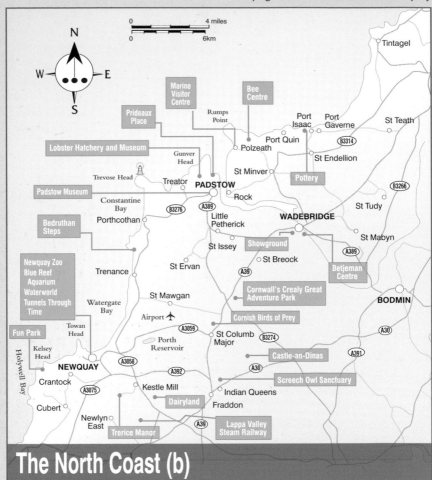

0   4 miles
0   6km

N
W   E
S

Tintagel

Marine Visitor Centre

Bee Centre

Prideaux Place

Rumps Point

Port Isaac   Port Gaverne   St Teath

Lobster Hatchery and Museum

Gunver Head

Port Quin
Polzeath
B3314

Trevose Head   Treator
PADSTOW
Rock

St Minver   St Endellion

Pottery

Padstow Museum

Constantine Bay
Porthcothan
B3276   A389
Little Petherick

WADEBRIDGE

B3266

St Tudy

Bedruthan Steps

St Issey

Showground   St Mabyn

Newquay Zoo
Blue Reef Aquarium
Waterworld
Tunnels Through Time

Trenance

St Ervan

A39   St Breock

A389

Betjeman Centre

St Mawgan
Watergate Bay

Airport   A3059

Cornwall's Crealy Great Adventure Park

BODMIN

Cornish Birds of Prey

Fun Park

Towan Head
Kelsey Head

Porth Reservoir

St Columb Major   B3274   A30

Castle-an-Dinas   A391

NEWQUAY   A3058

A30

Screech Owl Sanctuary

Holywell Bay   Crantock   A392

Kestle Mill   Indian Queens

A3075   Cubert

Dairyland   Fraddon

Newlyn East   A39   Lappa Valley Steam Railway

Trerice Manor

The North Coast (b)

Trerice Manor

Blue Reef Aquarium, Newquay

Black Cross and **White Cross**, which lie between Castle-an-Dinas and Quintrell Downs, could have been named as important stations for pilgrims to Holywell. Or perhaps they were depots for the black and white tin from the moorland. In either case Summercourt September Fair, one of Cornwall's oldest, would have been involved.

On the A3058 Summercourt to Newquay road, **DairyLand Farm World** offers an unusual look at country life. It is a working farm with 'space-age milking on a merry-go-round' where 120 cows are milked to music in one of Europe's most up-to-date modern rotary parlours. The museum of rural exhibits in another part of the farm displays tools and instruments used on farms in the past.

At **Kestle Mill** hamlet on the same road in the Newquay direction, a narrow lane winds steeply up to the charming National Trust property of **Trerice Manor**. Protective trees stand round this popular Elizabethan house, which is small enough to be a home, yet retains the quality and character of the Royalist Arundells who rebuilt it

Newquay Zoo

Tolcarne Beach, Newquay

Wild West hero

The hamlet of **Ruthvoes** about 6 miles (9.5km) east of Newquay was the birthplace of a man little remembered here, Deadwood Dick, folk hero of many Wild West stories. Born in 1847, Richard Bullock started work in the clay industry then, emigrating to South Dakota, became a bullion guard for the Homestake Mine owned by Senator Hearst. Richard's expert marksmanship earned him the nickname 'Deadwood Dick', but in spite of many hazardous journeys on duty, he died peaceably at the good age of seventy-three.

in 1571. This secluded manor house contains fine fireplaces and plaster ceilings, oak and walnut furniture, and tapestries; a small museum in the barn traces the development of the lawn-mower! A summer garden has some unusual plants and there is an orchard of Cornish fruit trees.

The **Lappa Valley Railway** at **Newlyn East** takes visitors in a miniature steam train along part of the original GWR Newquay to Chace water track. At the end of the short ride to a leisure park with various attractions, the historic engine house and stack of the disused East Wheal Rose can be seen. This was Cornwall's richest lead-producing works until a cloudburst brought disaster to the miners and closure to the mine. The handsome ruin is all that remains.

The road from Newlyn East to **Cubert** and **Holywell** is so straight that it probably follows an ancient pilgrim way. As you approach the coast, you will find **Holywell Bay Fun Park**, a popular family attraction with a wide range of rides and activities as well as its own golf course.

The well which gives Holywell its name is, in fact, not on the beach but about a quarter of a mile (400m) away at Trevornick Farm. This lies behind the extensive dunes set in a wide area of National Trust and Ministry of Defence land — footpaths are clearly defined. The Trust path leads to Kelsey Head and West Pentire on the Newquay side of **Porth Joke** and is strangely remote though so near to the busy holiday resort. Here the cliff flowers are especially delightful in spring and early summer while the little cove is ideal for families who want to avoid crowds. Porth Joke's unusual name comes from the fact that it was once the haunt of choughs — *chogha* being Cornish and the plural of jackdaw to which family the chough belongs.

It is pleasant to walk from **Crantock** to **Cubert Common**, one of the few enclosed commons in the country, now National Trust land. Another path to take follows the line of the Gannel to Trevemper and Newquay, and, though the beach of this inlet is good for children, it can be dangerous, as the river runs swiftly in under the cliffs of East Pentire. A short and different way back to Newquay at this point is by passenger ferry from West Pentire (summer only).

Padstow and Wadebridge

Padstow is the next holiday centre along this north coast and rests quietly on past memories. Buildings here date

---

Legend of the travelling saints

Crantock, just outside Newquay, is an attractive village centred on the Round Garden, the little orchard in the middle belonging to the National Trust. Its ancient collegiate church is on a hill overlooking the Gannel, a sandy estuary. St Carantoc and St Cubert are thought to have been missionary 'saints' who, like others of their kind, travelled in pairs and then settled near each other. The former founded a monastery here and the monks prospered by controlling the estuary trade. It was famed for its learning and had a library long before the days of Caxton. A house in the village – Great Weston – was named after one of the prebendaries who taught here in the collegiate days. In the late sixteenth century it was recorded that Crantock had seven churchyards and seven other parishes to administer. Some historians, however, believe that Langarroc was its original name and a legend of a wicked city buried beneath the sands may perhaps have some foundation here.

---

from the Middle Ages and are still relatively unspoiled, with slate-hung and stone cottages and their colourful sheltered gardens edging the one-way route to the harbour. Today, small coasters from the Continent berth next to gaily rigged yachts. It all looks so peaceful – a very different kind of activity from the scenes of several hundred years ago when Sir Walter Raleigh, then Lord Warden of the Stanneries, presided in the sixteenth-century courthouse on the south quay.

Overlooking the harbour is Rick Stein's famous **Seafood Restaurant**. Established in 1975, his television series twenty years later confirmed its status as one of Britain's leading fish restaurants. **The National Lobster Hatchery** can be found on the quay. Perhaps some of the young lobsters released from here into the wild return in catches for the restaurant.

The name of Thomas Martyn means little to most people but we should all be lost without the modern 1-inch maps he originated. Born in Gwennap in 1695, he came to Padstow to teach and pass on his scientific skills. After this he was employed to make surveys of large Cornish estates such as the manors of St Ewe and Tolverne and his work was so accurate that he was eventually prevailed upon to undertake a similar task for the whole of Cornwall. By 1748 he had issued his 1 inch to 1 mile map which was not only accurate but beautiful and sold for three guineas each, long preceding any similar publication.

St Petroc, Cornwall's chief saint, settled here in the sixth century and the church dedicated to him is still mostly unrestored from the building which dates from the fifteenth century. Notice its unusual font of blue-black Catacleuse stone from the nearby quarries at Harlyn Bay. The name can also be spelt Cataclew's, as seen on the map at Cataclew Point. The rock here is Palaeozoic but variable in character – dark grey or blue and sometimes even yellowish.

Behind the church and screened from the road by a castellated wall is **Prideaux Place**, one of the few Cornish manor houses still occupied by the family for whose ancestors it was built. In 1987 it was opened to the public for the first time in 400 years and visitors can wander round the 20-acre (8 hectare) deer park and marvel at the great chamber inside the house, gazing up at the embossed plaster ceiling which depicts scenes from the Bible. and dates from about 1585.

North of Padstow the public footpath leads to **St George's Well** and on to **Stepper Point** where the spectacular cliff scenery remains unspoilt. There are tracks all round past **Trevone Bay** to Trevose Head. Motorists have to shuttle to and from these coastal points as there is no connecting road. The fine farm-

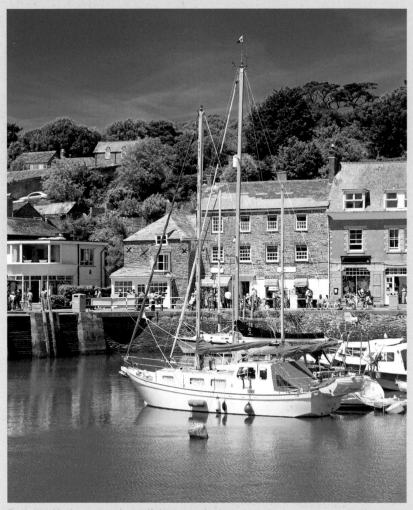

Padstow Harbour on a beautiful summer's day

stead at the entrance to the hamlet of **Treator** on the B3276 is the birthplace of Sir Goldsworthy Gurney, another great Cornish engineer.

After Trevone Bay, with its clean sand, where rock eddies can be dangerous, is **Harlyn**. It is interesting historically because of the gold lunulae and the many prehistoric remains discovered there early in the twentieth century when workmen, digging foundations for a house, uncovered a Neolithic cemetery. Some of the antiquities are to be seen in the museum at Truro.

The toll charged to drive to the point at **Trevose Head** is little enough to pay for some of Cornwall's wildest and roughest coastal views. Few golf courses can be as well sited as the links at Trevose. Open to the headland, with more than ten beaches and the ruins of the chapel where St Petroc converted Prince Constantine close by, they must be unique.

The coastal footpath is difficult to negotiate along these very exposed cliffs, and agile walkers who venture down the steep path to **Fox Cove** will find a delightful place of retreat even at the busiest times. The National Trust have saved the cliffs at **Porthcothan** and in 1966 also acquired 220 acres (89 hectares). That land stretches from

The Saints' Way

As you look across Padstow harbour you will be standing at the start of an ancient 26-mile (42km) track across Cornwall now known as the 'Saints' Way'. It was originally used by Bronze and Iron Age traders who preferred the land route to Fowey rather than the dangerous waters at Land's End when they travelled to Brittany from Ireland and Wales. Much later, Celtic Christians also travelled overland and followed the same way but they stopped to build churches, erect granite crosses and open up holy wells. It is in remembrance of them that this long walk has now been established as the 'Saints' Way'. This could well be the central point of an entire holiday because along the way there are so many different aspects of the Cornish scene to be enjoyed.

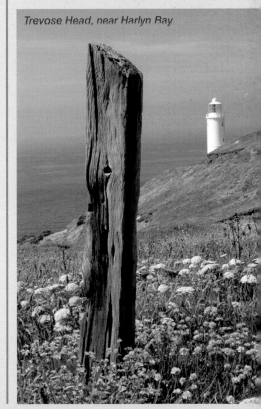

Trevose Head, near Harlyn Bay

155

Obby Oss festival

There is one special day – 1 May – when all the world seems to come to Prideaux Place at Padstow. That is when the 'Obby 'Oss festival takes place and the doors here are opened to the blue horse who dances in the staircase hall to the music of an old traditional tune.

Parking is not easy in Padstow during the season and on May Day it is impossible, especially with crowds lining the narrow streets waiting for the procession of this unique folk festival. It takes the form of a dance struggle between 'Oss and Teazer and is thought to represent the conflict between winter and summer or even good and evil, as seen in the story of St George and the dragon. A short distance from the town a spring dedicated to the saint is believed to have gushed forth from the rock immediately he set foot there. But whatever lies behind the old custom, the procession of horse, teazer, dancers, singers and musicians still makes its way annually between houses decked with flags and greenery.

Porth Mear, past several fine small coves, a fine rock arch and beyond Park Head to **Diggory's Island** at the north end of **Bedruthan Steps**. These rock stairs became eroded to danger point but have now been restored. There is an information centre, shop, tea-room and car park near this justly famous beauty spot with its spectacular cliff scenery.

Arable fields are under cultivation right to the cliff edge and flocks of sheep are surprisingly numerous. Tamarisk hedges, which are unusual in Cornwall, are planted here not for their beauty but because they afford the most effective protection from salt spray blown off the sea during gales.

After the pleasures of Padstow and its nearby coast, visitors will find it strange to be directed to a disused aerodrome. But it is a pity to miss the church at **St Eval** (pronounced as in 'ever'), standing lonely and surrounded by dreary concrete flats, once busy runways. The rather severe exterior of St Eval church belies its character. It is, in fact, one of the most friendly in Cornwall, with open doors for visitors.

In complete contrast, **St Ervan** church is hidden in the wooded seclusion of its churchtown at the end of a narrow lane between sections of the old aerodrome. It is built on a circular Celtic site high above a lush valley and a golden angel at the door – perhaps it is the saint himself – invites you to enter. Inside, there is the Lord's Prayer in Cornish, and some fine old slate headstones on the walls.

From here the lanes wind through Rumford and over the B3274 to the parish of **St Issey**. The rich brown and red-brown stone quarried nearby is used locally, its warm colours reflected from the walls of cottages whose bright gardens border on the road. Where the lane joins the A389 Padstow Road, there is another Ring o' Bells.

Little Petherick takes up a considerable amount of the A389 from here to

Padstow, but it is such a delightful village that no one complains. Old slate-hung houses lean towards the mill stream as if sharing a secret. The church is small and has been very Anglo-Catholic since the beginning of the twentieth century. There is little left of the tiny church that was here 600 years before – only two bells, some bench ends, a font and the thirteenth-century marble slab to Sir Roger Lemporu, unusually decorated with a human head and a foliated cross. Athelstan Riley became patron here in 1898 and restored building, furniture and vestments to former High Church traditions.

Wadebridge is interesting for several reasons – its name, its position, its bridge and its own pleasant character. Historians believe that 'Wade' indicates that it had probably been used by the Romans, who crossed the River Camel at that point because of the *vadum* or ford there. In the Middle Ages, before the bridge was built, there was so much traffic at this fording point that

RAF connection

During World War II, squadrons of Coastal Command flew from St Eval station; their badge incorporated a likeness of the church. In March 1959, 205 Squadron presented their standard to this place of worship, where it still hangs. The handsome font cover is an additional remembrance of that occasion. Today, padre and vicar share services as the congregation is drawn from RAF St Mawgan and the civilian homes in this scattered parish.

chapels were erected to greet travellers and pilgrims. **St Michael's** at the **St Breock** end was licensed as early as 1382 and about 1468 a bridge was built between it and the **King's Chapel** at the eastern end. They were both sold for secular purposes by Queen Elizabeth I in 1591.

So many tales exist about the construction of what Carew called 'the longest, strongest and fairest bridge that the Shire can muster' that more needs to be said about it. In 1538, Leland gave the following interesting account:

Wadebridge wher ther was a fery 80 yeres syns and menne sumtyme passing over by horse stoode often in great jeopardie, then one Lovebone, Vicar of Wadebridge, moved with pitie began the bridge and with great paine and studie, good people putting their help thereto finished it with xvii fair and great uniforme arches of stone. One told me that the foundation of certein of th' arches was first sette on so quick sandy ground that Lovebone almost despaired to performe the bridge untyl such tyme as he layed pakkes of wolle for fundation.

The Bridge on Wool inn sign agrees with this report and so do those who appreciate that wool solidifies when wet and compressed. Others believe that money to build the bridge came from wealthy sheep farmers in the area, especially those from Bodmin Moor – hence 'built on wool'. More recently the bridge has been widened on several occasions to cope with modern traffic, the latest in 1994.

Today those who stand by the river and gaze at the 13 arches of the old bridge looking downstream will see it overarched by the modern bridge over the bypass. This too is a feat of engineering and quite elegant but will it stand the test of time? While by the river look for the little egrets that can be seen there, an unusual bird in the British Isles.

The area around the bridge is depicted in a mosaic by Emma Spring (she also worked with the children on the mosaics at Saltash). It stands by the entrance to the Co-op car park and was presented to Wadebridge by the North Cornwall Visual Arts Project. The slate quays and stone wharves which can still be seen in places beside the river are, however, little more than ghostly reminders of the great trading days of the town, situated where the old pilgrims' way to the Mount crosses the trade route from Ireland to Europe.

Eventually, railways brought a dif-

Bedruthan Steps

Porthcothan Bay

ferent kind of traffic – holidaymakers and goods to Wadebridge and Padstow – but the line beside the Camel estuary is now only for pedestrians. It provides quiet walking or cycling on the **Camel Trail** – the raised swan-nesting mounds are of special interest. The station buildings remain and part of them house the **John Betjeman Centre** with its memorabilia of the poet.

To the south of Wadebridge, an extensive showground lies on high ground beside the A39 from St Columb. **The Royal Cornwall Show** is held here in June when Cornish talents compete in every field. Vintage car rallies and all the many other events taking place here are well advertised. The **St Breock standing stone** is also on these, the St Breock Downs. Wadebridge's **Parish Church of St Breock** lies in a tree-encircled valley a little out of the town. It rests peacefully away from the traffic.

Rather less peaceful, but highly popular, is **Cornwall's Crealy Great Adventure Park**, located just off the A39 at Tredinnick, 6 miles (10km) south-west of Wadebridge. Cornwall's biggest theme park offers a variety of rides, shows and animal displays to keep the whole family entertained, whatever the weather.

North of the Camel Estuary

To explore the area north of Wadebridge, begin at **Egloshayle** ('estuary church') on the A389 Bodmin road. The church itself lies on the corner of a lane but is impressive with its 80-foot – (24m) high tower. Inside there is a door which commemorates the fact that Vicar Loveybond (Elizabethan variant of Lovebone) gave both the tower and a grand east window of five lights. The dedication is thought to be to St Conan, which is unusual in Cornwall.

The lane climbs and twists away

to Above Town, turns left, then right at the next junction where it meets unexpected country. The bridge over the River Allen is scarcely a car's width, which indicates the narrowness of the way ahead to **St Mabyn**, a village of many footpaths – all worth exploring.

Three miles (5km) beyond lies well-kept **St Tudy**, where there is much of interest. Born and buried here was Richard Lower, the first to perform an operation of blood transfusion direct from one animal into the vein of another and then from man to man. He became the most noted physician in London and was in attendance on Charles II. Unfortunately his interest in politics was ill-timed and the Titus Oates affair caused him to lose everything – his position, his practice, his credit and his Fellowship of The Royal Society. He died at the age of sixty in 1691. There is a monument to Charles Bligh, a member of this St Tudy family, on the wall of St Tudy church, and Captain William Bligh of *Bounty* fame was born here.

North from here along the B3266 the village of **Michaelstow** shelters in a valley where the blue and white of wild bluebells and garlic make the church-yard a lovely sight in early summer. High above this protected community the Iron Age earthwork is named on the map as **Helsbury Castle**. Within it is the ruin of a chapel and not far away is Helsbury Farm and Helstone, recalling the possibility of an original cult that worshipped the sun (*howl* in Cornish). When Christianity came to the area, a chapel was built to exorcise the pagan associations and was dedicated to St Michael, whose name was also given to the place where people had settled

in the valley below.

It does not matter which of the narrow lanes you take from here to cross the A39 and reach **St Teath**. This is another village that has long since lost its former importance. The church, which is in the centre, was built within a circular Celtic site and so follows the worshipping tradition of centuries but there is now no trace of the collegiate institution once established here.

The countryside picture changes now with open land much more in evidence as the byways join the B3314 and climb to Tregeare Rounds where the lane before Pendoggett turns sharply towards the sea. As the road nears the coast, the number of footpaths increases – all leading down the valleys and along the cliffs towards Port Gaverne, Port Isaac and Port Quin.

Each of these places has a different history, and has been important in its own way since before Tudor times. **Port Gaverne** used to support a thriving pilchard industry that brought prosperity to the small community even as late as the nineteenth century. The National Trust now owns the beach and two groups of cellars where fishermen used to make and store their pots, nets, sails and gear as well as process their catch.

The name of **Port Isaac** often puzzles those unfamiliar with the Cornish language. It means simply the 'corn port' (*porthysow*) – although it once had additional trade in pilchards and supported a good trade in slate. Now its narrow, twisting streets tumble down to the postage-stamp beach where visitors pay to park their cars in season – at low tide of course. It is a place popular with artists, lovers of small buildings like doll's houses and those who like walking. On the west side of the tiny bay is **Port Isaac Pottery** in what was the United Methodist Free Church. The interior of the church remains intact with gallery and pulpit, both of which are used to great effect to display paintings. Hand-thrown and individually painted pottery is produced here.

From here the coastal footpath keeps faithfully to the cliffs but motorists have to run inland through **St Endellion**. The church is another of the various collegiate establishments in Cornwall and has both an interesting history and especially fine bench ends. The ringers' rhyme in the tower is noteworthy as it was written by Nicholas Roscarrock, a recusant whose manor, **Tresungers**, still retains its former Tudor grandeur and is considered by some to be Cornwall's finest seventeenth-century building, although it is not open to the public.

Port Quin is a sad, beautiful place – a place of tragedy. It now belongs to the National Trust, which has adapted the fishermen's cottages, and the tiny cove, once again, has a cared-for look. In the nineteenth century this hamlet was home to fishermen and others employed at the Doyden antimony mine. But eventually it failed and the miners emigrated to Canada. At a later date all the remaining men of the little port sailed out together to fish, were caught in a storm and none survived. Small wonder that Port Quin is known as the village that died, for that is exactly what it did do and it is only slowly coming to life again now.

Doyden Castle, which looks down

Witch hunt

Ann Jefferies, who was born at St Teath in the early seventeenth century when witch-hunts were beginning, is still remembered. She entered the service of Moses Pitt, a man unexpectedly well educated for those times. From him she learnt about the healing powers of herbs and helped many with her knowledge. Unfortunately, one of the harsh Tregeagles was jealous of her popularity and had her committed to Bodmin Gaol as a witch. But, though she was deprived of food, she survived her ordeal and was eventually released. Then she married a Padstow man and carried on with her work of healing until she died.

from the cliffs edging the cove, was built as a gambling retreat in 1839 by a colourful character called Samuel Symons whose home was near Wadebridge. The National Trust bought it and it is now available as holiday accommodation. Approaching Polzeath look for the **Porteath Bee Centre**, a living exhibition of bees with a shop full of products from the bee.

Just below lies **Polzeath Beach**, fine for surfing and consequently very popular. Beginners will find tuition at **Surf's Up Surf School** and may be lucky enough to spot the seals and dolphins who swim here regularly. Visitors can learn more about the marine life of the area at the **Polzeath Voluntary Marine Wildlife Area Visitor Centre**

View from the Camel Trail cycleway and footpath along a disused railway line

Above, below & right: Port Isaac

Below: Sea urchins for sale at Port Isaac

adjacent to the pitch and putt course. A series of events takes place over the summer to promote greater awareness of this fragile environment.

The **Doom Bar** opposite Daymer Bay is composed of sand which makes a good fertiliser and has its own legend. The story goes that a mermaid had once guarded the port of Padstow, but after being mortally wounded by a young man who was tired of her advances, she cursed the place, withdrew her protection and caused the sand to pile up and hinder shipping. It still does, but has now become a blessing as its benefits to farmers are a partial compensation for the loss of shipping revenue.

Rock has wide and beautiful sands and is an estuary beloved by both artists and yachtsmen because of its rare combination of colour and sheltered freedom. It is also a place for sportsmen who tire of the sea – **St Enodoc** has a golf course nearby. The little chapel at St Enodoc was buried in the sands but dug out and restored in 1863. It is mainly Norman but both tower and spire are unusual in Cornwall – the latter dating from the thirteenth century. Sir John Betjeman, the Poet Laureate who died in 1983, chose to be buried here because he loved Cornwall dearly and the area of the Camel estuary best of all.

The road back to Wadebridge lies through **St Minver**, another village famous for its bellringers. Like St Endellion, the church has a painted ringers' rhyme and, like Lostwithiel, a broached spire.

Trewornan Bridge, which takes the traffic over the River Amble, is of particular interest as it is perhaps the only one built after the Reformation that is worth looking at. It has all the appearance of a medieval design with similar pointed arches, but it is, in fact, little more than a century old and was built by the Georgian squires who found riches under the ground and controlled the destinies of Cornwall through their wealth.

Poet's memorial

The National Trust owns 700 acres (283 hectares) of the land from Trevan Point to **The Rumps** and Polzeath Beach. Saved from bungalow development by popular appeal in 1935, this fine historic promontory might be considered a poet's memorial. Lawrence Binyon sat on this headland and found inspiration for his famous poem 'For The Fallen', with the words that are quoted on Remembrance Day throughout Britain:

> They shall grow not old, as we that are left grow old;
>
> Age shall not weary them, nor the years condemn.
>
> At the going down of the sun and in the morning
>
> We will remember them.

May is the best time to come here for the flowers are especially lovely then and this is one of the few places where pillow-lava – a volcanic rock which looks like pumice stone – reaches the surface. Still quite visible are the ruins of an Iron Age cliff castle.

What to do if it rains

St Ives

St Ives Museum
Tate St Ives
St Ives Society of Artists

Hayle

Paradise Park and JungleBarn

St Agnes

Presingoll Barns
Parish Museum
Blue Hills Tin Steams

Perranporth

Perranzabuloe Museum

Newquay

Waterworld
Blue Reef Aquarium
Tunnels Through Time
DairyLand Farm World

Trerice Manor

Portreath

Treasure Park
Tolgus Mill

Padstow

Prideaux Place
Padstow Museum
National Lobster Hatchery

Wadebridge

John Betjeman Centre

Polzeath

Porteath Bee Centre

Places to Visit

St Ives & The Hayle Estuary

Leach Pottery

Higher Stennack, TR26 2HE
☎ (01736) 796398
www.leachpottery.com
Established by Bernard Leach in 1920. Still used as a pottery. His work is also on display. Open: 10am–5pm, Mon to Sat, all year.

Barbara Hepworth Museum and Sculpture Garden

Barnoon Hill, TR26 1TG
☎ (01736) 796226
Website and hours as Tate St Ives. Administered by the Tate Gallery, all in the sculptor's former home. Open: Mar to Oct, daily, 10am–5.20pm; Nov to Feb, Tue–Sun, 10am–4.20pm.

♛ <18

St Ives Society of Artists

Old Mariner's Church, Norway Square, TR26 1NA
☎ (01736) 795582
www.stivessocietyofartists.com
Gallery overlooking the harbour, committed to support of work with a bias towards the 'open air' principle of its founders. Open: 10.30am–5.30pm Mon–Sat and Mar to early Jan, 2.30–5.30pm summer Sun.

Lelant Bird Reserve (RSPB)

Ryan's Field
☎ (01736) 711682
Overlooking the Hayle estuary an open hide is available in the grounds of Quay House. Open: at all times.

Tate St Ives

Porthmeor Beach, TR26 1TG
☎ (01736) 796226
www.tate.org.uk/stives
Open: 10am–5.20pm daily, Mar to Oct. 10am–4.20pm Tue to Sun, Nov to Feb.

♛ 🏛 <18

St Ives Museum

Wheal Dream
☎ (01736) 796005
Unique collection of artefacts covering all aspects of local life. Open: 10am–5pm Mon–Fri, 10am–4pm Sat, Mon before Easter to Oct.

♛ (Limited) 🏛 ☂ 🐕

Paradise Park & JungleBarn

Hayle, TR27 4HB
☎ (01736) 751020
www.paradisepark.org.uk
Collection of the world's rarest birds, otter sanctuary, birds of prey. Open: 10am–6pm daily, closed Christmas day.

Ⓟ ♛ 🏛 <16 ☂

Around St Agnes

Healey's Cornish Cyder Farm

Penhallow
☎ (01872) 573356
www.thecornishcyderfarm.co.uk
Home of the Cornish Scrumpy Company, and voted 'The Nation's Favourite Farm Visit' for five years running. Tractor rides, cider tasting and farm shop. Open: daily all year except early Jan, 9am–6pm Apr to Sep; opening times vary at other times of year. Free admission.

Ⓟ 🏛 🐕

Places to Visit

St Agnes Parish Museum

Penwinnick Road, TR5 0PA

☎ (01872) 553228

Well-displayed collection of exhibits connected with local history. Open: 10.30am–5pm daily Easter to end of Sept. Free admission.

Tehidy Country Park

Best approached from B3301 at North Cliffs/Reskajeage Downs.
Free access. Visitor Centre on South Drive. Open: all day and every day for walks.

Presingoll Barns

St Agnes on B3277, TR5 0PB

☎ (01872) 553007

www.presingollbarns.co.uk
Cornish shopping experience. Open: 9am–5.30pm daily all year, 9.30am–4.30pm during low season. Off little interest to under 12s.

Ⓟ ♿ (Part only)

Perranzabuloe Museum

Ponsmere Rd, Perranporth, TR6 0BW

☎ (01872) 573321

www.perranzabuloemuseum.co.uk
Open: 10.30am–4.30pm (closed 1pm–2pm) Mon–Fri, and 11am–1pm Sat. Easter to end Oct. Free admission.

Ⓟ ♿ ⛹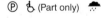

Blue Hills Tin Streams

Trevellas, near St Agnes, TR5 0YW

☎ (01872) 553341

Discover the skills of the ancient tinner on the journey from rock to metal on a tour of the works. Open: 10am–4pm Mon to Sat, Easter to end-Oct.

Treasure Park

Tolgus Mill, nr Redruth

☎ (01209) 218198

www.treasurepark.co.uk
All you want to know about gold. See goldsmiths and jewellers at work and pan for gold. Open: 9.30am–5.30pm Mon to Sat, 10.30am–4.30pm Sun all year.

Tolgus Mill and Redruth Old Cornish Society Museum

Within the Treasure Park complex

☎ (01209) 215815

http://tolgus-tin.org
The last large tin stream works in Cornwall. Open: 9.30am–5.30pm (dusk in winter) Mon to Sat, 10.30am–4.30pm Sun.

In & Around Newquay

Newquay Zoo

Trenance, Gardens, TR7 2LZ

☎ (01637) 873342

www.newquayzoo.org.uk
Wide variety of animals both large and small, animal encounter sessions, feeding times and keepers' talks. Open: 9.30am–6pm daily Easter to end-Sep, 10am–5pm daily Oct to Easter. Times may vary in winter. Closed Christmas Day.

Ⓟ (Nearby) ♿ ⛹ <16

Waterworld

Trenance Leisure Park, TR7 2LZ

☎ (01637) 853828

www.newquaywaterworld.co.uk
Fun pool, 25m pool, gym, sauna and solarium. Call for opening times.

Ⓟ ♿ ⛹ <17

Blue Reef Aquarium

Towan Promenade, TR7 1DU
☎ (01637) 878134
www.bluereefaquarium.co.uk
Underwater viewing and hands-on exhibits, Kingdom of the Seahorse, demonstrations, talks and special presentations. Open: 10am–5pm daily.

♿ <14 ☔ 🐕

Tunnels Through Time

St Michael's Road
☎ (01637) 873379
www.tunnelsthroughtime.co.uk
Lifesize characters bring to life stories of bygone days in a mix of fact and fiction. Open: 10am Sun–Fri, Easter to Oct. Also Sat during school holidays and bank holiday weekends. Closing times vary – call for details.

Ⓟ (Nearby) ♿ ☔
 (On quiet days)

*Sloop Inn, St Ives.
Note the date*

Cornwall's Crealy Great Adventure Park

Places to Visit

Holywell Bay Fun Park

3 miles (4.8km) south of Newquay,
TR8 5PW
☎ (01637) 830095
www.holywellbay.co.uk
Go-karting, fairground rides, play area
and pitch and putt.
Open: 10.30am (earlier in high season)
daily Easter to Sep.Weekends only after
first week in Oct.
Ⓟ ♿ 🚻

DairyLand Farm World

TR8 5AA
On A3058 Summercourt–Newquay
road
☎ (01872) 510246
www.dairylandfarmworld.com
Working farm and museum with
farmpark and playground, nature trail
and heritage centre. Open: 10am–5pm,
Easter to Oct, daily.
♿ 🚻 <3 Free 🌧

Trerice Manor

(National Trust)
SE of Newquay, TR8 4PG
☎ (01637) 875404
A very attractive National Trust property
– this small manor house was rebuilt in
1571. It has contemporary fireplaces
and plaster ceilings.
Open: 11am–5pm daily Sat–Thur.
Ⓟ ♿ 🚻 🌧

Lappa Valley Railway

St Newlyn East, near Newquay,
TR8 5LX
☎ (01872) 510317
www.lappavalley.co.uk
Steam train carries visitors along part
of GWR Newquay–Chacewater line.
Leisure park and East Wheal Rose

(engine house and tall chimney stack)
at end of journey. Open: 10am–5pm
daily Easter to Oct. Closed some
weekdays in Apr, May and Oct.
Ⓟ ♿ 🚻 <15

Screech Owl Sanctuary

Nr Indian Queens, Goss Moor,
St Columb, TR9 6HP
☎ (01726) 860182
www.screechowlsanctury.co.uk
Large collection of owl species,
pets' corner, play area.
Open: 10am–6pm daily, Feb to Oct.
Ⓟ ♿ 🚻 <14

Cornish Birds of Prey Centre

On A39 at Winnards Perch, nr St
Columb Major, TR9 6DH
☎ (01637) 880544
www.cornishbirdsofprey.co.uk
Sanctuary for birds of prey, flying
displays, coarse fishing lakes. Open:
Easter to end-Oct, daily, 10am–5pm.
Kennels available for dogs in car
park.
🚻 <14

Padstow & Wadebridge

Prideaux Place

Padstow, PL28 8RP
☎ (01841) 532411
www.prideauxplace.co.uk
An Elizabethan house (and deer park)
with a magnificent embossed ceiling.
Open: 12.30–5pm Sun–Thu, Easter
and mid-May to early Oct.

Padstow Museum

Market Place, PL28 8AH
☎ (01841) 532752
www.padstowmuseum.co.uk
An interesting collection of artefacts which give an insight into the history of the port of Padstow. Open: 10.30am–4.30pm Mon to Fri, 10.30am–1pm Sat, Easter to Oct.

 <16 Free

Carnewas & Bedruthan Steps

(National Trust)
Nr Bedruthan, St Eval, Wadebridge, PL27 7UW
Bedruthan Steps with beautiful coastal views, information room, shop and tea room.
☎ Shop (01637) 860563
☎ Tea room (01637) 860701
Open: shop, 10.30am–5pm daily, all year (10.30am–3.30pm Feb to Mid-Mar).
Tea room, 10.30am–5pm daily, Apr to Sep; 11am–5pm (4pm out of season).

Ⓟ ♿ ⋔ 🐕

The National Lobster Hatchery

South Quay, Padstow, PL28 8BL
☎ (01841) 533877
www.nationallobsterhatchery.co.uk
Aims to enhance lobster stocks around the coast. Visitor centre. Open: From 10am–4pm, daily, all year.

Ⓟ ♿ <15

Cornwall's Crealy Great Adventure Park

Tredinnick, PL27 7RA
A39 near St Columb, 6 miles (10km) south of Padstow
☎ 0870 116 3333
www.crealy.co.uk
Indoor and outdoor attractions for children. Shire horses and other farmyard animals. Open: 10am–5pm daily Apr to Oct.

Ⓟ ♿ ⋔ 🐾 (Free poop scoop bags)

John Betjeman Centre

Wadebridge, PL27 7BX
☎ (01208) 812392
www.johnbetjemancentre.org.uk
Former station houses memorabilia of John Betjeman. Open: Mon–Fri 10am–4pm, closed Bank Holidays. Little interest to under 7s. Free admission.

Ⓟ ♿ ⋔

North of the Camel Estuary

Polzeath Marine Visitor Centre

Wadebridge, PL27 6TA
☎ (01208) 863181
www.ncdc.gov.uk
Adjacent to pitch and putt course. Visitor Centre established to show in a graphic and original fashion most of the life on the seashore. Beach events/Rambles. Open: 10am–5pm most days, May to Sep. Free admission.

Ⓟ (Nearby) ♿ ⋔

Porteath Bee Centre

Nr Polzeath, PL27 6RA
☎ (01208) 863718
www.porteathbeecentre.co.uk
Learn about bees. Open: Exhibition, Daily Easter to Oct. Shop and Pooh Corner, open all year.

Port Isaac Pottery

Rosacrrock Hill, PL29 3RG
☎ (01208) 880625
www.portisaacpottery.co.uk
Working pottery and gallery of ceramics and paintings.
Open: 10am–4pm in summer.
Telephone first at other times. Poor disabled access.

7. Bodmin & The Moor

The town of Bodmin, Cornwall's geographical centre, stands on the Moor beside the River Camel where the twentieth-century A30 (bypassed in 1976) crosses the ancient trade route from Ireland to Europe. Its name means 'abode of monks', for the town grew up around the priory which had been built by St Petroc's followers who settled here in the fifth century.

Bodmin

In 1086, Bodmin was Cornwall's only town and it has since been a coinage centre, a meeting place for the Assize Courts (which have now been moved to Truro) and the home of Cornwall's Infantry Regiment. But when Truro became the cathedral city, Bodmin's importance rapidly declined and an air of regret for what might have been still seems to linger in the town.

There are, however, a number of interesting places to visit both in and around Bodmin. **St Petroc's** is an im-

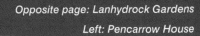

Opposite page: Lanhydrock Gardens

Left: Pencarrow House

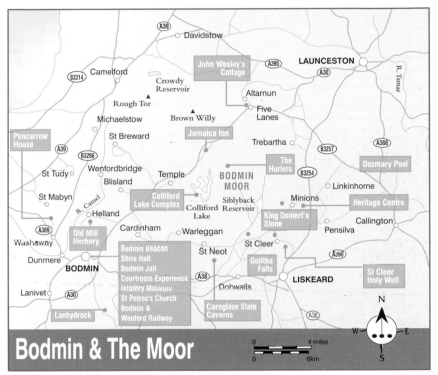

Bodmin & The Moor

posing building and the largest parish church in Cornwall. Under lock and key in an ivory casket, the relics of the saint are preserved – so precious that when a jeweller was asked to value them he said he could not because they were beyond all price. In 1177 these same relics were stolen by an Augustinian monk but were later recovered by Prior Roger of Bodmin after some brilliant religious detective work. Each year, at the annual mayoral elections, the treasures are taken out of the church and carried in procession through the town. At the lower end of the churchyard, down Priory Road, is **St Guron's Well**, set in the wall at the roundabout. This is believed to be named after a little-known Celtic saint who came here even before Petroc.

A few hundred metres up Turf Street is Mount Folly, probably the old friary garden, as Folly is a corruption of a Cornish word with that meaning. The **Shire Hall** was the Assize Court until 1988 and it has now been restored to reveal its architectural features of an extraordinary interior cantilevered staircase and the imposing solid granite front façade. The Tourist Information Centre is housed there now along with **The Courtroom Experience**. Visitors can watch a courtroom drama played out and sit as members of the jury.

In the nearby **Guildhall** are two relics from the past. One is a bell, the other a stone corn measure inscribed 'However ye sell – BF 1563 – your measure fyll'; perhaps a warning that the local Weights and Measures official was keeping watch for cheats. Close by is the Turret Clock, a reminder of what happened after the 1549 Prayer Book Rebellion. It was here that the mayor of Bodmin, Nicholas Boyer, was hanged for his part in the uprising.

The right fork at the top of Turf Street leads to the 160-foot (49m) **Beacon**, a pleasant picnic area with fine views. The 144-foot (44m) obelisk at its summit commemorates General Walter Raleigh Gilbert who was given a baronetcy by Queen Victoria for his distinguished service in India.

At the top of St Nicholas Street are the War Memorial and The Keep where the **Duke of Cornwall's Light Infantry Regimental Museum** is

Bodmin's famous sons

Today the names of Belling and Quiller-Couch are probably better remembered than that of Boyer. John Belling (1680–1761) was a burgess and clockmaker in the town. Today his descendants manufacture electrical equipment used throughout the world. Sir Arthur Quiller-Couch (1863–1944), known as 'Q', was the internationally accaimed author who was born in Bodmin. There is a memorial to him on Honey Street.

housed. Even for those with little interest in military matters there is much to catch the eye among the collection of guns, standards, medals and regimental memorabilia which covers 300 years.

From here, Halgavor Road leads down to moorland where a Mock Mayor's Court was held in medieval times. The name, translated from the Cornish, means 'fine for tin streaming and keeping goats' (therefore Goats' Moor). The latest OS map retains the old name in the area south of Bodmin and is marked 'Halgavor Moor' (SX 072652).

Beyond Halgavor Plantation lies **Lanhydrock** – 2 miles (3km) south-east of Bodmin. Here is everything that most visitors could wish for to enjoy a day of varied pleasure in and around the estate. It is a seventeenth-century house largely rebuilt after a fire in 1881, superbly sited above the Fowey valley and Respryn Bridge. There are fifty rooms open to view in the house alone and a splendid garden.

Respryn Bridge, east of the house, was one of the most important in Cornwall during the Civil War and was held for King Charles when Royalists were encircling the Parliamentarian troops at Lostwithiel in 1644. Four years later, however, although Cromwell's victory was not generally celebrated in Cornwall, Lord Robartes, who owned the estate and had made his fortune from tin, wool and banking, planted an avenue of trees at Lanhydrock and so proclaimed his allegiance to the Roundhead cause.

The Long Gallery at Lanhydrock was untouched by the fire and in this 116-foot (35m) long room the magnificent plaster ceiling depicting scenes from the Old Testament is still in perfect condition. The many acres of garden and woodland given to the National Trust – the latest as recently as 1970 by the 8th Viscount Clifden – are particularly beautiful with fine shrubs, formal gardens and woodland walks. They include Brownqueen Wood, which was the monks' deer park when Lanhydrock belonged to St Petroc's Priory before the Dissolution. The gatehouse (1651) and church are also interesting. There are open-air theatre and other events in summer and a music festival in July.

Take the Fletchersbridge turning at the first junction beyond Carminow Cross to find **Castle Canyke** (Grid Reference SX 087658), one of the chain of Celtic Iron Age settlements serving prehistoric tinstreamers and later used on the Ireland to Brittany trade route across mid-Cornwall.

The area south-west of Bodmin along the A39 is equally fascinating. **Lanivet**'s Panda Inn sign puzzles most people who see it for the first time. But the explanation is simple – the bamboos which thrive in this valley went to London Zoo to feed Chi-Chi, the famous panda. A chapel tower rising mysteriously behind a charming slate-hung house is another of this village's curiosities. It is, in fact, the remains of **St Benet's Abbey**, a leper hospital in 1411 and a Courtenay mansion in the sixteenth century.

The lane opposite the Panda Inn leads to the old Bodmin–Truro coach road – a straight up-and-over way with fine views at the top. Just beyond the farmstead of Mount Pleasant, as this road joins the A30, a lane on the right leads off into a mass of narrow byways

of peace and quiet. Through Lower Woodley and Ruthernbridge, with its ancient packhorse bridge, the lane climbs past peaceful farms, numerous little unnamed bridges and on to the old granite cottages clustering round **Withiel** church. In June a festival of flowers and music tempts visitors to linger in this remote village with its many footpaths branching away from the church.

A short distance on the right along the Roche road is another byway – this one leads to the tiny village of **St Wenn**.

The country all round here is green and uncluttered and the lanes meander across the valley past Rosenannon to St Breock Downs and the prehistoric longstone or, in the brilliance of furze and heather, to Nanstallon, Dunmere and Bodmin.

Along the road (A389 to Wadebridge) to **Washaway** is a sign to the award-winning **Camel Valley Vineyard**. Sit on the terrace and enjoy a glass of Cornish wine and during the afternoon in summer take a guided tour to see how that wine reaches your glass.

Pencarrow, one of the few fine mansions open to the public and still

---

Solemn warning

The church at St Wenn is another high and lonely place but is of special interest because of its sundial warning over the porch. Even on a bright day in summer, this place remains solemn. 'Ye Know Not When' say the letters on the face of the old timekeeper.

Walks

Roughtor

6–7 miles (9.5–11km) • easy climbing • about 4 hours
Map: OS 1:25,000 Explorer Series 109: Bodmin Moor
After exploring St Breward, the granite village and one of Cornwall's highest, drive down to Tuckingmill, then right at the junction following the mainly unfenced way to a No Through Road sign, passing another saying 'Roughtor 43rd Wessex Division War Memorial' and on into open woodland. The road is bordered by fir on the right till the sign of 'Private Access – No Admittance, Fern Acre Farm' on a huge block of granite shows the place to park the car. The walk begins gently up Alex Tor towards Stannon Clay Works. Leaving the farm track on the right make for Roughtor (Rowtor); in a direct route across the springy turf you arrive at Louden Hill with its Logan Rock (a rocking stone). On to the top with the bronze memorial tablet where once was a chapel dedicated to St Michael. Along this summit are remains of Bronze Age stone enclosures to be noted before descending to a little bridge at the south-easterly valley bottom. This crosses the De Lank River and a well-defined, zigzagging and steep path leads to the summit of Brown Willy with superb views. Follow the path back down to the bridge and head across the moor, keeping the farm track to your right.

Siblyback Lake to Golitha Falls

7–8 miles (11–13km) • easy • 4 hours
Map: OS 1:25,000 Explorer Series 109: Bodmin Moor
Park the car on the east side of Siblyback Lake, north of St Cleer. A lakeside path running south leads to the dam, passing many small sandy beaches on the way. Follow the path to Trekeivesteps, which winds through bracken and gorse before reaching a minor metalled road and a left turn. A pleasant downhill walk leads to Draynes Bridge, built for packhorses in the fifteenth century to cross the River Fowey. The walk downstream is beautiful at any time of the year and made interesting by the need to negotiate occasional stepping stones and footbridges. The sound of water pouring over rocks grows louder as the Golitha Falls are approached (note the pronunciation as 'Goleetha'). Walk into the sheltered glade of the falls, a series of small waterfalls and gorges with grassy banks suitable for peaceful picnics, and enjoy the beauty before returning to Draynes Bridge. Turn right towards the Doublebois to Minions road and there turn left in a roughly easterly direction. About 800 yards (730m) along this road is King Doniert's Stone, erected by the local Old Cornwall Society to remember the ninth-century king of East Cornwall who drowned just 800 yards (730m) away. Follow the road eastwards to a way on your left that leads back to the car park.

Lanhydrock

Distance and time to suit walkers • easy
Map: OS 1:25,000 Explorer Series 107: St Austell and Liskeard
The Lanhydrock Estate consists of nearly 1,000 acres (405 hectares) and the variety of walks through the park and woods offers all visitors a wide, personal choice. Look out for those that connect with the Camel Trail and the Bodmin–Wenford railway – three delights in one day.

Pencarrow House

lived in by the owners, lies a little further long the A389. It stands in a perfect setting of 50 acres (20 hectares) of formal and woodland gardens cared for by the owners, the Molesworth-St Aubyns. The house is at the end of a mile- (1.6km) long drive (which was cut through an ancient British en-campment) past fine rhododendrons, camellias and hydrangeas – all under the shelter of towering beech trees. It was probably built about 1771, but the estate has actually been in the family since the reign of Elizabeth I. The owners are often about the grounds and always have a welcome for visitors, which is something that should put it at the top of anyone's itinerary.

Bodmin Jail on Berrycoombe Road

An ancient custom

Bodmin is where one of Cornwall's ancient customs used to be celebrated and has now been revived. This was the Bodmin Riding, a horseback procession in July, when guildsmen rode to the priory, received garlands and, after a church service, proceeded to take part in various sporting events. The revival has been extended to include mock battles, re-enactments and pageants and is called Bodmin Riding and Heritage Day. (See www.bodminridingandheritage. org.uk)

The famous park in Lanhydrock Castle

The mystery of Bodmin Jail

One intriguing story, still shrouded in secrecy, tells that the Crown Jewels and the Domesday Book were stored here for safety during World War I. The idea was that if an invasion were to take place the treasures could easily be taken to Falmouth and shipped to the secure haven of America. No one knows just how true the story is but, in spite of all doubt, local people accept it as a fact.

is an award-winning museum where models of inmates 'stare' at you from narrow windows. There is also a res-taurant and shop. The prison is almost 200 years old and was built because Launceston Jail, apart from being too small and dilapidated, was not central enough. Former days are made very real now by the skilful use of models and properties from the Royal Shakespeare Company while clever lighting and sound effects have been incorporated to recreate startling scenes. At strategic points round the prison complex large information boards not only explain the numerous tableaux but also give background details about life in the gaol at the relevant periods.

Since its closure, Bodmin Jail has been used for purposes varying from manufacturing engineering products to a nightclub. Now its present use as a museum is probably better suited to its structure, although the château-like main gates are so handsome that they seem almost a misrepresentation of the tragic events once enacted within the walls.

Bodmin Moor, western side

It is easy enough to reach the centre of Bodmin Moor by driving straight along the A30. Much more interesting is the route through lush valleys making the Moor itself seem even starker by comparison when it is reached at last. Opposite the Hole in the Wall public house (once Bodmin's Debtors' Prison) on the A30 ring road, Pool Lane leaves the town through Berry Lane and quickly away from the general hustle and bustle. The high land here gives views over the River Camel as does the village of **Helland**. This small place has a church with one of Cornwall's oldest memorials and an old mill house with a delightful herb garden, **The Old Mill Herbary**. Here about 3 acres (1 hectare) of semi-wild terraced gardens and a mini arboretum are home to a large variety of herbs, unusual and rare species of wildflowers, shrubs, trees and climbers.

Deep in the valley below is an early fifteenth-century bridge in fine condition (probably because it is away from main roads). For centuries, every donkey in Cornwall was known as the miner's friend but there are few to be seen here today. Memories of former days are still alive at Helland Bridge – nearby there is a place where these gentle animals were once kept. It is called Donkeys' Pool.

Not far from the Longstone cross-roads on the B3266 is **Colesent**. Although this is a dead end it is worth the short detour to see the woods below. There are views from here over the Camel but motorists will have to make other choices. One way is through the tiny hamlet of **Merry Meeting** – a place to visit just for the name, though it is quiet and charming. Upriver lies **Wenford Bridge**, so small that many pass it by, but for many years, until his death in 1983, it was home and workshop to the internationally famous potter Michael Cardew. Still active in his eighties he had enough energy to create works of art envied by many and right up till his death his enthusiasm and fascination for the craft of pottery remained undiminished.

Moorland travel consists very much of criss-crossing rivers or avoiding them altogether. From Wenford Bridge it is a question of taking the short route south on the east of the Camel and passing china clay works, then crossing the De Lank River to **Blisland**. Much has been written about this village because it looks so different from every other one in Cornwall. Granite cottages, the Manor House and the old inn are set round what is almost a village green. The dedication of the church to St Protus and St Hyacinth is rare. So is the building's beautiful interior with its breathtaking rood screen, restored in 1896 in pre-Reformation style and one of the finest in Britain.

Away from the village, on Pendrift Common, is **Jubilee Rock**. It is 700 feet (213m) above sea level and so the views from here are excellent. In 1809 a Lieutenant Rogers made a place for himself in history by carving this great boulder with coats of arms of royalty and noble families as well as various symbols of agriculture and industry.

From Blisland, beside the Manor House, two other roads twist to the north and climb higher to moorland. Here visitors can find a place to picnic and get a different view of the Camel before taking the Bradford road to **Kerrow Downs**, a wild area, but not literally Robert Louis Stevenson's 'naked moor' because the boulders and heathers provide a low landscape that is so characteristic of Cornwall's moorland regions. There is an old clapper bridge at **Bradford** and it is tempting to sit beside it and think of the days when it was busy with sheep, shepherds and wool merchants with their packhorses laden for market.

There is another clapper bridge at **Dulphy** which carries the narrow road over boulder-strewn moorland to **St Breward** which, at 720 feet (219m) above sea level, is Cornwall's highest village. This whole area was more thickly populated by prehistoric man than anywhere else in the region. Hut circles, stripple stones, stone circles and the unexcavated King Arthur's Hall are all within walking distance. There is plenty of scenery here to fire the imagination. Like Luxulyan (see chapter 2), this is a granite village, solidly built against all weather. The stone for the houses and cottages came from nearby De Lank quarries which also sent granite to London's Blackfriars Bridge, the Wolf Rock, Eddystone and Beachy Head Lighthouses, as well as harbours and other buildings in distant parts of the world.

There are various ways from here to Roughtor including several moorland paths. The quickest for motorists is to drive down the steep hill into the woods at **Tuckingmill** and turn either left or right. The latter route, which passes eventually through **Watergate**, is for those prepared to brave some very narrow but lovely lanes. The more straightforward road over the Gam Bridge goes right along the B3266 near to Michaelstow, but at **Valley Truckle** just before Camelford, turns to Watergate and the moor again. Truckle is a misformation of Tucking with its wool trade associations.

Roughtor, sometimes spelt Rowtor, is understandably popular and in the season the small car park is rarely empty. Here Forestry Commission woods are pleasing to the eye in this barren treeless locality. Near the stream is a monument marking the spot where the un-fortunate eighteen-year-old Charlotte Dymond was murdered in 1844 by her lover who was hanged at Bodmin for his crime. The National Trust own 174 acres (71 hectares) of the land about Roughtor which, rising to 1,300 feet (400m), is the second highest point in Cornwall. It was a Bronze Age settlement and remains include hut circles and enclosed fields with signs of lynchet cultivation. This tor was given to the Trust in 1951 by Sir Richard Onslow, as the 43rd (Wessex) Division memorial to its men who died in World War II. The bronze tablet is set within foundations of the ruined chapel of St Michael.

The signpost at the crossroads along Jubilee road past Roughtor Farm points to Davidstow. About 1 mile (1.5km) along is **Crowdy Reservoir** which

Above: Horses on Bodmin Moor

Opposite page: A Celtic wayside cross on Bodmin Moor

shines a deep aquamarine on bright summer days. There are opportunities here for windsurfing, and birdwatching from a special hide, but permission must first be obtained from the South-West Lakes Trust.

The Central Moorland

The sudden flatness of the road through Davidstow Woods is a strange contrast to much of the countryside. Crossing a deserted airfield it skirts the northern edge of Bodmin Moor along softer lanes leading to **Altarnun**. Here the old Launceston to Bodmin road used to carry coaches over the picturesque fifteenth-century bridge in the centre of this tiny village, the heart of Cornwall's largest parish. Beside it is the **Cathedral of the Moor**, a handsome building dedicated to St Non, mother of the Welsh St David. The church is as fine inside as out, with 79 Tudor bench ends and massive piers, each pillar made from a single piece of moorstone. Northey Burnard's slate carvings in the churchyard are said to equal the best in Europe.

The highest place in Cornwall, **Brown Willy** (1,375ft/420m), lies behind **Jamaica Inn**, an eighteenth-century coaching stage made famous by Daphne du Maurier's novel of the same name, in the tiny hamlet of **Bolventor**. The hill is reached only by footpaths, as the nearest road stops at Codda, about 1 mile (1.5km) in from the A30. The source of the River Fowey is between nearby Maiden Tor and Buttern Hill. Opposite Jamaica Inn there is a road that leads to one of Cornwall's mysteries – **Dozmary Pool**. In the midst of nowhere it seems, this area of water is reminiscent of those lines by R L Stevenson about 'a naked moor, and a shivering pool.'

In 1533 Dozmary was reported to be fourteen fathoms deep but no one knows how it exists as no stream flows into it and it drains no part of the moor. One legend says that there is an underground connection with the sea, possibly because the name means 'drop of sea'. It has a strange unearthly beauty and an exhilarating brilliance that attracts people whether they want to solve its riddles or not. Two legends remain very firmly associated with this interesting place: one about King Arthur and Excalibur, another how the villain Tregeagle lost mansion and parklands beneath these waters and was condemned to empty Dozmary using only a limpet shell with a hole in it.

A short distance away at **Colliford**, beside a reservoir completed in 1983, is the **Colliford Lake Park Complex** where many endangered species of animals can be seen in the 60-acre (24 hectare) conservation area. Of different interest is the twelfth-century Cornish Long House, a single-storey dwelling with a thatched roof and cob walls typical of the period – a rare sight in the region.

Walkers can cross the moor to **Temple**, but motorists have to return to the A30 and drive towards Bodmin, turning left onto the old coach road to this hamlet. From the china clay works at **Hawk's Tor** there is a track which leads through Temple. It was the old way for tinners who, having won their ore from that great granite outcrop, guided laden packhorses down the Warleggan Valley to the harbour of Lostwithiel. The simple church stands on the site of a house built by the Knights Templar as a hospice for pilgrims on their way to the Mount. It

John Wesley

At Five Lanes, near Altarnun, lies Trewint and **Wesley Cottage**, famed for its associations with John Wesley. A Burnard carving of Wesley's head should be noticed on the façade of the Methodist chapel at Altarnun. This cottage lies in a lane which runs parallel to the A30 and it was here that Wesley stayed six times with the hospitable Elizabeth and Digory Isbell, conducting services from the stone porch and on one occasion baptising one of their babies.

He journeyed to Cornwall in an endeavour to bring people back to the Anglican Church, which he begged them never to forsake. But events took quite a different turn, resulting in the establishment of the Methodist movement, causing the great eighteenth-century schism in the Church of England. After some time the Trewint rooms fell into decay but in 1948–50 they were restored to their eighteenth-century style. Now a special service is held here annually on Wesley Day, 24 May, with others on Sunday afternoons during July and August. Open to the public (see p.189).

Selected Car Drives

Bodmin to Pencarrow and return

Take a lane off the A389 in central Bodmin towards Berry Tower, passing the cemetery on the left, making for Helland. At Helland Church, take the left turn where the junction road falls down to Helland Bridge. It rises on the other side, crossing the B3266 to St Mabyn, then down across the River Allen. Immediately left follow a very minor road over a disused railway line to Castle Killibury, an ancient earthwork seen on both sides of the lane which meets the A39. Take the left road towards Croanford and Pencarrow where the 1-mile- (1.5km) long drive flanked by huge rhododendrons, specimen conifers and blue hydrangeas leads to the Georgian house. The Washaway road and A389 takes you back to Bodmin.

Bodmin to Jamaica Inn, the Eastern Moor

About 12 miles (20km) north-eastwards from Bodmin along the A30 lies Jamaica Inn and Daphne du Maurier country. At Bolventor the road is signed to Dozmary Pool with its alleged connections with King Arthur. On the road leading to St Neot the moorland views are very fine. Colliford Lake Country Park lies to the right. The stained glass windows at St Neot should be seen before driving across the river to Pantersbridge and Warleggan then round the lanes to Cardinham. Join the A38 in the lovely Glynn Valley where a right turn leads back to Bodmin.

was that foundation which eventually put it outside episcopal jurisdiction to become Cornwall's Gretna Green with an unsavoury reputation. That extra-legal status continued until about 1744.

The Moorland East of the River Fowey

To explore the southern area it is advisable to start from Bodmin where the A38 dips into the Glynn Valley woods; there has been a considerable amount of road-widening here but it is still delightful, especially in spring and autumn. The road runs close to the

River Fowey and provides easy access for fishermen.

At the far end of this valley, from Doublebois, narrow, bouldery lanes, colourful in spring, climb to the quiet grey village of **St Cleer**. It has several interesting features, its handsome church tower, and the roadside holy well carefully restored by Captain Rogers in 1864 as a memorial to his grandfather, the Reverend John Jope, vicar of St Cleer, 1776–1844.

From St Cleer, the road leads to **Trethevy Quoit**, an ancient monument standing in a field at the back of some cottages – seeming to guard them. It is a megalithic chamber, 7 feet (2.1m)

long and about 9 feet (2.7m) high. The shape is that of a capstone supported by five uprights. It is believed to have been constructed some 4,000 years ago by Bronze Age people for use as a burial chamber for their tribesmen. These huge granite slabs were probably taken from the moor but it is not yet known what method was used to place such great weights into position.

Beyond the Crow's Nest hamlet more narrow lanes climb up to open moorland below Caradon Hill. In this landscape of deserted mines, **Pensilva** seems to be at the top of its own quiet world. Yet in the mid-nineteenth century it and the surrounding villages were so crowded that they looked more like the mining camps of Colorado and the far West. Today the moors are for sheep and those who enjoy walks away from roads. It is a pleasant, easy path up to **Caradon Hill** where, as well as views to Brown Willy, Plymouth and Dartmoor, there are blueberries to pick in summer.

North of Pensilva are **Caradon Town** and **Linkinhorne**, once both busy mining centres, but the former is now only a handful of houses. Linkinhorne church, set in its frame of trees, has an unusually handsome granite tower and fine wall paintings rediscovered as recently as 1891 and representing the Seven Works of Mercy and the Seven Deadly Sins.

Beyond Coad's Green on the B3257, a narrow lane on the left leads downhill to Trebartha and East Moor. From Trebartha Barton, a lane ends in lonely moorland high among prehistoric hut circles. There are paths everywhere and numerous places to explore, **Smallacombe Downs** being particularly exciting with its views over King Arthur's Bed and the River Fowey on the far side.

Twelve Men's Moor is here, too, an ancient tin-streaming area known

Altarnun Church

Memorial to a mathematician

Daniel Gumb's memorial can be found at Linkinhorne. He was a unique Cornishman who lived with his wife and children in a house built under a granite slab near the Cheesewring on the moor. But he was no idler. He taught himself mathematics and the works of Euclid in order to study astronomy, working out the more complicated geometric problems on rocks. His carvings can still be seen by those with really keen eyes.

Above: Pew ends at Altarnun Church

Below: Jamaica Inn

for seven centuries by that name. History records that in 1284 the prior of Launceston granted a lease there to 12 hard-working tinners. Among them were men with names that deserve to be recorded, such as Boglawoda, Cada, Foth, Trewortha and Broda. The road from Berriowbridge to Henwood, so busy in the past, is wooded and delightful, climbing up again to moorland. It is so peaceful yet so full of memories, with old engine houses and mine chimneys.

At **Minions**, parts of an old mineral railway track can still be seen and in numerous places nearby there are Neolithic and Bronze Age monuments. Paths from this hamlet lead to the **Cheesewring** where, until the 1950s, quantities of silver-grey granite were quarried and sent to Liskeard and Looe to be exported. The main fascination of this place for most people is the strange stone formation called the Cheesewring. It is the remains of a cairn where large thick oval slabs balance precariously. The rocks, about 22 feet (6.7m) high and 17 feet (5.2m) in diameter, have been formed by nature and weathered over the years to the fantastic shape that remains.

Beside Minions is **Caradon Hill** – its modern television mast at the top of the 1,210-foot (369m) hill. On the right, past the houses is a notice to **The Hurlers Stone Circles**. These strangely-shaped stones have, not unnaturally, given rise to local legends. Whatever the legend says, the facts are that these shapes suit their environment and add to the feeling of Cornwall's past that lingers still on Bodmin Moor. Archaeologists tell us that these ancient

megaliths are excellent examples of three Neolithic or very early Bronze Age circles. Excavation at the nearby Rillaton Barrow revealed a gold cup which is now in the British Museum.

At Common Moor, a lane on the right leads to **Siblyback Lake**, one of the best recreational reservoirs in Cornwall. Those who want to fish or sail need permission from the South West Lakes Trust but otherwise there are walks and picnic areas for the general public.

The Moorland West of the River Fowey

Redgate lies at the crossroads where there is a signpost to the hamlet of **Draynes** (originally Drayness) – its bridge probably the first over the Fowey. It was recorded in 1362 and carries a very ancient track from Caradon to Bodmin. Here a car park is close to the footpath which leads

King Doniert Stone

There is another English Heritage site, King Doniert Stone, at the roadside just beyond Common Moor. Here, however, are actual historical records carved on two granite monoliths. One is inscribed with the Latin words Doniert Rogavit Pro Anima – 'Doniert prayed for his soul'. Doniert is thought to have been Durngarth, King of Cornwall in the latter half of the ninth century.

through dense beech woods to the **Golitha Falls**. The water cascades for over 800 yards (800m) of twisting cataracts and the Fowey is seen in majestic splendour. The pronunciation is 'Goleetha', which means obstruction.

The Draynes to **St Neot** road is undulating, sloping steeply to this remote village. High beside the road stands the church, dedicated to a kindly dwarf. The interior is famous for its well-preserved fifteenth-century and early sixteenth-century stained glass conveying the impressive beauty of pre-Reformation windows. They tell the story of the Christian religion from the Creation but the windows of St Neot and St George were later additions. Look for the five historic crosses in the churchyard.

Although there is little now to indicate a busy industrial past, St Neot and the Loveny Valley were much involved with the wool trade as well as silver, copper, tin and slate. A short distance down the wooded valley are the **Carnglaze Slate Caverns**, known to have been worked from ancient times. Visitors taken round on guided tours can see another aspect of the Cornishman's skill when confronted with the need to 'win' any substance from under the surface. One of the surprises is the great lake, a sight as dramatic as the Blue Grotto on Capri.

During World War II the Royal Navy used the first cavern at Carnglaze as a rum store. In 2001 it was converted to a 400-seat auditorium called the **Rum Store** and during the summer a variety of performances are held here. The shape of the cavern ensures that the acoustics are outstanding.

The road back to the moor leaves St Neot and climbs to Goonzion Downs and **Pantersbridge** – a name with a double meaning, appropriate for a double bridge. A charter of 1241 mentions a place on the high road to Bodmin called Pontiesu, named by the Knights Templar as 'Jesus Bridge' or Pontjesus and later corrupted to Pantersbridge. It has charm in its own right, and the second roadway, which eventually took the increasing traffic from Liskeard to Bodmin, is something that adds to its character.

Due north is a farm track to **Warleggan** – one of the names Winston Graham used in his *Poldark* books. The village is today a desolate, ghostly place, almost deserted, perhaps because the last resident vicar, disapproving of the congregation, locked them out of the church and afterwards preached to cardboard figures.

The way back to Bodmin passes through **Mount** and **Cardinham**. Here, two ruined castles and echoes of the ancient nobility still remain.

Places to Visit

In & around Bodmin

St Petroc's Church

☎ (01208) 73867
Largest parish church in Cornwall.
Open: 11–3pm daily Apr–Sep. Other times by arrangement with the clergy and churchwarden.

Duke of Cornwall's Light Infantry Regimental Museum

The Keep. PL31 1EG
☎ (01208) 72810
Cornwall's premier military museum. Military exhibits. Open: 9am–5pm Mon–Fri all year and Sun in Aug and Sept.

Ⓟ 👫 <16 Free ☂

Bodmin Jail

Berrycoombe Road, PL31 2NR
☎ (01208) 76292
www.bodminjail.org
A chilling exhibition of prison life with pillory, stocks, dungeon and execution block, well presented and maintained. Shop and restaurant.
Open: 10am–dusk daily, all year.

Ⓟ 👫 <16 Free ☂ 🐕

Shire Hall

Mount Folly, PL31 2DQ
☎ (01208) 76616
www.bodminmoor.co.uk/bodmintic
Fine building that houses The Courtroom Experience, a Tourist Information Centre and a Town and Countryside exhibition. Open: 10am–5pm, Mon–Sat. Courtroom Experience hourly 11am–4pm, Mon–Sat in summer, Mon–Fri in winter.

Ⓟ (Nearby/Charge) 👫 <17 ☂ 🐕

Lanhydrock

(National Trust)
PL30 5AD
2½ miles (4km) SE of Bodmin
☎ (01208) 265950
A seventeenth-century house, largely rebuilt after fire in 1881. The gatehouse (1651) and north wing are unaltered. Good restaurant facilities. Open: 11am––5.30pm late Mar to Oct daily except Mon (closes 5pm in Oct). House open Bank Holiday Mondays at same times. Garden open throughout the year 10am–6pm.

Ⓟ 👫 <16 Free ☂ 🐕 (Park/Woods)

Bodmin and Wenford Railway

Bodmin, PL31 1AQ
☎ (0845) 125 9678 or (01208) 73666
www.bodminandwenfordrailway.co.uk
From Bodmin Parkway to Boscarne Junction. Many special events. Open: Mar to 1 Jan. Trains every day end of May–end-Sept and school holidays, less often at other times. Timetable varies with season; telephone or check website for details.

Ⓟ 👫 <16 ☂

Camel Valley Vineyard

Nanstallon, PL30 5LG
☎ (01208) 77959
www.camelvalley.com
Wine sales and guided tours at award-winning Cornish vineyard. Open: Sales,10am–5pm Mon to Fri, all year. 10am–5pm on Sat, Easter to Sep. Mon–Fri in winter 10am–5pm. Tours, 2.30pm Mon–Fri, 1 Apr to 30 Sep. Charges for tours only. Little interest for children.

Ⓟ 👫 ☂

Above: Golitha Falls

Below: Bodmin Moor

Pencarrow

PL30, 3AG, Off the A389 and B3266 at Washaway

☎ (01208) 841369

www.pencarrow.co.uk

Historic Georgian mansion owned and occupied by the Molesworth-St Aubyns. Refreshments. House open: 11am–5pm Apr–Oct, Sun to Thu. Gardens open daily 9.30am–5.30pm Mar to Oct.

  ⅋ <17 🌧 🐾

The Moorland East of the River Fowey

Trethevy Quoit

Near St Cleer

A handsome prehistoric burial chamber of five standing stones and a capstone. There is free access at all times.

Minions Heritage Centre

Minions, Liskeard, PL14 5LE

☎ (01579) 362350

Former mine engine house that describes 4,000 years of history on nearby Bodmin Moor. Open: All year round, 10am-5pm (often late in summer), admission free.

⅋ (By arrangement) 🌧

Siblyback Lake

PL14 6ER

1 mile (0.6km) through Common Moor

☎ (01579) 346522

An extensive recreational area with space for walks and relaxation.

(Charge) ⅋

The Moorland West of the River Fowey

Golitha Falls

3 miles (4.8km) N of Dobwalls

www.golithafalls.co.uk

Here the River Fowey cascades through deep woodland over shelves of smooth rock once obstructing its path. Parking facilities by the road at the entrance to the Falls. The path starts across the road and entrance is free. Toilet facilities.

Carnglaze Slate Caverns

Near St Neot, PL14 6HQ

☎ (01579) 320251

www.carnglaze.com

Underground slate caverns of unknown extent though work has been done here for over 200 years. Guided tours to the famous subterranean lake with its blue-green water. Jumper and sensible shoes advisable. Music performances of all kinds in the Rum Store. Open: 10am–5pm, Mon–Sat, all year. August until 8pm. Little interest to under 7s.

  <15 (Part outside) 🐱

Bodmin Moor Western Side

Crowdy Reservoir

Off A39 Camelford–Bude road

Walks all round but for other pursuits permits are needed.

Old Mill Herbary

Helland Bridge, Bodmin, PL30 4QR

☎ (01208) 841206

www.oldherbary.co.uk

Camomile lawn and unusual culinary,

medicinal and aromatic herbs. 5ac garden. Open: 10am–5pm daily except Wed, Apr to Sep. Free admission.

Ⓟ 👫 <15 🐕

Central Moorland

Wesley Cottage

Trewint, off A30
☎ (01566) 86158
www.wesleycottage.org.uk
A place of pilgrimage for Methodists. On 24 May open-air services are held here. This cottage is not a museum but has many treasures. Summer opening: Tue, Fri and Sat, 10.30am–3pm. Call to check winter opening times. Free admission.

♿ (Ground Floor Only) 👫

Jamaica Inn

Bolventor, PL15 7TS
☎ (01566) 86250
www.jamaicainn.co.uk
Now a popular restaurant. Buildings genuinely Georgian but spoilt inside with simulated Tudor. Still retains some old-world charm. Daphne du Maurier room.

Smugglers Museum

Jamaica Inn, Bolventor, PL15 7TS
☎ (01566) 86250
www.jamaicainn.co.uk/Smugglers_museum.htm
The Jamaica Inn story told in tableaux, sound and light. Collection of smugglers' relics. Open: Feb, Mar, Nov, Dec 11am–4pm; Apr, May, Jun, Sep 10am–5pm; Jul and Aug 10am–7pm.

Colliford Lake Park Complex

PL14 6PZ, A30 Bodmin to Launceston follow signs to right
☎ (01208) 821469
www.collifordlakepark.com.
A delightfully sited area of 60 acres (24 hectares) with rare breeds of birds, cattle, poultry, sheep and twelfth-century Cornish Long House. Lakeside walks, pets' corner, picnic areas, indoor play areas. Refreshments. Open: 10.30am–5pm daily Easter to Oct. Call for winter opening times.

Ⓟ ♿ (Most Areas) 👫 <12

What to do if it rains

Bodmin
Duke of Cornwall's Light Infantry Museum
Lanhydrock
Bodmin Jail
Shire Hall

Washaway
Pencarrow

Wenford
Bodmin and Wenford Railway

Nanstallon
Camel Valley Vineyard

Trewint
Isbell Cottage

Bolventor
Jamaica Inn and Museum

St Neot
Carnglaze Slate Caverns
Minions
Heritage Centre

Opposite page: Cornish Coast at Tintagel

Left: Launceston Castle

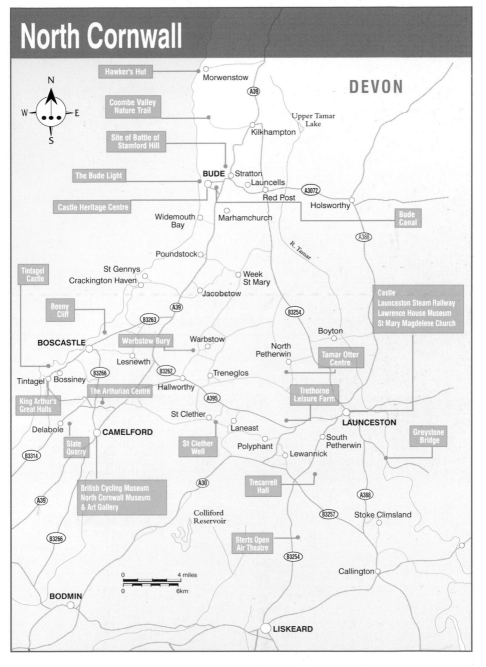

North Cornwall

Hawker's Hut

Coombe Valley
Nature Trail

Site of Battle of
Stamford Hill

The Bude Light

Castle Heritage Centre

Tintagel
Castle

Beeny
Cliff

BOSCASTLE

Warbstow Bury

Tintagel — Bossiney

King Arthur's
Great Halls

The Arthurian Centre

Delabole

Slate
Quarry

British Cycling Museum
North Cornwall Museum
& Art Gallery

CAMELFORD

St Clether
Well

Trecarrell
Hall

Sterts Open
Air Theatre

BODMIN

DEVON

Morwenstow

Kilkhampton

Upper Tamar
Lake

BUDE — Stratton

Launcells

Launcells

Red Post

Holsworthy

Bude
Canal

Widemouth
Bay

Marhamchurch

Poundstock

St Gennys

Crackington Haven

Week
St Mary

Jacobstow

Warbstow

North
Petherwin

Boyton

Castle
Launceston Steam Railway
Lawrence House Museum
St Mary Magdelene Church

Tamar Otter
Centre

Lesnewth

Treneglos

Hallworthy

Trethorne
Leisure Farm

St Clether

Laneast

LAUNCESTON

Polyphant

South
Petherwin

Greystone
Bridge

Lewannick

Colliford
Reservoir

Stoke Climsland

Callington

LISKEARD

A39
A3072
A388
A39
B3263
B3254
B3266
B3262
A395
B3314
A39
A30
A388
B3257
B3266
B3254

0   4 miles
0   6km

Robert of Mortain established Launceston as Cornwall's northern gateway and ancient capital when he built his strategic keep in about 1067 at the top of precipitous slopes overlooking the Tamar. He probably built Polston Bridge at the same time, thus rerouting the ancient pilgrim way from Kilkhampton. The first charter of Launceston's Borough Archives proudly calls the new road *Via Regalis Cornubiensis* – The 'Royal Cornish Way'.

Ownership of land was still a feudal matter in Norman times, especially in the case of Polston Bridge. Estates in Cardinham were only given conditionally – the condition being that when the Earl of Cornwall crossed the Tamar at this point, the Lord of Cardinham would meet him and, bearing his riding cloak, stay with him for 40 days or as long as he was in Cornwall. This ancient feudal custom still holds good, though today's dues are different. Prince Charles, who is Duke of Cornwall, went to Launceston in 1973 and received his rights from the Lord-Lieutenant. They were a brace of greyhounds called Whisky and Soda.

Memorial church

The church of **St Mary Magdalene** in Launceston was built under tragic circumstances by Sir Henry Trecarrel who owned an estate a few miles south of the town. While engaged on building his manor house there, he lost both his wife and little son and, grief-stricken, gave up all thought of completing his home and devoted his life to building the church and all matters concerning it. Particularly notable is the superbly carved granite exterior with not an inch of this hard stone undecorated. The motifs vary from prayers and angels to roses, pomegranates and coats of arms – those of Trecarrel and Kelway are on the upper storey of the south porch. The church was probably completed by Kelway who, it is believed, married one of Trecarrel's daughters.

Launceston

English Heritage is responsible for the upkeep of **Launceston Castle** which is a fine monument overlooking the town and the surrounding countryside. A cylindrical keep and ruined curtain walls are all that remain, but it is still worth a visit if only to understand its importance as a strategic site.

Immediately below, in Castle Street, is **Lawrence House Museum**, a handsome period house full of exhibits relating to the history of the town and neighbouring places. It is one of Cornwall's best museums – its moulded plaster ceilings are particularly fine. A steep road – with one-way traffic down – leads to the parish church.

A stroll around the town through its narrow streets reveals examples of architecture from Tudor times to the modern day. Look upwards to see the town clock and old signs such as the boot above a former shoe shop. Streets in Launceston are short and, although **Southgate** is two roads away, it is, in fact, reached in a minute. This handsome Norman arch, all that remains of the walled town defences, has been widened to accommodate increasing traffic. Above the arch and up a flight of extremely steep steps are rooms with a history, as they were originally for soldiers on guard duty and later housed the town's criminals.

Visitors who see Launceston on market day will be very much aware of the **White Hart Hotel** with its sturdy door. Historians believe that not only the door but the entire doorway, complete with columns, may have been rescued from the chapel of the castle, possibly when the stronghold fell to Cromwell in 1646.

Around Launceston

This pleasant town is a good holiday centre for studying the old packhorse bridges crossing the Tamar, Kensey and Inney Rivers and the neighbouring picturesque valleys where quiet corners of countryside are still to be found. The B3362 Tavistock road from just south of Launceston leads immediately to leafy lanes, some unusually narrow for motorists used to motorways. This way lies **Greystone Bridge** (1439), described by Cornwall's historian, Charles Henderson, as 'the fairest bridge in the two shires which it links together… for beauty of situation and perfection it

> ### Stoke Climsland Post Office
>
> Low beams and small cool windows are part of the charm of this cottage, also one of the oldest post offices in the country. Little can have changed here since it held the important position as an early Penny Post receiving house in 1839. Formerly, it had been a dwelling for workers attending to church repairs.

has no superior in the Western Counties'. Today, it is frightening to watch juggernauts roll across but in spite of everything the structure, which has a Grade 1 listing from English Heritage, stands firm. This proves the skill of medieval builders who were paid with indulgences – the conscience money of sinners who repented, hoping to buy their way to Paradise.

The sharp slate hedges of this area are screened by ferns and the lanes meander peacefully by remote places like **Lowley Bridge** and **Bealsmill**, to **Tutwell** and **Horsebridge**. After Greystone, the Tamar winds through some of the finest inland scenery in Cornwall, mainly woods once belonging to the great Benedictine house of Tavistock. The name Horsebridge has no animal origin but is a corruption of Hautes Brigge, then Hawte Brig. The flat wide meadows on either side are a great contrast to the wooded valleys of the upper and lower Tamar.

Since 1337, **Stoke Climsland** and much of the surrounding land has been Duchy of Cornwall property, including the church patronage. The first duke, the Black Prince, was a good landlord,

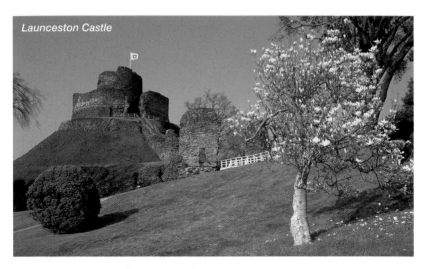
Launceston Castle

much concerned with the responsibilities of his estates, and in 1354 he gave six oaks from this deer park (now a farm) towards the construction of **Stoke church**. This old building stands central to the village, which is high above rolling pasturelands and rural countryside and there is a quiet contentment about the lane running between it and the village shop opposite.

A footpath opposite the church leads to Duchy Home Farmland where many prize-winning cattle are now bred. At the left of the road towards Kelly Bray is **Shutta**, which many miss because it is set a good way back. This is a privately owned sixteenth-century farmhouse which incorporates some interesting features of local history such as a huge granite bowl used for cider-making and doors from Whiteford, one of Cornwall's oldest manors. Seven entrances, 52 doors and 365 windows were built into Whiteford. Nothing remains of it apart from the name of a nearby farm, the doors here, others on Duchy property and some Adam chimney pieces in Buckingham Palace.

About a mile north of Bray Shop (on the B3257) a lane leads to the quiet countryside of **Trebullett**. Trebullett comprises two hamlets – Lower Trebullet is near Trecarrell Bridge, from which a steep lane leads to the other group of houses not named on the map. A left turn at the crossroads in their midst goes to **Trecarrell Hall**. Charles I stayed at the hall on his way to do battle at Liskeard. The bridge is not the one he crossed – that was swept away by floodwaters in 1847.

Visitors may see Sir Henry's great banqueting hall at Trecarrell. He built it to last – the great beams on its cradle roof are as strong as when they were first lifted there. This might have been another Cotehele but for the deaths of his wife and child that changed everything. The chapel is also here, with its gallery where the lord of the manor and his lady attended Mass. Perhaps the saddest sight is the pile of great stones lying by the farm gate where they were left almost 500 years ago.

The B3254 runs back to Launceston through the broad open fields of **South**

Petherwin. Before completing the return, turn south to see the **Sterts Theatre**. Established in 1982, this spectacular, covered open-air theatre is open all year and houses a gallery and runs a full programme of workshops. Performances are held throughout the summer months. Returning to Launceston visitors will pass **Botathan farmhouse**, which witnessed scenes of ghosts and exorcism in the seventeenth century.

The hilltop church at **Lewannick** is built of a stone which is not seen in many other parts of Cornwall. It is dark green and was quarried at **Polyphant** village across the A30. The almost circular churchyard indicates a very early Christian site, possibly fifth century AD. Here are two 'gravestones' with inscriptions in Latin and Ogham (an ancient British alphabet which consists of only twenty letters). Today people go blackberrying among the neglected stone outcrops. A visit to this place is worthwhile.

Not many visitors go further along the lanes to **Laneast**, though Sir John Betjeman called the church an unspoiled version of Altarnun. A Norman foundation, it was reconsecrated in the fifteenth century when the 38 pew ends were carved. Today it is very much loved and cared for, with fresh flowers to scent the building. John Couch Adams was born in the parish of St Sidwell's, Laneast in 1819 and a black tablet on the wall names him as the greatest astronomer since Newton. It also recalls his discovery of the planet Neptune. Truro cathedral also has a memorial to him and in Launceston Museum there is a bust by the sculptor Northey Burnard.

There are walks from here to **St Clether**, but for the motorist the road runs along a ridge, dropping a little to the church, its holy well, a small hall and one house. This well building is the oldest in Cornwall with its own chapel and stone altar. There is a serenity, too, which draws people to this remote place. The Lord's Prayer in Cornish is to be found in the church, and there is a stained glass window of the saint.

As you drive along the A395, stop at **Trethorne Leisure Farm** near Piper's Pool. Youngsters enjoy it here with pony rides (shire horses for the adults to ride), animals to feed, indoor and outdoor play areas, falconry displays and tenpin bowling.

Sheep are very much part of the landscape round Launceston, especially north of this road at **Treneglos** hamlet, where the old Cornish 'trev' is no more than a triangular green beside a church and two or three houses. It is almost as high as nearby **Wilsey Downs** where there are walks to prehistoric tumuli. Celtic tribes were forced to seek safety and live above the wooded valleys – Warbstow Bury, north from Wilsey and Treneglos, is a good example of this and ranks with Castle-an-Dinas and Chun Castle as one of Cornwall's largest ancient sites. Choose this place for a picnic and walks on a sunny day.

From this expanse of fields and farms, the lane plunges deeply down between hedgerows not despoiled by harsh council machines to **Tuckingmill** near Canworthy Water on the River Ottery. Fleeces from farms on the high ground once kept the local woollen mills busy and villagers in full employment. Now the cottages are quiet, those beside the river reflecting on their changed position in life.

The road from **South Wheatley** to **North Petherwin** is narrow and undulating but wooded and pleasant. After much study, St Paternus came to this place in the sixth century and the small churchtown remains apart from the main group of houses at Petherwin Gate in a typically Cornish manner. There is a poignant memorial here to three sisters – Susanna, Margaret and Ann – who died young in the seventeenth century.

The **Tamar Otter and Wildlife Centre** is nearby and in the 23 acres (9.3 hectares) of this, which was the first branch of the Otter Trust but is now in private ownership, there are British and Asian otters. Deer run wild and there are peacocks, wallabies and numerous waterfowl.

Boyton, once a thriving town, has now shrunk to a hamlet. It stands on high ground overlooking the wide and lush valley of the River Tamar. The parish is proud of Agnes Prest of Northcott, a Protestant martyr, burned at Southernhay in Exeter in 1557 for refusing to accept the doctrine of transubstantiation. She shares a memorial with Thomas Benet outside Maynard School in that city. There are numerous walks here, some on high ground and others down in the valley. Either way, it's a tranquil area for rambling.

Motorists returning to Launceston pick up the B3254 road at **Ladycross**, probably once associated with Tavistock Abbey, and return to Launceston over the **Yeolmbridge**. This is Cornwall's oldest and most perfectly finished bridge, the only one with a ribbed vault and pointed arches, similar to that of the north gate of Launceston Castle.

On the hill north of the River Kensey and level with Launceston Castle is **St Stephen's**, once a collegiate establishment and consecrated in 1259, which makes it the mother church of Launceston. The original borough of St Stephen's grew up around the monastery below the present church and from it Launceston's old name originated – Lanson or Dunheved. There are arguments for both but the former is more Celtic as it comes from Lan Stephen's town, *lan* being Cornish for holy ground.

Today, this area of the Kensey Valley keeps a little of its past – a packhorse bridge, slate-hung cottages overlooking the mill complex and a toll house, where Launceston's wealth once lay. The building of St Thomas was formerly the chapel of St Stephen and stands as the lone reminder of Launceston's pre-Conquest religious past.

In the Kensey Valley, the **Launceston Steam Railway** will take you back into history as Victorian locomotives pull their coaches through two and a half miles (4km) of beautiful scenery along the track of the old North Cornwall Railway. Among the museum's many exhibits is a restored 1905 Robey horizontal steam engine and tours of the workshops are on offer.

Camelford

The rest of north Cornwall can be divided into two sections, each with a character of its own. **Camelford**, about 16 miles (26km) west of Launceston along the A395, can be a base for seeing King Arthur country. Motorists driving north from Wadebridge on the

Walks

Week St Mary (5 miles/8km south of Bude)

5 miles (8km) • some hills • 2½ hours
Map: OS 1:25,000 Explorer Series 111: Bude, Boscastle and Tintagel
At Week St Mary's village square head south then turn right toward the Lambley Park hotel (badly fire-damaged in 2004). After 800 yards (730m) take the footpath through the gate at the left of the hotel. Follow it to Ashbury Farm, through the yard, out at the far gate, along the track to your left then down to the woods. Ashbury Iron Age fort is on your right as the path drops to a stile by a stream. Over the bridge turn right, follow the hedge and stream to a stile leading to the remains of Burycourt medieval manor. Leave by the gate to a forest track which comes to a road where you turn left up the hill, and past the house at the top go through a gate on the right. Go on by the hedge to a track above forestry and walk to a gate into a lane. A sunken lane lies to the right – the old road to Week St Mary and a mill – not a public right of way but the owner allows walking. At the bottom go left across a stream into a field and through a right hand gap to follow the hedge up into a lane and past a farm to the road. Turn left and beyond the road junction go over a stile on the left to the return path to the village.

Bude Canal

5 miles (8km) • moderate • 2½ hours
Map: OS 1:25,000 Explorer Series 111: Bude, Boscastle and Tintagel
From Bude Visitor Centre (Crescent car park) go along the canal towpath inland until Whalesborough Wood where the route crosses the main A39. In front is Hele Bridge: turn left here and over it to the path, following it beside the canal and up the inclined plane to Marhamchurch. At the pumping station leave the towpath and go down the lane to the left, following it downhill and across the river where ahead of you, after turning right, is Hele Mill. Before the mill turn left; join the path up the steps where a gate on the right at the top of the field leads to the old road. Turn left past the farmhouse to a gateway with a fine view of the Bude valley then retrace your steps past the houses and turn left into a lane. Cross the A39; go down to the Bude sewage works as this track leads to the old railway. Go for a short way then turn left down embankment steps to a fenced path beside a ditch. By the railway bridge turn left at the minor road, crossing the field on the right, respecting any stock in there. The road leads to Rodd's Bridge and so to Bude.

Left & below:
Tamar Otter &
Wildlife Centre

A39 approach this quiet market town through the lovely Allen valley, a route starred with primroses and bluebells in spring. A peaceful place now, Camelford was once a lively pocket borough, busy with wool and cloth-making as indicated by the nearby hamlet of Valley Truckle (Cornish for tucking-mill).

Well signposted from the A39 and worth a visit is the **North Cornwall Museum and Art Gallery**. This exhibition opened in 1974 in an old coach house to display a collection of items reflecting rural life in north Cornwall. A section of the building has been constructed to resemble a typical moorland cottage interior and in addition, changing craft and painting exhibitions are held throughout the season. Those who have seen it are not surprised to learn that it has been featured on both television and radio as well as being given the Pilgrim Trust Award for the best small museum in Britain.

Camelford is also the home of the **British Cycling Museum**, housed in the old station just north of the town, with more than 400 bicycles and a huge collection of cycling memorabilia.

The westward coast roads from Camelford all pick up the B3314 where **Delabole**, about two and a half miles (4km) away, is well signposted. The village is clean and attractive but the focal point is the slate quarry which has been producing fine slate for many centuries. Look out for the millennium clock beside the road in the village, made entirely in slate.

Northwards along the B3266, the road crosses the high plateau of **Waterpit Down**, pleasant with extensive views and the ubiquitous sheep. A roadside cross here is a tenth-century stone carved with interlaced ornamentation. It has weathered considerably since it was set up as a pilgrims' waymarker. A maze of narrow lanes leads eventually to **Lesnewth**, very remote but once an important place where Cornish kings and chieftains held court (*Lis* means court/palace and *Noweth*/*Newith*, new). The church of St Michael is securely built into the hillside opposite a farm and easily missed as the roof is at road level.

Boscastle and Tintagel

Walkers will find that several paths lead away from this unusual churchtown into the lovely **Valency Valley** but motorists have to cross the latter for the B3263 Boscastle road at the head of the valley, partly owned by the National Trust. The drop down to **St Juliot's church** is steep but typical of roads in this area.

At **Boscastle**, the original inner harbour was built by Sir Richard Grenville in 1584; with 61 acres (25 hectares)

Selected Car Drives

Tintagel to Widemouth Bay

From Tintagel the B3263 to Boscastle is very pleasant but for a different view do not take the left turn downhill to the village but carry on for about a mile (1.5km) then take the first left – a secondary road which will carry you up and down steeply to Lesnewth. About a mile (1.5km) past the church a sign to Tresparrett is the one to follow, then on to Tresparrett Posts. There the minor road crosses the B3263 to Higher Crackington, Middle Crackington and for drivers with good brakes on to Crackington Haven. Steep and narrow are the lanes into and out of this cove between Cambeak and Pencarrow Point where fierce cliffs have wrecked many a ship. After St Gennys Church, a place of peace in its own grassy square, pass left for Coxford and Millook. Here the views are magnificent: the road is narrow and steep but rising out of it the undulations of Penhale Cliff lead to the ease of a road by the sands of Widemouth Bay. Follow that cliff road and Bude awaits you. Then the A39 will offer a wide safe way to your holiday centre.

Around Bude to the north

From Bude follow the A39 a very short distance south but watch for a left turn to Marhamchurch. Stop and see the church if it is open. Drive straight through Hobbacott to the Buttsbear Cross T-junction and there turn left along the B3254, crossing the A3072 at Red Post to Launcells Cross. Here your way is left and first left to Launcells Church. Return up out of that valley and turn sharp left into Stratton and the site of the Battle of Stamford Hill. About a mile (1.5km) along the A39 in the Kilkhampton direction, turn left for Poughill. Then follow signposts for Stibb and Coombe. Continue on to Crosstown and Morwenstow – a cluster of houses centred on the Bush Inn and Hawker's Church. Leave Morwenstow through Gooseham towards Woolley but turn right in the village towards the A39 junction where a left turn would take you into Devon. Your way is to the right for Kilkhampton. Turn left onto the B3254, and make for Thurdon, Dexbeer and Broomhill, then take the right turn at the village junction after a steep road up from the Tamar Valley. It will take you through Rhude Cross and along the river valley to Bush and the A39, Stratton and Bude.

of adjoining cliffs, it is National Trust property. There is an NT information centre open in the summer in the Old Smithy and a cafe in a former pilchard cellar. It is hard to believe that it was once Launceston's port for shipping slate, corn and tanning bark. Cargoes of food and coal were imported here. Today, few would care to negotiate even a small motor yacht between the sharp, twisting rocks of this narrow inlet, but local boatmen, who know the dangers, take visitors out to see a different view of the cliffs, especially the one some call King Arthur's Head. Before leaving Boscastle pause at the **Museum of Witchcraft** to learn about the ancient rites.

Steep, heather and gorse-clad cliffs and a narrow strip of water make Boscastle. Little enough, but it is very popular and no doubt the Valency Valley adds to its appeal. It runs inland for 5 miles (8km) and in spring it is a delight – in autumn, unbelievably beautiful.

On Monday 16 August 2004 the narrowness of this lovely valley was the cause of a devastating flood in Boscastle. Some five inches of rain fell in a very short time on ground that was already saturated. The resulting flash flood swept through the village, wrecking many houses and shops, destroying the bridge and washing around 80 cars into the harbour. Miraculously no one was killed or badly injured. A year later the village was bustling with visitors again, due in no small part to a great community effort by the local people.

Motorists climb out of Boscastle to pass Trevalga and arrive at **Trethevy** (the head of Rocky Valley) along the B3263. Walk down the valley to the

Delabole Slate Quarry

Pack saddle donkeys were first used to remove the rock: horses were next and now lorries provide the transport. The great quarry is 500 feet (152m) deep and over one and a half miles (2.4km) round. Richard Carew included it in his 1602 Survey of Cornwall, John Wesley wrote about it in the eighteenth century and Eden Phillpotts made it the subject of his novel Old Delabole (1915). The skills they all admired are still practised today and masons produce items such as church altars and fine flooring, memorial stones and plant holders. The name of the local inn has strong links with the quarry, being known as the Bettle and Chisel. After learning about the names of various slate tiles – Ladies, Countesses, Duchesses, Queens, Rags and Imperials – it is interesting to see them on the old cottages and walls for many miles round about.

cliffs and look for the maze: two rare labyrinth pattern carvings.

Bossiney village is now a quiet hamlet but in 1584 it was the centre of a 'rotten' borough whose MP was Sir Francis Drake. Long before that, Bossiney Court was mentioned in the Domesday Book. It stands on ground once owned by the first Duke of Cornwall, the Black Prince.

It is difficult to know where Bossiney ends and **Tintagel** begins because of recent buildings. Many suggest that Tintagel should be avoided as commercialism spoils the memory of King Arthur. Perhaps there are too many gift shops here but there is also much to enjoy. **King Arthur's Great Halls** tells the story of King Arthur and his

Round Table in a modern, electronic show while also on display are examples of the art of stained glass and the craft of the local stonemasons.

In the centre is the **Old Post Office**, one of the National Trust's most picturesque properties. This small fourteenth-century stone house with an ancient slate roof of fairy-tale curves was built on the plan of a medieval manor with a large hall. It is called the Old Post Office because it was the letter-receiving office for the district, opened by the GPO in 1844.

A dusty, easy slope (a Land Rover is also available in summer for those who prefer it) takes visitors to the foot of **Tintagel Head**, which is Duchy of Cornwall property. On this magnificent promontory are the well-preserved remains of a Celtic monastery as well as the ruins of one of the Black Prince's castles.

English Heritage has charge of another castle – on the land overlooking the narrow division between cliff and headland. This is the remains of a medieval stronghold built by Earl Reginald of Cornwall. On the other side of the valley is **Camelot Castle Hotel**, an outstanding place built to accommodate holidaymakers flocking here as a result of Alfred Tennyson's Arthurian poetry. Even in 1897, this building was thought to detract from the spirit of the area and the 14-acre (6 hectare) headland was eventually bought for the National Trust as a memorial to the Poet Laureate. Away from the village is the **Church of St Materiana**. It is a fine Norman building and should be visited when walking along Glebe Cliff, which has a viewpoint with wheelchair access.

After leaving Tintagel by the B3263, there is a lane to the left beyond Penpethy Farm which is worth exploring. For archaeologists, the lonely mound of **Condolden Barrow** is an intriguing monument, as some people believe Queen Iseult to be buried there.

Across the B3266 at **Slaughterbridge** is **Worthyvale Manor**, an ancient and beautiful place on an estate crowded with history. Worthyvale Manor was recorded in the Domesday Book of 1086, but was important even before that, when in 823, a decisive battle took place in Worthyvale fields. The Saxon leader Egbert was victorious and later became the first king of all England. The house is not open to the public.

Slaughterbridge is now the site of the **Arthurian Centre** for it was here that King Arthur is said to have led his Celtic forces into battle against Mordred, where the lane crosses the River Camel. Both were killed and a large stone inscribed in Latin still lies on the riverbank, giving the name Slaughterbridge an irrevocable link with the past, even though historians consider it to be merely legendary.

Glorious cliff walks

The cliff walks from Trethevy to Tintagel are nothing less than splendid, especially on a fine spring day when there is a profusion of wild flowers and a mass of seabirds. In June, puffins can be seen on Long Island but not, alas, without binoculars. **Rocky Valley**, the walk from these cliffs to **Trevalga**, is one of exceptional beauty. In fact a day spent here would not be wasted.

There are walks to the stone and to the battlefield and the Land of Arthur Exhibition is nearby.

Bude

Those who live in **Bude** do not consider their pleasant town to be at all remote or forgotten, but in the far north of Cornwall, it is an area with its own special character and quite different from any other part of the Duchy, a friendly, attractive place offering a warm-hearted welcome to visitors.

In the 1830s, Sir Goldsworthy Gurney built the toy-like **Castle** beside the beach. Today it houses a **heritage centre**, opened in 2007, with exhibits focusing on Bude and its maritime history as well as a gallery dedicated to the castle's builder and his many inventions. Gurney invented the Bude Light to illuminate the castle. He created a bright light by injecting a stream of oxygen into an oil flame and then reflected this single light throughout the castle by means of mirrors. He went on to improve the lighting in the House of Commons by means of three Bude Lights, a system used for 60 years until the coming of electricity.

To celebrate the millennium and Gurney's invention the **Bude Light** was erected in front of the castle. Using coloured concrete and fibre optic lighting the sculptors crafted a slender cone, some 29 ft (9m) high, set in a paved area and small amphitheatre. At night the cone lights up to show the patterns of the constellations in the sky above.

Bude could have become a canal port, but instead developed into a quality holiday resort, probably best known for some of Cornwall's finest

Museum of Witchcraft

Compass Tower in Bude

surfing beaches. Visitors fish the canal because it is regarded as one of the finest coarse-fishing waters in the west. A 2-mile (3km) stretch of quiet level walking along the towpath is not only pleasant but of special interest for lovers of wildlife. About half a mile (1km) along, a bird hide has been erected. A major regeneration project commenced in 2007 with the aim of fully restoring this section of the canal and, despite a setback in March 2008 when a storm damaged the gates of the sea lock, it is hoped that the work will be completed during 2009.

Ebbingford Manor, the town's oldest house, dating from the twelfth century, is off Vicarage Road, which runs

Boscastle harbour

beside the canal. This small but charming building was at one time home of the Arundells, who were related to Henry VIII and Lord Baltimore, the founder of Maryland, and is said to have the smallest chapel in England. It is not open to the public, but part of the house is available as a holiday let.

It is hard to believe that wrecks were a terrifying commonplace in the early days of the nineteenth century, for the pleasures of Bude, which include golf and tennis courts for visitors, are only for relaxation. There is safe saltwater swimming in the **Splash Leisure Pool**, while beyond the castle are sands and surf comparable to those of South Africa and Australia!

Marhamchurch lies south of Bude and across the A39 through high banked hedges and narrow, climbing lanes. It is an unusual rectangular village set on a ridge and seems to be keeping watch over the surrounding farmland. Its wide central road leads to the Norman church, low and square near the war memorial. The solid fifteenth-century oak door is usually open and is one of its interesting features, as is the encased sanctuary knocker. A former rector, Brother Peter, came from the Girondist House of the Holy Cross at Bordeaux and was the incumbent of Marhamchurch in 1458. His service here was so happy that after

his death his ghost returned to the old rectory, where he has apparently often been seen, even in recent times.

Village celebrations are the same here as at all other churches with Celtic origins – their feast day usually follows the church festival. The tradition at Marhamchurch is a rare one. On **Revel Day** – after 12 August – Father Neptune crowns a local schoolgirl, who then rides through the village on a white horse.

The narrow lanes to the south are undulating and delightful, with the high views showing the agricultural nature of the region. Take your time and enjoy a slow, relaxing drive south, through Week Orchard, Week St Mary, Treforda and into **Jacobstow.** Here the church, embraced by trees in a roadside dell, is easily missed and the unspoiled hamlet is charming because of its very solitude. Nearer the coast the wooded lanes are lost in high open fields again.

Wainhouse Corner is a junction on the A39 where the way leads to the fearful cliffs of **Crackington Haven** and for a considerable distance, north and south, the coastal footpath crosses

Camelot Castle Hotel, Tintagel

National Trust land. This tiny cove was a harbour for colliers in the eighteenth and nineteenth centuries and their captains must have been intrepid sailors to navigate here. **Cambeak** promontory on the southern arm of Crackington Haven stretches into the sea like a great lizard and gated paths lead to **Trevigue**, a sheltered farm. Cars may be left here for a further walk to **High Cliff**. This is Cornwall's highest coastal point and the views are typical of this northern area.

Northwards, on the cliff out of the Haven stands **St Gennys Church**. It is almost alone in its fold of green fern on the cliffside and ornamental cherry trees give it a fairy-tale look in spring. One of the treasures here is the altar tabernacle, a splendid piece of church furniture. Handsomely embroidered kneelers also add to the glory of this Celtic church where prayers have been said since St Gennys established his humble cell on these cliffs.

The road to **Millook** is narrow, steep and badly cambered in places but it can be negotiated with good brakes and the use of bottom gear. Once safely out of the valley, the wide road past the Common falls away to a startling panorama across Widemouth Bay and north to Morwenstow. The spectacular sands of **Widemouth Bay** stretch away almost endlessly. Once they were dreaded by sailors but now visitors can enjoy adventure holidays here and learn canoeing and windsurfing.

North of Bude

Cornwall has not revealed all its treasures yet – there is much to see between Bude and Morwenstow. Some say that this area is the best of all. The A3072

Poundstock Church

Dedicated to the dwarf hermit, St Neot, this building is beautifully sited in a dell away from the main road. Murals and exceptionally handsome bench ends are among the interesting features. Beside the churchyard the Gildhouse of stormy history is used for parochial church meetings.

It seems gentle enough now but it was not so in the fourteenth century. Then local villains were commissioned as Collectors of Subsidies and lawbreakers wielded more power than good citizens. Affairs reached a climax in 1357, however, when armed men swarmed into the church as a priest was celebrating Mass, killed him at the altar and desecrated the vestments and sacred vessels. It was not long before the killers were caught and punished and Poundstock returned to peace again. It still retains much of its medieval beauty. The Gildhouse served many purposes: poorhouse, school, and substitute church. The windows are original and worth studying.

road goes to **Stratton**, which, though it has fallen below Bude in status, was important in Roman times. Its character, however, is quite different.

Stratton is rightly proud of Anthony Payne, the Cornish giant who was born at The Tree Inn, and died there too. This huge man weighed 532lb (240kg). His portrait by Kneller is in the Royal Cornwall Museum in Truro. He devoted his life to the service of his master, Sir Bevil Grenville, whose

The Thomas Hardy Connection

In 1870, at the age of 30, the writer Thomas Hardy was sent to North Cornwall to draw up plans for the restoration of St Juliot's Church. At that time he was working as an architect, specialising in church architecture. The building was in a ruinous condition when he arrived to inspect it but following renovation work, which he organised, it was reopened two years later.

St Juliot's Church, an isolated building dedicated to St Julitta, still stands at the head of Valency valley. The brass and ruby oil lamps Hardy installed in the church during restoration are now to be seen in the Wellington Hotel, Boscastle. St Juliot Rectory remains, a reminder of when Hardy stayed there to continue the work on the church and court his Emma. Lovers of Hardy's works will know how the famous man returned again and again to court the rector's sister-in-law, Emma Gifford, and how she persuaded him to leave architecture for literature and later married him in 1874.

Although he is better known for incorporating the Dorset landscape into his works, these early visits to North Cornwall also had an influence. Beeny Cliff, Buckator, Penally and Pentargon are among the places he loved and incorporated in his second novel, *A Pair of Blue Eyes*. Beeny Cliff at Boscastle was loved by Hardy and Emma – she sketched it and he wrote from there. Hardy's poem *Moments of Vision* describes the cliff outline of Penally Point, the northern arm of the Boscastle harbour – resembling the neck, head and beak of a bird of prey. Many years later he wrote a poetic drama, *The Famous Tragedy of the Queen of Cornwall*, in which Condolden Barrow featured.

Today this area offers much to enjoy and the features that Hardy and Emma visited are still there. There is a nature walk, mostly alongside the little river, from the church of St Juliot down to the harbour, and the Valency Valley, some 5 miles (8km) long and partly owned by the National Trust, remains lovely and unspoilt.

troops defeated the Roundheads at the Battle of Stamford Hill in 1643. A plaque on the wall at Stamford Hill marks the site.

Away from the main road, but worth seeing, is **Poughill** (pronounced 'Puffle') **Church**, dedicated to St Olaf, a Dane. There are two large wall representations of St Christopher, repainted by Frank Salisbury, and a Tazza Cup and Paten, beautifully shaped and richly decorated. The clock in the tower has a memorial tablet which is rarely seen but worth mentioning. It says of Sir Goldsworthy Gurney: 'His inventions and discoveries in Steam and Electricity made communication by land and sea so rapid that it became necessary for all Britain to keep uniform clock time.'

Those following the coastal walk will have increasingly fine views, especially near **Stowe Barton** where the road dips into the Coombe valley. This handsome farm was built on the site of Sir Richard Grenville's home, unfortunately pulled down in 1739: today only the stables remain.

The bridge at **Coombe** carries a tablet – now very weathered – which commemorated King William IV's contribution to its building. In the early days of the nineteenth century, the ford here was a danger to the lives of men and animals so the Reverend R S Hawker of Morwenstow appealed to the king for financial help and eventually a bridge was built. **Duckpool** is a good place to swim and the National Trust cliff, **Steeple Point**, affords an ideal vantage point for walkers. The nearby Coombe Valley is also Trust land. The cottage at the entrance to this valley is of special interest, though people rarely notice the cross-shaped window above the door. Here Hawker spent his honeymoon and began writing *Trelawney*, the poem which is now considered to be Cornwall's anthem.

As the road climbs out of this valley, it continues north past the dish aerials of the Government's GCHQ Composite Signals Organisation Station – an imposing sight. Beyond is **Morwenstow**, which is almost the end of Cornwall but is full of history and known as Hawker country. For 40 years, till 1875, this famous parson-poet was vicar here. Wrongly styled an eccentric, he startled his fellow churchmen by righting many wrongs and frequently risking his life to rescue shipwrecked sailors and give Christian burial to the bodies of the drowned. In the churchyard is what might be a memorial to his brave dedication – the figurehead of the *Caledonia*, wrecked on the rocks below in 1842, leaving only one man alive. Petitioner for his parishioners' cause at a time of dire poverty, and restorer of the harvest festival, Robert Stephen Hawker's achievements will long be remembered. He wrote fine poetry in a hut on the cliff top, now owned by the National Trust, and his unique vicarage chimneys, modelled on church towers, can just be glimpsed in the woods below the church.

The Bush Inn, a few hundred yards away from the churchtown, is unusual in retaining the traditional sign, the sign of a bush, once given to all taverns to signify where drinks were sold. It is an old inn where the Morwenstow Union Friendly Society probably met in the late eighteenth century. It had a thatched roof until a fire in 1968, but now that has gone and some of its charm has disappeared as well.

The end of Cornwall is reached where Marsland Mouth lies below Marsland Cliff – the scene of many shipwrecks in days of sail – but the lane turns inland to **Woolley**, where there is not an end but a beginning. For among the marshes at Woolley Barrows, Cornwall's River Tamar, which marks the boundary with Devon, has its source. The A39 road south, which was the pilgrim highway to St Michael's Mount, goes to **Kilkhampton**. The church here is worth a visit because it has a splendid lychgate, good pew ends and numerous Grenville monuments.

From the B3254, the road leads to the **Tamar Lakes** with fly-fishing on the upper, coarse on the lower and walks, picnics and much else to enjoy in beautiful surroundings. The first of these reservoirs, Lower Lake, was created in 1820. From here the river flows south to join the sea at Saltash where this journey around Cornwall began.

Places to Visit

In & Around Launceston

Launceston Castle

(English Heritage)
Launceston, PL15 7DR
☎ (01566) 772365
www.english-heritage.org.uk
A fine ruin overlooking the town. It was the chief seat of Robert of Mortain, brother of William I. Views are impressive. Open: Daily 10am–5pm Apr to Sep (6pm in Jul and Aug, 4pm in Oct. Last entry 30 mins beofre closing.

ᵻᵻᵻ<16

Launceston Steam Railway & Museum

Below the castle, PL15 8DA
☎ (01566) 775665
www.launcestonsr.co.uk
Five miles (8km) round trip through the Kensey valley on the trackbed of the old North Cornwall Railway, Victorian locomotives pull coaches which allow passengers to enjoy the scenery. Museum of Vintage Transport. Open: From 10.30am. Late May bank holiday and Jun, Sun to Wed. Jul, Aug and Sep Sun–Fri. Also Easter holiday, and Oct half-term Sun–Fri.

Lawrence House Museum

(National Trust)
Castle Street, PL15 8BA
☎ (01566) 773277
A Georgian town house given to the National Trust in 1964 to preserve the character of the street. The moulded plaster of the ceilings is exceptional. It is let to the local Town Council as a museum. Collection of childrens' toys, exhibition on WWI &II. Open: 10.30am–4.30pm Mon to Fri from Apr to end–Oct. Other times by appointment. Free admission.

Ⓟ(Nearby) ♿ (GF only) ᵻᵻᵻ ☔

Warbstow Bury

3 miles (4.8km) N of A395 Launceston-Camelford road (SX 201909)
An impressive prehistoric defensive earthwork: fortress, double-walled and two gateways protecting barrows. King Arthur is said to be buried there.

Trethorne Leisure Park

Kennard's House, A395, PL15 8QE
☎ (01566) 86324
www.trethorneleisure.com
Ideal for young children, with animals to see and ponies to ride. Four lane ten-pin bowling alley. Open: 10am–5pm (6pm in summer) daily all year (bowling/Restaurant). Leisure Park daily Feb–Nov, weekends Dec–Jan.

Ⓟ ♿ ᵻᵻᵻ<15 ☔

Sterts Theatre

Upton Cross, Liskeard, PL14 5A2
☎ (01579) 362382
www.sterts.co.uk
Covered open-air theatre, studio and gallery. Open: Easter–Sept; theatre performances in summer only.

Ⓟ ♿ ᵻᵻᵻ<16

Tamar Otter and Wildlife Centre

North Petherwin, PL15 8GW
☎ (01566) 785646
www.tamarotters.co.uk
Enjoy a sight of British and Asian otters, golden pheasants, wallabies and water deer roaming free. Tearoom and shop. Open: 10.30am–6pm 1 Apr (Good Friday if earlier) to 31 Oct daily. Full charge to over 3s.

Ⓟ ♿ ᵻᵻᵻ<16

Places to Visit

Around Camelford

British Cycling Museum

The Old Station, Camelford, PL32 9TZ
☎ (01840) 212811
From 1881 to present-day machines on display. Open: 10am–5pm Sun to Thu all year.

Ⓟ ♿ 🛉🛉 <18 ☂

North Cornwall Museum and Art Gallery

The Clease, Camelford, PL32 9PL
☎ (01840) 212954
Open: 10am–5pm Mon to Sat Apr to Sep. Of little interest to under 7s. Not suitable for wheelchair access.

Ⓟ (Opposite) 🛉🛉 ☂

Delabole Slate Quarry

Follow AA signs from Camelford, PL33 PAZ
☎ (01840) 212242
www.delaboleslate.co.uk
Open: Tours Mon to Fri at 2pm, May through to Sep, except bank holidays. All other times by appointment. Of little interest to under 7s.

Ⓟ ♿ (Limited) 🛉🛉 <18

In & around Boscastle & Tintagel

The Arthurian Centre

B3314, Slaughterbridge, PL32 PTT
☎ (01840) 213947 or 212450
www.arthur-online.com
Land of Arthur Exhibition on the site of Arthur's last battle. Walks, play area, shop and refreshments. Open: 10am–5pm Easter to late Oct.

Ⓟ ♿ 🛉🛉

National Trust shop and information centre

The Old Forge, Boscastle,
☎ (01840) 250353
Open: 10.30am–5pm mid-Mar to Oct.

Museum of Witchcraft

Boscastle , PL35 OHD
☎ (01840) 250111
www.museumofwitchcraft.com
World's largest collection of witchcraft-related artefacts and regalia Open: 10.30am–6pm Mon–Sat, 11.30am–6pm Sun, from Easter to Halloween.

Ⓟ (Nearby) ♿ (Limited) 🛉🛉 <16 ☂ 🐕

Tintagel Old Post Office

(National Trust)
Fore Street, Tintagel, PL34 0DB
☎ (01840) 770024
A small fourteenth-century stone house built as a medieval manor, with a charming garden. Open: 11am–5.30pm Apr to Oct daily.

Ⓟ ♿ (Ground Floor Only) 🛉🛉

Tintagel Castle

(English Heritage)
PL35 OHD
☎ (01840) 770328
www.english-heritage.org.uk/tintagel
Cliffside remains of a medieval castle built on prominent site in mid-twelfth century by Reginald, Earl of Cornwall. Open: 10am–6pm daily Apr to Oct, (5pm in Oct) 4pm Nov to Mar.

Ⓟ (In Village) 🛉🛉 <16 🐕

King Arthur's Great Halls

Fore Street, Tintagel
☎ (01840) 770526
www.kingarthursgreathalls.com
Tells the story of King Arthur and also

displays local craftsmanship. Shop.
Open: Daily, all year.

†i† (Family Ticket)

Bude

The Castle Heritage Centre and Gallery

The Castle, Bude, EX23 8LG
☎ (01288) 357300
Opened in 2007 in Sir Goldsworthy Gurney's castle, the centre houses an exhibition of Gurney's inventions, as well as focusing on the maritime history of Bude. There is also a shop and restaurant. Open: daily, 10am–6pm Easter to end Oct; 10am–4pm Nov to Easter. Off little interest to under 7s.

Ⓟ (Nearby) ♿ †i†<16

Splash Leisure Pool

Stucley Road
☎ (01288) 356191
33m leisure pool with wave machine, plus health spa facilities. Open every day. Please call for opening times.

†i†

Bude Canal

A remarkable piece of engineering in being the longest tub boat canal in Britain – and with inclined planes – but it was a project devised before engineers had power and the materials to make it successful. Today, Sir Thomas Acland's brilliant scheme is a place of recreation for visitors, especially anglers and walkers.

The Bude Light

Bude Castle
Spectacular sight at night especially when the sky is clear.

North Of Bude

Hawker's Hut

(National Trust)
Vicarage Cliff, Morwenstow
Perched on the edge of the cliff overlooking the fearful rocks where so many ships foundered and whose men he saved, Parson Hawker built his shelter. Access by footpath from churchyard gate.

Tamar Lakes

Off A39 near Kilkhampton
☎ (01288) 321712
80 acres (32 hectares) for watersports and trout fishing. Hire of dinghies, canoes, kayaks and wetsuits.

What to do if it rains

Launceston
Lawrence House Museum
Steam Railway and museum
St Mary Magdalene Church

Camelford
North Cornwall Museum and Art Gallery
British Cycling Museum

Boscastle
Visitor Centre by the harbour
Witchcraft Museum

Tintagel
Old Post Office
King Arthur's Great Halls

Slaughterbridge
The Arthurian Centre

Bude
Splash Leisure Pool
Heritage Centre and Gallery

Morwenstow
Church

Opposite page: A white boat floating on a clear sea, Isles of Scilly

Left: New Grimsby, Tresco

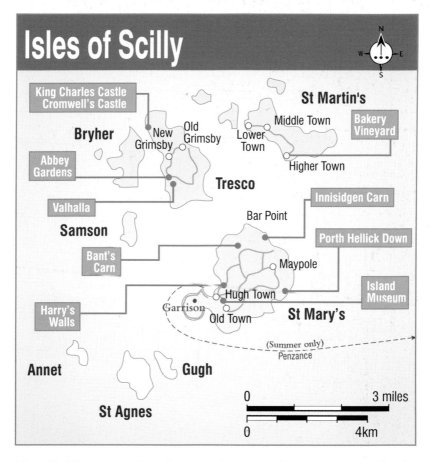

Isles of Scilly

King Charles Castle
Cromwell's Castle

Bryher

New Grimsby
Old Grimsby

St Martin's

Middle Town

Bakery
Vineyard

Lower Town

Abbey Gardens

Higher Town

Tresco

Valhalla

Innisidgen Carn

Samson

Bar Point

Porth Hellick Down

Bant's Carn

Maypole

Island Museum

Harry's Walls

Hugh Town

Garrison

Old Town

St Mary's

(Summer only)
Penzance

Annet

Gugh

St Agnes

0 ——— 3 miles

0 ——— 4km

The Scillies consist of more than 300 islands but only six are inhabited. These are St Mary's, Tresco, St Martin's, St Agnes, Bryher and Gugh and they have a total area of only 4,400 acres (1,780 hectares). St Agnes, though almost the smallest, has the special distinction of being the most southerly inhabited point in Great Britain. Situated about 26 miles (42km) west of Land's End, this interesting geographical grouping is unique in its relationship to the mainland.

Though associated with Cornwall, the people are not part of it, as any true Scillonian will stoutly maintain. Nor do they belong to the rest of England, in spite of the imposition of taxes that would make it appear so.

Getting there

There are three ways of getting to the islands :

Helicopter

British International offer a year-round scheduled service from Penzance to either St Mary's or Tresco. Flights are approximately 20 minutes.

Fixed-wing aircraft

The island's own airline, the 'Skybus' offers year-round scheduled services from Land's End and Newquay (and seasonal flights from Exeter, Bristol and Southampton) to St Mary's with connections at Newquay to/from London.

Ship

The *Scillonian III* passenger ferry provides daily sailings (except Sundays) from Penzance to St Mary's. The crossing takes around 3 hours and can be rough (No service in winter months).

'Isles of tranquillity'

The first sight of the islands seems to contradict the various names given to them over the centuries – Isles of the Blest, Paradise Islands and the Lotus Isles. The immediate impression is of rocky outcrops with scarcely any vegetation in sight, but soon the unusual peace and quiet, which is part of Scilly's charm, takes over and the almost complete absence of vehicles

makes itself felt. As a result, it is easy to relax and enjoy the startling blue of the sea, silver sands on empty beaches with birds and flowers that are so different, not to mention the stone 'library' of prehistory which consists of more than 150 Bronze Age relics. The fact that all the inhabited islands have maintained their reputation as a lifeline to tranquillity is largely the result of extremely careful administration by their owners, the Duchy of Cornwall and their tenants, the Island Council, who have prevented any development that might spoil the unique beauty of the Scillies.

When to go

Unlike anywhere else in the British Isles, Scilly, with its exceptionally soft climate, is the ideal place for open-air holidaymakers to visit in late February or early March. This is the time when the flower harvest is at its height and the fields of floral 'sunshine' rival even the brilliance of the sun. The atmosphere is different from that of the summer season and visitors enjoy being part of the concentration on flower exporting which pervades the islands in early spring. The flower show, which takes place in March, is, of course, connected with the seasonal business but it is no ordinary one and claims to be the oldest in the country, because Scillonian growers were among the first to promote the growing of flowers as an industry.

The flower-growing industry began here in a somewhat strange manner when one William Trevillick, who farmed on Rocky Hill, St Mary's, packed a few blooms in his Aunt Ellen's

Walks on St Mary

Porth Hellick

3 miles (5km) approx • easy • 1½ hours
Map: OS 1:25,000 Explorer Series 101: Isles of Scilly
Take the road past the lifeboat slip, then turn to the right past Parting Carn. By turning right again at the second turning arrive at Salakee and on to Porth Hellick beach. Follow the coastal footpath from here, past a deep point curving to Pelistry Bay. Here you return to Hugh Town by way of Holy Vale.

The Telegraph Walk

5 miles (8km) • easy • 2 hours
Map: OS 1:25,000 Explorer Series 101: Isles of Scilly
Start again on the road past the lifeboat slip, then join the footpath along the shore by Porthmellon. This skirts the uncompleted sixteenth-century fortifications known as Harry's Walls, soon joining the Porthloo road up to the golf course beyond which is Telegraph Tower, the island's highest point. North of this tower a lane leads near Bant's Carn Burial Chamber (about 1800BC) and the excavations of a village (about 200BC–AD300) on Halangy Down. Follow north-eastwards to Bar Point and on to two Bronze Age burial chambers at Innisidgen. Continue to Watermill Cove and Pelistry so that you can make your way back to Hugh Town via Holy Vale.

The Peninnis Walk

2 miles (3.5km) approx • easy • 1½ hours
Map: OS 1:25,000 Explorer Series 101: Isles of Scilly
Follow the road up the hill from the Church of St Mary the Virgin and turn sharp right just before reaching the top. A fork to the right 50 yards (46m) along this road leads to the hospital and beyond it, Buzza Tower, an old windmill adapted to commemorate King Edward VII's visit in 1902. The left fork is King Edward's Road which leads to Peninnis with its lighthouse, a gate and a Cornish stile giving access to the headland. Here rock formations such as Pulpit Rock, Tuskless Elephant and the Walrus are subjects for artists and photographers: all will follow the coastal path to Porthcressa and back to Hugh Town.

hatbox and, as an experiment, sent them to Covent Garden. The date of that inspired idea is thought to be as early as 1867, but it makes little difference. What is important is that it came at a time when the islanders were desperate for a new source of income.

Old industries had gone – kelp-making, which ended with the intro-duction of synthetic iodine in 1835, was superseded by boat-building. But this, in its turn, ended in about 1870 when sail gave way to steam; so the flower industry which resulted from Trevillick's brainchild was greeted with considerable enthusiasm.

It was further encouraged by Augustus Smith of Herefordshire who leased the islands between 1835 and 1872 and became, in fact, a self-appointed Lord of the Isles and benevolent landlord, using all his resources for the good of the community. Not only did he help the incipient flower industry, but he also fostered the potato trade and brought Guernsey cattle over to improve the quality of the milk. He is also acknowledged to be the one who pioneered compulsory education here long before it appeared on the mainland – altogether a remarkable man whose enthusiasm and foresight undoubtedly saved the Isles of Scilly from the fate suffered by some Scottish islands where inhabitants were forced to leave their homes for lack of employment. But the flower-growing industry, too, is unfortunately in decline, although many of the fields are still golden in the spring. Today's industry is tourism.

Boat trip to Bishop Rock Lighthouse

St Mary's

St Mary's is the main island. **Hugh Town** – that rather grand name for such a small 'capital' – is built on the isthmus which separates the Garrison area from the main part. It is here that many visitors stay after their arrival at the air terminal near Old Town or at the harbour of Hugh Town. In this small capital there are numerous shops, two banks, the main post office and three churches, each of a different denomination. The Town Hall serves a dual purpose as it shares its officialdom with performances of concerts and plays during the season. **The Isles of Scilly Museum** has a variety of interesting displays which cover the archaeology, wildlife and history of Scilly. Its central feature is a fully-rigged pilot gig (a Scillonian speciality) and there are also an appropriate number of wreck relics.

The fast, slim gigs also had other uses. The *Klondike*, for example, which is now in the museum at St Mary's, usually went out on coastguard duty and was the vessel involved in the changeover of crewmen on the Bishop Rock Lighthouse. Another one, however, had a much more romantic task – to transport wedding parties – and this pleasant work carried on till 1929 when the last bride to travel to her wedding by gig went to Tresco from her home on Bryher.

There are numerous dramatic accounts, too, of gig crews, employed in work on salvage operations, who returned with unusual cargoes. On one particular occasion, goods listed after a wreck were stated as 'lard, frozen geese, turkeys and two hundred fat bullocks'.

The origin of gig-racing

Naturally there is a considerable amount of boating and fishing here, and from St Mary's Quay, the popular sport of gig-racing can be watched and enjoyed every week during the summer. The history of these unique craft apparently began in 1790 when 'a gentleman in holy orders' placed an order for one to be built at the Peters boatyard of St Mawes. He specified a six-oared boat that could be used for saving life on the treacherous north coast of Cornwall. Tradition has it that this vessel was the first Padstow lifeboat and members of the old shipbuilding fraternity there say that a six-oared gig would certainly fill the role.

St Mary's harbour

Not the romantic kind of underwater treasure that most people envisage in these circumstances but nevertheless there must have been a profit for someone. With their capacity for greater speed than most vessels, it is only to be expected that when smuggling was part of life, these gigs should have been used for illegal purposes. And this was

The Bant's Carn burial chamber, St Mary's

indeed the case, for records show that trips involving contraband goods were made regularly from Scilly to the port of Roscoff in Brittany.

But this specially designed island craft also suited local pilots who were more interested in legitimate business and they would race their boats out into the Channel, each hoping to gain the fee by being the first to reach any sailing ship needing guidance through the dangerous coastal waters. And from that, the idea of racing for fun evolved, especially when the prize was more golden guineas than the crew could earn in a week as pilots. Sometimes the men would row many miles, even after work, to take part in one of the many regattas which were held all round the Cornish coast in the nineteenth century. These lapsed after World War I, however, and no more gigs were built. It was not till the 1950s that gigs were seen again: a Newquay man decided to encourage the revival of building these special vessels and eventually there were four gigs from Scilly fully restored. In the early 1960s, races began on the islands and are now a familiar part of the summer scene. It is good to know, too, that the knowledge of gig-building has not disappeared and that the skills are being passed on at Cornwall College in Falmouth.

Inter-island trips

St Mary's Quay is also the point of departure for inter-island boat trips. These are particularly delightful in the spring when the seabird sanctuaries can be seen at close quarters (the Island of Annet is closed to all visitors from mid-April to late August so that nesting birds may be protected). Atlantic grey seals can also be seen easily from these inter-island launches. It is easy to understand why some visitors consider these particular boat trips to be the highlight of their holiday on Scilly.

Beaches

Perhaps one of the greatest attractions of the Isles of Scilly is the seclusion of its sandy beaches. They are all safe for bathing and even in high summer remain uncrowded. There are, however, two danger spots. The sand bars connecting St Mary's with Toll's Island and St Agnes with Gugh are unsafe when the water flows over the two bars, but that is only at high tide. The clear waters attract skin-divers particularly, on account of the marine life and the numerous wrecks. The authorities, who know the swell conditions and tidal streams, recommend divers to operate in groups under supervision, particularly as the nearest decompression chamber is at Plymouth, some 120 miles (190km) away.

Garrison walls & gate

If the weather is right, visitors usually take a short circular walk around the Garrison walls on their first evening as the fine sunsets over Samson are not to be missed. This is when they begin to appreciate the wisdom of the local council ruling: 'Caravans, motorised caravans and similar vehicles may not be brought to the islands. Private cars are most unwelcome and are quite unnecessary for the enjoyment of a holiday in the islands' (there are approximately 9 miles (15km) of road on St Mary's). Taxis and bus services cater for all necessary transport.

Garrison Gate was not built till 1742 although **Star Castle** (a hotel since 1933) was constructed in 1593 at the top of the hill as a defence against possible Spanish attack. The population then moved from Old Town to greater safety near the castle.

There is a coast path here as elsewhere on the island, but another leads straight down to **Woolpack Point** where two rusty old cannons still point seawards as if awaiting the enemy. From here, if the weather is good, there is a fine view across St Mary's Sound to the islands of St Agnes and Gugh, but it is a place to be avoided during a north-westerly gale.

Exploring the rest of St Mary's

Returning to Hugh Town, the road passes the Duchy of Cornwall's Land Steward's impressive granite offices. They overlook Porthcressa, St Mary's central and most popular beach.

The exploration of the main part of the island begins at **Peninnis Head**. The shorter way leads to the church, begun by King William IV and finished in 1837 by Augustus Smith. Past the vicarage is the island power station, skilfully built in an old quarry, and at the top of the hill is **Buzza Tower**. This was constructed in 1821 as an old Spanish-style windmill to grind corn; after which it was converted into a tower to commemorate King Edward VII's visit in 1902. It now has an even more useful role as a landmark for shipping. A bumpy track along a granite-walled lane leads eventually to **Peninnis Head**, a magnificent, rugged promontory at this southern extremity of St Mary's. Here, even the granite has been smoothed and weathered by storms; the resulting shapes deserving names such as the Tuskless Elephant, the Toastrack and the Kettle and Pans (where shrimps are plentiful).

Old Town

The path to Old Town and its bay passes the medieval church, now only fragmentary remains of a once large cruciform building. The churchyard is full of memorials to Scillonians and other seamen wrecked off this coast. Some of the men were from Sir Cloudesley Shovel's ill-fated fleet, notably Henry Trelawny, son of the famous bishop from Pelynt, near Looe, captain of one of the ships. Here, too, the victims of the HMS *Schiller* disaster (1875) are buried. A memorial for those who died in both World Wars and a monument to Augustus Smith are also to be found in the cemetery.

From Hugh Town the road goes past the lifeboat slips and turns right at Parting Carn for **Porth Hellick**. The coast path also reaches this point. Here is the quartz monument to Sir Cloudesley Shovel whose flagship *Association* was wrecked in 1707; the most valuable underwater treasure ever located round the British Isles, which belonged to it, was discovered in 1967. Since then the *Romney*, *Eagle* and *Firebrand* have been found, the last-named as recently as 1981. The admiral's personal plate alone would be worth a small fortune today, but the hazardous diving conditions have clearly hindered recovery operations, although divers still persevere.

On these downs is a group of five chambered tombs, all very close together. Most of these 4,000-year-old passage graves are crumbling; the best preserved is maintained by English Heritage.

Augustus Smith

In the 1830s, a wealthy merchant banker from Hertforshire was granted the lease of the Isles from the Duchy of Cornwall. In 1834 he made Tresco his home and built a huge Victorian house, 'Tresco Abbey', alongside the ruins of an old Benedictine Abbey dating back to the twelfth century. In time, the isles were ceded back to the Duchy, with the exception of Tresco which remains in the ownership of the family today. This extraordinary man with the very ordinary name was a far-sighted visionary who gave the islands new life and prosperity simply by rooting out the cause of their deterioration – an ancient system of land tenure.

These old ways had resulted in serious unemployment caused by a surplus population so he put the men to work building roads and the wall boundaries which were the beginning of the famous Tresco Abbey Botanical Gardens. Smith created them on the site of the old priory and in the mild climate and natural shelter of Tresco, made the island blossom with subtropical plants.

Isles of Scilly at sunset

Pelistry Bay

The coastal path carries on to **Pelistry Bay** where the sand is especially beautiful (felspar and quartz) and the sea views hard to beat. This is where swimmers need to avoid bathing when the sea

covers the bar. Inland is **Holy Vale**, believed to have been the site of either a convent or a monastic cell and the path continues to picturesque **Watermill Bay**, past coastal indentations, before returning to Hugh Town.

Porth Harry

Telegraph Walk, in Hugh Town, as it is called, starts at the lifeboat slips and leads to Porthmellon. Here are the uncompleted sixteenth-century fortifications – **Harry's Walls**. Visitors can enjoy the facilities of the golf course beyond Porthloo Beach, but coastguards at Telegraph Tower are always on watch and also send meteorological readings to the London Air Ministry for weather forecasting. On the rough cliff slopes near **Bant's Carn** is another English Heritage property. This encompasses a prehistoric burial chamber and village

A stone maze, Bryher

Cows and calves, St Agnes

of the Roman period.

Bar Point

At the pine-fringed northern tip of St Mary's lies **Bar Point** where there is some of the best bathing. Here are two more English Heritage monuments, the Innisidgen prehistoric burial chambers.

Before leaving St Mary's, Scilly's main island, there is an interesting point to consider about the western lighthouses. Eight of them can be seen from here on a clear night. Bishop Rock, Peninnis Head, Sevenstones and Round Island are in the locality. Further away are Wolf Rock and Longships off Land's End, while on Cornwall's mainland, Pendeen and the Lizard are also visible.

Tresco

The 750 acres of Tresco might well be considered a complete nature reserve, the population living mainly in a line of hamlets across the central neck of the island. It differs from the other islands as it is leased privately from the Duchy by Robert Dorrien-Smith who owns and runs the island as a business: the 'Tresco estate'.

There are no cars, caravans or motorcycles (with the exception of estate vehicles and golf buggies for those with limited mobility), nor is camping allowed. The beauty of this place, and probably the conservation of the entire group, is due to the vision of Augustus Smith.

Tresco today has a thriving community of approximately 150 permanent residents, some families going back generations, but the island is also run as a business providing holidaymakers with luxurious accommodation at the Island Hotel, at the more informal and cosy New Inn pub or on a self-catering basis in one of the many timeshare and rental

Tresco

holiday cottages. A recent re-development of an area south of New Grimsby has resulted in 'The Flying Boat Club', offering 12 beachfront holiday cottages and a members' clubhouse with restaurant, indoor swimming pool and leisure facilities.

Although many holidaymakers choose to travel to Tresco in style via helicopter direct from Penzance, those arriving from St. Marys via the Skybus or *Scillonian* ferry, along with day-trippers from other islands, usually arrive at New Grimsby quay or, depending on the tides, at the other quays at Old Grimsby to the north-east or Carn Near to the south.

South from Timothy's Corner on the west coast, the road leads past the hub of the Island - Tresco Stores, the Post Office, the estate office, and the 'Bike Shed' for rental bikes, and on past old farm buildings (now converted to holiday cottages) and skirts the silver sands of Appletree Bay. At low water it is possible to walk across the flats to Samson and Bryher though speed (and directions!) are essential to avoid being cut off – this can be a dangerous activity if not done properly! Here, above the road, stands a granite monument to Augustus Smith and his successors. He designed it, intending it to stand beside his grave at St Buryan in West Penwith, but there was insufficient space so it remains here.

Inland lies the **Great Pool** which, with the smaller **Abbey Pool**, occupies about 46 acres (19 hectares). A great concentration of birdlife on these waters attracts bird lovers, who come especially to see the rare migrants that breed here. About fifty species nest in the island

and probably more are seen here than anywhere else in Europe.

Tresco is an island of two halves, the more sheltered south surrounded by almost deserted beaches of fine white shell sand accessed via numerous footpaths. Rough roads lead up past Borough Farm on the east coast to **The Old Blockhouse**, an old artillery battery built in the sixteenthth century and on to Old Grimsby where the road heads back towards New Grimsby, passing the church of St Nicholas and the island school.

The northern part of Tresco has cliff walks on heather, ling and short springy grass which lead to **Cromwell's Castle.** This substantially built round tower with its 12-foot (3.6m) thick walls was erected in 1651 as a defence against the Dutch. Sited on the hill above, there are the remains of **King Charles' Castle** built in the mid-1550s – a long, low oblong fort but so badly sited that the guns could not operate. Castle Downs has early tin-workings, and on the headland at Piper's Hole there is evidence of three more. Intrepid and agile visitors may scramble down this gully at low tide and find a large freshwater lake. Candlelight turns this unexpected discovery into a miniature fairyland, but it is only for experienced climbers!

Tresco Gardens

The world-famous **Abbey Gardens** are unique. Originally built by Augustus Smith amongst the ruins of the old Benedictine Abbey, they have been extended by family members ever since. They are a vast collection of exotic plants from all over the globe, that thrive in the mild, virtually frost-free climate of the Isles of Scilly; plants that would not normally grow even on the Cornish mainland just 30 miles away!

The gardens have been carved into three south-facing terraces and encompass more than 20,000 species from 80 countries and from every climatic region in the world – many brought by Scillonian seamen returning home from their voyages.

A visit to the Abbey Gardens must also include the **Valhalla museum** – a strange and eerie place displaying a collection of figureheads and other relics washed ashore from over seventy ships wrecked in the area.

The Gardens are open daily and refreshments are available at the garden Visitor Centre, gift shop and café.

The other Isles

The other 'off islands' are even more peaceful and sparsely populated, so much so that some have called them 'The Lotus Isles', and it is well worth taking one of the inter-island launches to explore their varied attractions. Accommodation on the other islands is more limited than on St Mary's, although there are excellent hotels on several of them, as well as self-catering and camping.

Bryher

Bryher (meaning 'Place of Hills' in Celtic) is the smallest of all the inhabited islands, and walking the entire coastline takes only a couple of hours. It has some of the best panoramic views and dramatic scenery of all the islands. From the quay, the lane heads up a hill past All Saints' Church which leads to **Hell Bay**, a wild and battered place on a stormy day due to its position on the Atlantic coast, and the luxurious Hell Bay Hotel. The **Great Pool** which is a popular place for birdwatchers, is here and to the south is the small and beautiful **Rushy Bay**. A pretty lane winds north past The Vine Café and on towards the Island pub and restaurant, Fraggle Rock, shop and Post Office. A campsite is situated up on the hill not far from **Watch Hill** which offers breathtaking views.

St Martin's

The island of St Martin's is renowned for its long, white sandy beaches which provide excellent and safe bathing. Most visitors will arrive by launch to the southernmost quay at Higher Town, where a shop, Post Office and tea-rooms can be found at the top of the hill. Also situated near here are the popular award-winning Bakery and the ecologically run **Little Arthur Café** and farm which are both well worth a visit, as is the **St Martin's Vineyard**. Tracks and footpaths provide excellent walking around the coastline where one can not only take in the breathtaking views but also stumble across prehistoric burial sites. One of the most distinctive features of St Martin's is the prominent red and white daymark at the north-eastern point of the island. A stroll along the pretty central lane passes Middle Town and the island campsite and onto Lower Town where visitors will find Lower Town quay, the Seven Stones Inn and a luxurious hotel.

St Agnes and Gugh

This beautiful, tranquil island is just one mile (1.5km) in diameter and the most westerly of all the islands. It has a community of around 70, many of whom are involved in the flower-growing industry as well as providing tourist accommodation in the form of guest houses, self-catering cottages and a campsite. This is the only island that does not have a hotel but it does have a public house, The Turk's Head, which is proud to be the most south-westerly pub in Britain. The small island of Gugh with its prehistoric standing stone is linked to St Agnes by way of a sand bar which can be crossed at low tide but care must be taken not to get stranded. Visitors to St Agnes will be dropped by launch to the Old Quay at the bottom of a hill which, to carry on up the winding road will lead to Higher and Middle Town and its café and craft shop and the well-stocked Post Office Stores. The old disused lighthouse with its distinctive white tower dating back to the seventh century is also situated near here. The tracks then lead to Lower Town and the **Big Pool**, a popular place with birdwatchers and onto **Troy Town Farm** where the campsite has magnificent views over to the western rocks, the Bishop Rock Lighthouse and the bird sanctuary island of Annet.

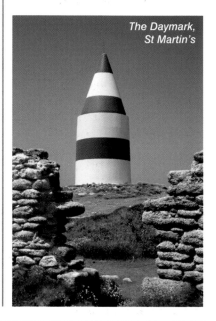

The Daymark, St Martin's

What to do if it rains

What to do if it rains – wear a waterproof!? It doesn't rain in the Isles of Scilly… Plenty of galleries and workshops. St Mary's Museum, churches. Local restaurants, cafés and pubs.

Cycling

Bike hire on St. Mary's and Tresco

St Mary's

Hire a bike, Porthcressa, ☎ 01720 422289

Tresco

Bookable through the estate office
The islands are small enough to easily explore by bike with peaceful lanes, off-road tracks and very limited traffic.

Places to Visit

St Mary's

The Garrison & Star Castle Hotel

TR21 OJA

☎ (01720) 422317 or 423342

www.star-castle.co.uk

Garrison Gate was built in 1742 as part of the garrison wall extending round the promontory. Today there are batteries, a park and promenade. Star Castle was a fortress erected by Elizabeth I and has walls projecting at eight salient angles. The inner building had two upper storeys and a bellcote.18ft-thick ramparts and a dry moat surround it. Since 1933 it has been a hotel.

Island Sea Safaris

'Nowhere', Old Town, TR21 ONH

☎ (01720) 422732

www.islandseasafaris.co.uk

Diving and snorkelling safaris. Novice dives. Wreck and reef diving for qualified divers. Assortment of organised underwater explorations for the totally inexperienced diver.

 <12

Isles of Scilly Museum

Church Street, Hugh Town, TR21 OJT

☎ (01720) 422337

www.iosmuseum.org

Built in 1967, it displays all facets of past and present life on the islands.Open: Mon–Sat 10am–4.30pm Easter to Sep. 10am–12pm Oct–Easter.

 <16

Isles of Scilly Pottery

The Garrison, TR21 OLS

☎ (01720) 422741

Open: 9am–12noon Mon to Fri.

Phoenix Stained Glass Studio

Porthmellon, TR21 OJY

☎ (01720) 422900

www.phoenixstainedglass.co.uk

See stained glass artefacts being made or join an afternoon workshop. Open: 10am–12.30pm and 1.30–4.30pm, Mon–Fri, 10am–12.30pm on Sat.

Harry's Walls

(English Heritage)

1/4 mile north-east of Hugh Town

Begun about 50 years before Star Castle. Originally square with four bastions.

Bant's Carn

(English Heritage)

1 mile north of Hugh Town

This burial chamber was probably built about 2000BC. It remained in use for 500 years.

Innisidgen Burial Chambers

(English Heritage)

1 ¾ miles east of Hugh Town

There are two monuments, upper and lower. The former is a mound about 26ft (8m) in diameter.

Cont'd overleaf

Places to Visit

Tresco

Abbey Pool

A 12-acre (5 hectare) area populated with geese and ducks. Popular with bird lovers.

Great Pool

A similar place to the above.

Tresco Abbey Gardens

☎ (01720) 424108
www.tresco.co.uk
Subtropical shrubs, palms and vegetation. Open: 10am–4pm all year. Shop and café open mid-Feb to early Nov.
👪 <17 Free

Valhalla

A museum for the preservation of carved, wooden figureheads and other carvings from over seventy ships wrecked in Scilly. It is housed in a building especially constructed by Augustus Smith about 1860, within the Abbey Gardens.

Cromwell's Castle

(English Heritage)
Palace Lane, Tresco TR24 0QL
On the shoreline, approach with care, ¾ mile (1km) north-west of New Grimsby Built in 1651 by Admiral Blake of the Republican forces, a 60-foot (18m) circular tower and granite platform commands the channel between Bryher and Tresco. Well preserved and finely situated. Entrance high up and reached by ladders. On the roof are six gun ports. Free access.

King Charles' Castle

(English Heritage)
Located ¾ mile (1km) north-west of New Grimsby. Coastal location, approach with care. This earthwork is of similar design to others in the period. A pentagonal fort was added in the Civil War. Free access.

The Old Blockhouse

(English Heritage)
This was built at the end of the sixteenth century as an artillery battery. It is above Old Grimsby.

St Martin's

St Martin's Vineyard

St Martin's, TR25 0QL.
☎ 01720 423418
Open throughout the summer months, this vineyard has been producing wine since 1996, when it was just a holiday hobby for the owners. Now they produce and bottle their own wine on the island and offer a tour of the vineyard where the opportunity to taste the wine is available.

St Martin's Bakery and Bakery Courses

Highertown, St Martins
www.cookingholidays.co.uk
Winner of the 'Best UK Food Retailer 2002'. Wide variety of stunning food made by hand on the premises, using mainly locally sourced organic ingredients.

Little Arthur Café and Farm

Higher Town, St Martin's, TR25 0QL
☎ 01720 422457
www.littlearthur.co.uk
A family owned and run eight-acre (3 hectare) site based on ecological and self-sufficiency principles. Serves food produced from local, organic produce where available and home-grown ingredients.

Getting There

By Air

There are several flights a day from London Stansted and London Gatwick to Newquay and others from regional airports around the UK, Europe and Ireland.

Newquay Airport: ☎ (01637) 860600 www.newquaycornwallairport.com

Flights are available from a number of UK airports to Plymouth.

Plymouth City Airport: ☎ (01752) 204090 www.plymouthairport.com

Car hire is available at the airports.

By Road

The M4, M5 and M6 motorways have made travel to Cornwall simple and straightforward, while within Cornwall itself, the two major holiday routes, the A30 and A38 continue to improve, with fast dual carriageways to beyond Bodmin and most of the way to Penzance. If you enter Cornwall via North Devon, then there is the Atlantic Highway, the A39, which you can join via the A361 from junction 27 on the M5.

By Coach

National Express offers direct services from London, the South-East, the North-East, the Midlands and from Yorkshire. The service from London Victoria and Heathrow Airport runs up to five times a day. For tickets and credit card bookings ☎ (08705) 808080 www.nationalexpress.com

By Rail

There are regular intercity services from London (Paddington), the Midlands, Northern England and Scotland, stopping at Plymouth, Bodmin, Liskeard, Truro and Penzance. The Night Riviera Sleeper service also runs between London Paddington and Penzance, calling at all mainline stations in Cornwall, every night except Saturday. For bus links to other places in Cornwall ☎ (0870) 608 2608.

National Rail Enquiries – train times and fares information ☎ (08457) 484950 www.nationalrail.co.uk. From overseas ☎ 020 7278 5240.

Accommodation

A wide range of all types of accommodation, from camping and caravan sites, self-catering flats and cottages, youth hostels, family holiday parks, bed and breakfast establishments to luxury hotels, is available in Cornwall.

Extensive and up-to-date lists of serviced accommodation such as hotels, family holiday parks and bed and breakfast establishments can be obtained from any Tourist Information Centre listed in this FactFile. For the County Accommodation Guide ring the Cornwall Tourist Board on ☎ 01872 322900

Information on self-catering holidays

Cornish Traditional Cottages

Blisland, Bodmin, PL30 4HS

☎ (01208) 821666 Fax (01208) 821766 www.corncott.com

Cornish Cottage Holidays

The Old Turnpike Dairy, Godolphin Road, Helston, TR13 8GS

☎ (01326) 573808 Fax (01326) 555929 www.cornishcottageholidays.co.uk

Details of camping and caravan sites may be obtained from Tourist Information Centres listed in this Fact File.

Youth Hostels

There are 11 youth hostels in Cornwall at Boscastle, Boswinger, Coverack, Golant, Land's End, Lizard, Penzance, Perranporth, Portreath, Tintagel and Treyarnon Bay. For further details contact the YHA, Trevelyan House, Dimple Road, Matlock, Derbyshire DE4 3YH ☎ (01629) 592700 or (01629) 592627 www.yha.org.uk

Birdwatching

Cornwall is one of Britain's best areas for watching seabirds. There is also a good variety of inland birds and the possibility of rare species that have been blown off course during storms. Recommended viewing points are:

Seabirds

Godrevy Point; The Island, St Ives; Pendeen Lighthouse; Gwennap Head; the Promenade from Newlyn to Penzance; Scilly Isles.

Inland

West Penwith Moors especially inland from the B3306 between Gurnard's Head and Morvah.

Wading birds

Hayle estuary; Marazion marsh.

Waterfowl

Drift reservoir west of Newlyn; Stithians Reservoir, south of Redruth.

Boat Trips

Boat trips are on offer from almost every harbour around the Cornish coast. Some of the most popular are listed here. NB All are subject to tide and weather conditions.

Enterprise Boats

Prince of Wales Pier, Falmouth and Town Quay Truro.

☎ (01326) 374241 or 313234 (seasonal only)

www.enterprise-boats.co.uk

Run return trips from Falmouth to Truro and Falmouth and St Mawes, Daily Apr–Oct.

Plymouth Boat Cruises

Phoenix Wharf, Plymouth or Ashtorre Rock Community Centre, Saltash

☎ (01752) 408950/671166

www.soundcruising.com

Dockyards and Warships or Tamar Valley cruises. Operates: Apr to Sep.

St Mary's Boatmen's Association

The Quay, St Mary's, Isles of Scilly
☎ (01720) 423999 www.scillyboating.co.uk
Variety of trips to other islands and to view wildlife.

Coastguard

To report an emergency incident at sea dial 999.

Cycling

There are a number of designated off-road cycle routes in Cornwall, as well as miles of quiet country lanes. The following suggestions may be helpful. For more information visit www.cyclecornwall.com.

Near St Agnes the **Tehidy Country Park Trail** has over 3 miles (5km) of cycle paths, ☎ (01209) 714494 for details.

The **Great Flat Lode Trail** between Redruth and Camborne explores one of the greatest concentrations of historic mine buildings anywhere in the world. $7^1/_2$ mile (12km), circular trail. Leaflet available from local TICs or information boards on route.

A trail linking the historic mining harbours of Portreath on the north coast to Devoran in the south is the **Coast to Coast Trail**. It runs for 11 miles (18km), closely following the line of two early horse-drawn tramways. Leaflet available from TICs.

The **Mineral Tramways Heritage Project** is opening up a number of new trails based on these former mining tracks. The two-mile (3km) **Tresavean Trail** was opened in 2007 near Redruth, and there are four more trails scheduled to open by the end of 2009. A map and guide to the trails is available from TICs or can be downloaded from the project web page on the Cornwall County Council website (www.cornwall.gov.uk). The website also carries information on many of the other cycle trails in the county.

The **Camel Trail** is a 17-mile (27km) flat trail on a disused railway track which runs from Padstow via Wadebridge to Bodmin and on to Poley's Bridge. Most of it is suitable for disabled access. Parking is available in Padstow, Wadebridge, Bodmin and Poley's Bridge. ☎ (01872) 222000 for further information.

The **Cornish Way** is a much longer route, 180 miles (290km), running from near Bude all the way to Land's End and forming part of Route 3 of the National Cycle Route. Uses mainly minor roads and traffic-free off-road routes. A special map is on sale at TICs, from Sustrans ☎ 0845 113 0065 www.sustrans.org.uk or Cornwall County Council ☎ (01872) 222000.

Cycle Hire

Bissoe Tramways Cycle Hire

Off A39 just north of Devoran.
☎ (01872) 870341
www.cornwallcyclehire.com
Open: 9.30am–6pm daily, summer;
9.30am–5pm daily, winter.

Bridge Bike Hire

Wadebridge
☎ (01208) 813050
www.bridgebikehire.co.uk
Open: 9am–5pm daily, all year.

East Rose Farm

East Rose, St Breward, Bodmin.

☎ (01208) 850674

www.eastrose.co.uk

Open: Daily, all year, dawn to dusk.

Padstow Cycle Hire

South Quay, Padstow

☎ (01841) 533533

www.padstowcyclehire.com

Open: 9am–5pm daily.

See also www.visitcornwall.com – click on 'Activities'

Dialect

abroad	(scat abroad) broken in pieces	klidgy	sticky
bal	a mine	launder	gutter
beal	beak of a bird	logan-rock	a stone that can be moved
belong	(he belongs to go) he is accustomed to go	lurgy	illness of unknown type
		muryans	ants
brave	well, in good health	oggie	pasty
bulhorn	a snail	passage	ferry
bussa	large earthenware pot	praze	small common
cloam	crockery	pen	head
croust	elevenses	proper	good
direckly	later	quilkin	frog or toad
fairmaids	cured pilchards	scat	break
figgy-duff	plum pudding	shute	a stream of water
flasket	two-handled basket for washing	smeech	a disagreeable kitchen smell
		soused	marinated
fogou	cave	tre-	settlement, homestead,
hoggan	a heavy cake		farmhouse
kievea	large tub		

Dogs

Dogs are banned from many beaches in Cornwall because of the risk to health from fouling. Visitors should check before allowing a dog onto a beach. TICs have details in an excellent leaflet, which can also be downloaded at www.caradon.gov.uk – follow the link to 'Tourism'.

Eating Out

Cornwall offers vast opportunities for eating out from the simple pasty bought at the local baker's shop to top-class restaurants. No attempt has been made to list any particular establishments here but Tourist Information Centres will be very pleased to make recommendations.

Facilities for the disabled

Most visitor attractions offer facilities for the disabled wherever possible. Please telephone the attraction concerned for up-to-the-minute information. Tourist Information Centres will also be able to advise on accommodation and attractions that offer suitable facilities.

Fishing

There are excellent opportunities for all types of fishing in Cornwall: deep sea fishing, boat angling, fly fishing, coarse fishing, rock fishing, beach fishing. Digging for bait is now banned from a number of harbours and estuaries. Consult local tackle shops for information about this and where to fish and obtain licences or permits if necessary. Always take local advice when fishing at the coast, either on shore or from a boat, as the area can be affected by heavy Atlantic swells even in the height of summer.

Deep Sea Fishing

Boat trips are available from Bude, Newquay, Hayle, St Ives, Penzance, Falmouth, Mevagissey, Fowey and Looe for full-day, half-day or evening deep sea fishing. Details are available at the harbour side or from local tackle shops.

Boat Angling

There are boat launching facilities at most harbours but permission should always be sought from the harbourmaster, as should local advice on weather and sea conditions.

Fly Fishing

Argal Reservoir
West of Falmouth. Fly fishing, picnic area. Open all year.
☎ (01237) 471291 or (01209) 860301

Stithians Reservoir
About four miles west of Penryn. Open season Apr to Oct.
☎ (01209) 860301

Drift Reservoir
Three miles west of Penzance on A30. Season: Apr to Oct.
☎ (01736) 786613
www.driftflyfishing.co.uk

Siblyback Water Park and Colliford Lake
Bodmin Moor. Season: Apr to Oct.
☎ (01579) 346522

Coarse Fishing

Argal
Near Penryn
All year. ☎ (01237) 471291 or (01209) 860301

Boscathnoe
Nr Penzance
All year. ☎ (01237) 471291 or (01209) 860301

Bussow
Nr St Ives
All year. ☎ (01237) 471291 or (01209) 860301

Porth
Newquay
All year. ☎ (01237) 471291 or (01209) 860301

Tamar Lakes
Nr Bude
All year.
☎ (01288) 321712
(see www.swlakestrust.org.uk for more information)

Golf

Full details of golf courses may be obtained from local tourist offices. A free guide entitled *Golf in Cornwall* is available from Tourist Information Centres. See also www.golfincornwall.co.uk.

Horse Riding

Efford Down Riding Stables

Bude
Beginners and experienced riders welcome.
☎ (01288) 354244
www.efforddown.co.uk

Lower Tokenbury Equestrian Centre

Caradon Town, Upton Cross, Liskeard
Beginners or experienced riders welcome. Booking essential.
☎ (01579) 362747
www.lowertokenburyequestriancentre.co.uk

Newton Equestrian

Polhorman Lane, Mullion
Beginners or experienced riders welcome.
☎ (01326) 240388
www.newtonequestrian-leisurecentre.co.uk

St Veep Riding Stables

South of Lostwithiel
Beginners or experienced riders welcome. Livery available.
☎ (01208) 873521
www.stveepridingstables.co.uk

Timberdown Riding School

Stoke Climsland
Beginners or experienced riders welcome. Riding holidays.
☎ (01579) 370577

Denby Riding Stables

Denby Farm, Nanstallon Farm, Bodmin
☎ (01208) 72013

Karting

Cornwall Karting

Wadebridge
☎ (01637) 860160
www.cornwallkarting.co.uk
Open: Mon to Sat 9.30am–6pm.

Kartworld

Liskeard
☎ (01579) 347229
Open: daily 10am–6pm May to Sept.
Call for winter opening times.

Leisure Centres/Indoor Pools

Bude Haven Leisure Centre

☎ (01288) 353714

Carn Brea Leisure Centre

Pool, nr Redruth
☎ (01209) 714766

Dragon Leisure Centre

Bodmin ☎ (01208) 75715

Lux Park Leisure Centre

Liskeard
☎ (01579) 342544

Penzance Leisure Centre
☎ (01736) 874744

Phoenix Leisure Centre
Launceston
☎ (01566) 772551

Polkyth Leisure Centre
St Austell
☎ (01726) 223344

Saltash Leisure Centre
☎ (01752) 840940

Ships and Castles Leisure Pool
Falmouth
☎ (01326) 212129

St Ives Leisure Centre
☎ (01736) 797006

The Splash Leisure Pool
Bude
☎ (01288) 356191

Truro Leisure Centre
☎ (01872) 261628

Waterworld
Newquay
☎ (01637) 853828

Maps

The best maps to use are Ordnance Survey Landranger Series 2cm to 1 km 1:50,000 numbers 190, 200, 201, 203 and 204; Ordnance Survey Explorer Series 4cm to 1km 1:25,000 numbers 101, 102, 103, 104, 105, 106, 107, 108, 109, 111, 112 and 126.

Public transport in the area

Travel Southwest Public Transport Information Line

☎ 0871 200 22 33 www.travelinesw.com

The *Cornwall Public Transport Guide* covering bus, ferry, plane and train is available free from TICs or online at www.cornwallpublictransport.info. ☎ 01872 322003

Buses

Locally, an extensive network of bus services is run by **First**.

☎ 0870 608 2 608 or 0845 600 1420 www.firstgroup.com

Trains

First Great Western operate mainline services throughout Cornwall. Customer Services ☎ 08457 000 125. Rail enquiry line ☎ (08457) 484950 www.firstgreatwestern.co.uk. They also operate the Looe Valley Line from Liskeard to Looe and the St Erth to St Ives branch line.

Park and ride schemes operate in season at Liskeard (for Looe) and Lelant Saltings (for St Ives). Parking is not easy at either resort and the park and ride schemes are well recommended.

www.carfreedaysout.com www.nationalrail.co.uk www.railaletrail.com

Ferries

Ferries operate across a number of estuaries in Cornwall, regularly in summer, often less so in winter, subject to tide and weather conditions. More information can be found at www.cornwall.gov.uk under 'Public Transport'.

Torpoint to Plymouth*
Mount Edgcumbe to Plymouth
Cotehele Quay to Calstock
Fowey to Polruan
Fowey to Bodinnick*
Fowey to Mevagissey
Padstow to Rock
Falmouth to St Mawes
Falmouth to Flushing
Feock to Philleagh (King Harry Ferry)*
St Mawes to Place
Helford to Helford Passage
Helford Gardens Ferry (Helford Passage to Trebah and Glendurgan)
Smugglers Cottage, Tolverne to Falmouth
* Vehicles carried.

Falmouth has a unique Park and Float scheme. During the summer cars can be parked at Ponsharden between Penryn and Falmouth and the journey completed by classic wooden launch. Passengers alight outside the National Maritime Museum.

Aqua Cab operates around the Fal estuary from 10am to midnight, daily. Just call ☎ (07970) 242258 or visit www.aquacab.co.uk

There is also a shuttle from Mylor to Falmouth three times daily. www.falriverlinks. co.uk. ☎ 07970 242 258

Isles of Scilly

There are helicopter flights (20-minute flight) to the Isles of Scilly daily except Sunday, with **British International** from Penzance Heliport. ☎ (01736) 363871 Fax (01736) 332253 www.islesofscillyhelicopter.com

A fixed-wing air service (15-minute flight) is operated all year by **Isles of Scilly Steamship**, Monday to Saturday to the Isles of Scilly from Land's End. A similar service operates from Newquay but with a reduced service in the winter months, and there are also flights from Exeter, Bristol and Southampton. Isles of Scilly Travel Centre ☎ (0845) 710 5555 www.ios-travel.co.uk

The sea crossing to the Isles of Scilly on *Scillonian III* leaves from Penzance and takes two and a half hours. Contact the Isles of Scilly Travel Centre as for fixed wing above. For ferries between the islands contact the local TIC as these vary with the weather and tides. ☎ (01720) 424031 www.simplyscilly.co.uk

Rock Climbing

West Cornwall is the foremost sea-cliff climbing area in Britain with the most popular cliffs being found at Bosigran, Sennen and Chair Ladder. There are granite, greenstone and killas cliffs offering climbs from Difficult to E8 grade for the experienced climber. **It is essential that climbers remember that these cliffs are affected by tidal movements and that Atlantic swells can hit the cliffs with explosive force, even in summer.**

Great care should be taken at all times.
It is also important to bear in mind environmental considerations concerning flora and fauna, especially at bird nesting sites. The used of fixed gear such as bolts or drilled pegs is not acceptable here.

British Mountaineering Council
☎ 0161 445 6111 www.thebmc.co.uk

Climbing courses/guiding:

Compass West
Sennen
Operates June to September
☎ or fax (01736) 871447
www.compasswest.co.uk

Sailing

All types of sailing are available from reservoir sailing and small dinghies to sea cruising, creek hopping to voyages to France and Ireland, and excellent facilities abound in Cornwall. Many yacht clubs offer temporary membership to visitors. Amongst the many available are:

Helford River Sailing Club	☎ (01326) 231460	www.helforddriversc.co.uk
Looe Sailing Club	☎ (01503) 262559	www.looesailingclub.co.uk
Newquay Sailing Club	☎ (01637) 878574	
Pentewan Sands Sailing Club	☎ (01726) 67802	www.pentewansailingclub.org.uk
Royal Cornwall Yacht Club	☎ (01326) 312126	www.royalcornwallyachtclub.org
St Mawes Sailing Club	☎ (01326) 270696	www.stmawessailing.co.uk

Amongst companies which offer sailing tuition are:

Classic Sailing
St Mawes
☎ (01872) 580022
www.classic-sailing.co.uk

Cornish Cruising
Falmouth
☎ (01326) 211800
www.cornishcruising.co.uk

Windsport International
Falmouth
☎ (01326) 376191
www.windsport.co.uk

Stithians Reservoir
near Redruth
☎ (01209) 860301
www.swlakestrust.org.uk

Or contact the Royal Yachting Association ☎ (0845) 3450400 www.rya.org.uk
Visitors' moorings are available at most harbours; contact the appropriate harbourmaster.

FactFile

Tourist Information Centres

Further information on any specific activity or event may be obtained from the appropriate Tourist Information Office. * means open in summer only.

Bodmin
Bodmin Shire Hall, Mount Folly Square
☎(01208) 76616
bodmintic@visit.org.uk

Boscastle
The Harbour
☎ (01840) 250010
boscastlevc@btconnect.com

Bude
The Crescent Car Park
☎ (01288) 354240
budetic@visitbude.info

Camelford*
North Cornwall Museum, The Clease
☎ (01840) 212954
manager@camelfordtic.eclipse.co.uk

Falmouth
11 Market Strand
☎ (01326) 312300
info@falmouthtic.co.uk

Fowey
5 South Street
☎ (01726) 833616
info@fowey.co.uk

Hayle*
The Library
☎ (01736) 754399
hayle.library@cornwall.gov.uk

Helston
Tyacke Road
☎ (01209) 614000
Mon to Fri only.

Isles of Scilly
Hugh Town, St Mary's
☎ (01720) 424031
tic@scilly.gov.uk

Launceston
Market House Arcade, Market Street
☎ (01566) 772321
launcestontic@btconnect.com

Liskeard
Foresters Hall, Pike Street
☎ (01579) 349148
tourism@liskeard.gov.uk

Looe*
The Guildhall, Fore Street, East Looe
☎ (01503) 262072
looetic@btconnect.com

Lostwithiel
Lostwithiel Community Centre, Liddicoat Road
☎ (01208) 872207
tourism@lostwithieltic.wanadoo.co.uk

Mevagissey
St George's Square
☎ (01726) 844857
info@mevagissey-cornwall.co.uk

Newquay
Municipal Buildings, Marcus Hill
☎ (01637) 854020
info@newquay.co.uk

Padstow
Red Brick Building, North Quay
☎ (01841) 533449
padstowtic@btconnect.com

Penzance
Station Road
☎ (01736) 362207
pztic@penwith.gov.uk

Perranporth
Tywarnhale Square
☎ (01872) 575254
info@perranporthinfo.co.uk

Redruth
The Cornwall Centre, Alma Place
☎ (01209) 219048
cornishstudies.library@cornwall.gov.uk

St Agnes
5 Churchtown
☎ 01872) 554150
ticstagnes@yahoo.co.uk

234

St Austell
Bypass Service Station, Southbourne Road
☎ (01726) 879500
tic@cornish-riviera.co.uk

St Ives
The Guildhall, Street an Pol
☎ (01736) 796297
ivtic@penwith.gov.uk

St Just
The Library, Market Street
☎ (01736) 788165
stjust.tic@btconnect.com

St Mawes
The Roseland Visitor Centre, The Square
☎ (01326) 270440
manager@roselandinfo.com

Tintagel
Bossiney Road,
☎ (01840) 779084
tintagelvc@btconnect.com

Truro
Municipal Buildings, Boscawen Street
☎ (01872) 274555
tic@truro.gov.uk

Walking

Coastal walking is excellent in Cornwall but there are opportunities to explore inland as well. Here you will find heritage trails, pilgrim routes and riverside walks as well as wild moors with ancient sites to visit. For more information, visit www.walkcornwall.com.

The South West Coast Path long-distance footpath, which celebrated 30 years in 2008, runs for some 630 miles (1,014km), 268 of those miles (431km) around the coast of Cornwall. Many sections can be walked as day walks, using public transport to return to base in the evening. The South West Coastal Path Association produce a guide to the route with details of accommodation, transport, ferries and tide tables.

South West Coast Path Association ☎ (01752) 896237
info@swcp.org.uk   www.swcp.org.uk

In addition there are the Coast to Coast Trail, the Saints' Way, St Michael's Way, The Tinners Way and the Mineral Trackways (see cycling above). The National Trust publish leaflets detailing walks on all the coastal properties belonging to the Trust in Cornwall. Leaflets for all of these and many other walks in Cornwall may be obtained from all local tourist offices or downloaded from www.nationaltrust.org.uk.

Watersports

Facilities for Bodyboarding, Surfing, Windsurfing, Canoeing and Diving are excellent in Cornwall. The Cornwall Tourist Board, www.visitcornwall.com ☎ (01872) 322900, can supply very good information on all aspects of watersports. It is essential that those who are new to these activities and to the area seek local advice in order to undertake the sports safely.

Surfing

British Surfing Association
Newquay ☎ (01637) 876474 www.britsurf.co.uk

Harlyn Surf School
Padstow ☎ (01841) 533076   www.harlynsurfschool.co.uk

Sennen Surfing Centre
Sennen Cove ☎ (01736) 871227 or 871561 www.sennensurfingcentre.com

Canoeing

Falmouth Canoe Club
www.falmouthcc.org.uk

Diving

British Sub-Aqua Club
☎ (0151) 350 6200 www.bsac.com.
Specific information for Cornwall:
www.cornwall-online.co.uk/waterside

Falmouth Diving Club
☎ (01326) 376928

Porthkerris Divers
St Keverne
☎ (01326) 280620
www.porthkerris.com

Seaways Diving and Marine
Penryn
☎ (01326) 375544
www.seawaysdiving.com

Inland waters offering a variety of watersports – tuition available.

See www.swlakestrust.org.uk

Roadford Lake
nr Launceston ☎ (01409) 211507

Siblyback Watersports Centre
nr Liskeard ☎ (01579) 346522

Stithians
nr Helston ☎ (01209) 860301

Upper Tamar Lake
nr Bude ☎ (01288) 321712

Weather

Cornwall is a very narrow peninsula and the weather is much influenced by the sea. In winter, temperatures rarely fall below 32°F (0°C) and thanks to the Gulf Stream the area is usually warmer than the rest of mainland Britain. The driest months are likely to be in early summer and May tends to be the sunniest. The weather here can change very quickly and sunshine is never very far away.

Weathercall ☎ 09068 500 404 www.metoffice.gov.uk

Websites

Cornwall Tourist Board www.visitcornwall.com
Cornish Riviera www.cornish-riviera.co.uk
North Cornwall www.northcornwall-live.com
West Cornwall www.go-cornwall.com
All Areas www.cornwall-online.co.uk
Scilly Isles www.simplyscilly.co.uk

Index

Index

Published in the UK by
Landmark Publishing Ltd
The Oaks, Moor Farm Road West, Ashbourne, DE6 1HD
☎ 01335 347349 Website: www.landmarkpublishing.co.uk

11th Edition 2009
ISBN 13: 978-1-84306-440-4

© **Rita Tregellas Pope 2009**

The right of Rita Tregellas Pope as author of this work has been asserted by her in accordance with the Copyright, Design and Patents Act, 1993. All rights reserved. No part of this publication may be reproduced, stored in a retrieval system or transmitted in any form or by any means, electronic, mechanical, photocopying, recording or otherwise without the prior permission of Landmark Publishing Ltd.
British Library Cataloguing in Publication Data: a catalogue record for this book is available from the British Library.

Print: Gutenberg Press Ltd, Malta
Design: Michelle Hunt
This edition was updated and edited by Ian Howe. Isles of Scilly text updated by Angela Olley.

Photo Captions:
Front cover: The Fishing village of Polperro (© elena moiseeva)
Back cover, Top: The Three Musketeers, Minack Theatre (© Minack Theatre)
Back cover, Middle: Eden Project (© Nathalie Banaigs)
Back cover, Bottom: Coastline at Newquay (© Joop Snijder jr.)
Back Cover Right: Scones Jam Clotted Cream and Strawberries with Afternoon Tea
(© Monkey Business Images)

Picture credits:
All photographs are supplied by Lindsey Porter except the following:
Newquay & the Cornish Riviera Tourist Dept: 162 middle right, 151 bottom; **YHA:** 203 top;
The Monkey Sanctuary Trust: 31 bottom; **NMMC:** 7 Right, 79; **Caerhays Estate:** 70 top;
National Seal Sanctuary Gweek: 102 top; **Roskilly's:** 107 bottom left; **Penlee House:** 114 top right;
Trevarno Gardens: 91 mini pic, 95 bottom left; **Minack Theatre:** 119 top & middle right;
Michelle Turton (Newquay Zoo): 7 middle top, 151 middle; **Newquay Blue Reef Aquarium:** 151 top;
Crealy Great Adventure Parks: 7 middle bottom, 167 bottom; **Pencarrow House:** 171 mini pic, 175 top;
Tamar Otter and Wildlife Centre: 198; **Museum of Witchcraft:** 202 top

All images below from Shutterstock with Copyright to:
Stephen Aaron Rees: 10 bottom, 74 top, 98 top right, middle & bottom, 103 right, 118,
119 bottom left, 127 bottom, 126, 119 bottom right, 222 top middle & bottom left, 214, 218, 219 top, 222, 215 top, 215 bottom; **Credit 954831545:** 62 **Kevin Britland:** 6,139;
Jaroslaw Grudzinski: 134, 146 bottom, 147; **David Quixley:** 59;
Samot: 11, 170, 175 bottom, 110 **David Hughes:** 90, 162 top, 47 bottom, 95 top ;
Monkey Business Images: 10 top; **M Willis:** 55 bottom; **Elena Moiseeva:** 7 left, 39 mini pic, 42 top,
Jenny Horne: 71 bottom; **Jaroslaw Grudzinski:** 175 bottom **9548315445:** 71,51;
Steve Roche: 122 bottom; **Harvey Fitzhugh:** 154; **Gary Dyson:** 155;
Sandy Maya Matzen: 202 bottom; **Rachelle Burnside:** 190; **Nathalie Banaigs:** 38;
Mary Lane: 50 top right; **David Woolfenden:** 50 middle left; **John Guard:** 67 bottom, 70 middle, 71 top;
Elisa Locci: 74 bottom, 75 bottom; **Joop Snijder jr:** 75 top, 114 bottom;
David Peta: 79 top; **E. Sweet:** 82 top; **Joe Gough:** 127 top; **Adrian Hughes:** 127 bottom

DISCLAIMER
While every care has been taken to ensure that the information in this book is as accurate as possible at the time of publication, the publishers and authors accept no responsibility for any loss, injury or inconvenience sustained by anyone using this book.